Think of a Garden

The playwright in the garden of his home in Olo, American Samoa, 1986. (Jeff Van Kirk)

Think of a Garden

and Other Plays

JOHN KNEUBUHL

Talanoa

Contemporary Pacific Literature

University of Hawai'i Press

Honolulu

97 98 99 00 01 02   5 4 3 2 1

Library of Congress Cataloging-in-Publication Data
Kneubuhl, John.
Think of a garden and other plays / John Kneubuhl.
p.   cm. — (Talanoa)
ISBN 0–8248–1773–7 (alk. paper). — ISBN 0–8248–1814–8 (pbk. :
alk. paper)
1. Hawaii—Drama. I. Title. II. Series.
PS3561.N417T48   1997
812'.54—DC21   96–39137
CIP

"Think of a Garden" is included here by permission of O Le Si'uleo O Samoa.

The publisher is indebted to the following individuals
for Hawaiian and Samoan translation assistance:
Carol Silva, Jackie Pualani Johnson, Haunani Bernardino,
Victoria Kneubuhl, Ernest Betham, Pia Jamieson,
Naomi Losch, and Fata Simanu-Klutz.

Designed by Paula Newcomb

Contents

Editor's Note   vii

Think of a Garden   1

Mele Kanikau: A Pageant   97

A Play: A Play   177

Afterword: A Portrait of John Kneubuhl
Jackie Pualani Johnson   251

Glossary   267

Production Credits   269

Editor's Note

Not until 1990, when I was studying at the East-West Center in Honolulu, did I hear about the playwright John Kneubuhl. I was writing my dissertation on clowning and comedy in Polynesia, and a friend had mentioned this fascinating part-Samoan playwright at the Hilo campus of the University of Hawai'i; he was directing his latest play, in which clowning and comedy played an integral part. Someone must have mentioned my name to John Kneubuhl, because soon after I received a letter inviting me to fly over to Hilo to see his play. There was also a prepaid ticket in the envelope. How generous of the man, I thought. How could I refuse?

The play in question was *A Play: A Play*. I was so impressed with the style and theatricality of Kneubuhl's direction that I ended up seeing it three times. Prior to this Hilo experience, I had never seen a play fuse traditional and modern ideas and techniques in a manner so confident and so outrageous. Here was a playwright and director who was master of the avant-garde as well as the comedic traditions of ancient Samoa. And I was seeing a play that was a culmination of more than two decades of playwriting for television and the stage. I felt honored.

Kneubuhl's health was declining during this time when I met him, and I was certain that *A Play: A Play* was his swan song. Thus when I learned that he was trying to complete the manuscript for another play as he lay dying in a hospital in Pago Pago I was incredulous. Kneubuhl died in 1992, a few hours before the curtain opened for the production of his last and most personal play, *Think of a Garden*.

Since its first performance in Pago Pago, *Think of a Garden* has been produced in Auckland (1993), Wellington (1994), and Honolulu (1995). Part of the play's appeal is the author's frank and moving portrayal of his own bicultural upbringing—the basis of this work of fiction. The emotional and psychological intensity unleashed during the climax of the play creates one of the most powerful scenes ever written by a Pacific playwright.

Mele Kanikau is yet to be realized on stage. I hope that its publication here will spur a director to stage this fine play, the most political of the trilogy. More detailed information on the plays and the playwright may be found in the afterword at the back of this book. Jackie Pualani Johnson, a close friend of Kneubuhl's and chair of the Theater Department at the Hilo campus, has written an eloquent piece that sets these three plays in their proper literary and cultural context.

Kneubuhl didn't particularly care about publishing his plays, which is probably why I had never heard of him during my time in the South Pacific. For him, production equaled publication. Though I understand and respect this view, there is something to be said for being able to hold a volume such as this in your hand, to read it at your leisure, and to be able to send it to a friend or colleague at the other end of the world. Classes in colleges and universities will now be able to study Kneubuhl's work, and all those interested in playwriting and the Pacific can now ponder the personal, cultural, and political issues that are central to these plays.

"If you want to be in theater, then you have a responsibility to be theatrical." This piece of advice from Kneubuhl is one that I will always remember. These three plays are a testimony to Kneubuhl's belief in the magic of theater, and how theater can touch our lives in ways that are personal and profound.

VILSONI HERENIKO

Think of a Garden

A PLAY IN FOUR SCENES

CAST

THE WRITER

PITO

DAVID KREBER

LU'ISA KREBER

BROTHER PATRICK

FRANK KREBER

LILO

HOUSEGIRLS

Place: Leone, American Samoa
Time: The late 1920s

Although based on historical fact, this play is guilty of many sins of omission; heroes and martyrs in Western Samoa's struggle for independence are not mentioned. I hope that the love and admiration I have for them are, even in my silence about their names, clamorous.

The play also flirts with autobiography and, I'm afraid, flirts outrageously at times. For the reader and for the actors, let it remain a flirtation only.

JAK
Olo, Tutuila
American Samoa
January 1991

2

SCENE ONE

(The backyard and porch of an old, large, tropical house: Victorian, iron, wood, cement. The L-shaped porch runs parallel to the back wall, then, at upstage right, turns and extends downstage right. An ornate wooden railing. Two or three steps lead from the ground to the porch stage right where a wide door, now open, provides entrance into the house. Wicker furnishes the porch, wrought iron the yard, everything white. An ornately decorated artificial Christmas tree stands at the upstage left end of the porch; Japanese lanterns hang along the eaves. At stage left, the yard melts into tropical foliage, a high hedge dominating. On a long white table, downstage right, are beautiful artificial flowers, loose and in bowls; this is the work table. Other flower arrangements, in vases and bowls, have been placed around the porch and yard.

At the start: WRITER *enters, fortyish, a softspoken, introspective man. He faces the audience.)*

WRITER: The place: the village where I was born, Leone, on the Polynesian island of American Samoa, in the South Pacific. . . . The scene: the back porch and yard of the house my mother's father built in the late 1870s.

His grandfather was one George Griffith, a Congregational missionary from Birmingham, England, who served in Western Samoa, across the channel, both as missionary and British Consul. It was there his son, Bradford, was born; Bradford married a highborn Samoan lady, and their son was my mother's father. He, too, married a highborn Samoan lady. They had two children: my mother and, four years later, my Uncle Lilo, who, perhaps intimidated by his mother and grandmother, never married. . . . Those were the days when Samoa was undivided among foreign powers, its many islands a unified country. . . . The family had homes and vast lands in Western Samoa and on this island which, in 1900, was ceded by its chiefs to the United States of America. Still, my mother always thought of herself as a Western Samoan, and acted like one. In fact, she was supposed to marry into a noble family there. Instead, she met and married my father, an American who became very successful with copra and cocoa plantations. He was also something of a lawyer, and with skillful management of my mother's land, he became even more successful.

My grandparents both died a few years after the wedding. A boating accident in mid-channel. They drowned. . . . My mother and father moved here soon after that sad time. . . .

My room was upstairs, where, throughout my childhood, my one view out of the house—that view that shapes one's world forever—was of this garden. . . . It was closed in on three sides by the house and on the fourth side by a tall hedge. *(He points to stage right.)* Along the front of the house with its Victorian porch was the main village road—sand, nothing else—and, on the other side, the steep sloping beach, the beautiful wide bay with its reef a quarter of a mile out, and the surf, pounding high on windy days. I used to think of wild, plunging horses, their white manes shredding in the wind behind them. *(He looks around the garden, touching the table at stage center, remembering. Then:)* Unless you lived in the house, you should never suspect the garden was here. And, even if, passing by, you saw it from a break in the hedge, you would not think it a garden. . . . Sand, like the whole village around the house, brown sand, tamped hard and flat into the brown earth, everywhere, by generations of brown ancestors, walking through their lives. . . . Not a shrub, not a blade grew here—could grow—but there were always flowers, beautiful artificial flowers that my mother would bring back from New Zealand, which she visited often. It was all magical to me, especially when my friend Veni came to play, or when I would sit with my old nurse, Pito, out here, on moonlight nights, and she would tell me the old stories, with the songs of grief in them. . . .

(PITO, *an old Samoan woman, comes out from the house, bringing an empty bowl. She wears a* puletasi. *She goes to the table downstage right, arranges flowers in the bowl. Meanwhile:)*

WRITER: So then, I ask you to think of that garden now as if it existed in your minds as truly and as beautifully as it did for me. And think of it now, as it was then: late afternoon, the day before Christmas, in the year nineteen hundred and twenty-nine.

(A boy, almost ten, DAVID KREBER, *comes out to the porch, perches on the rail, and watches* PITO *at her work. He is a rather frail boy physically, but there is nothing frail about his behavior. He wears a short-sleeved shirt, short pants, no socks, no shoes.)*

DAVID: Mānaia au teu, Pito.[1]
PITO: *(Goes right on working.)* Oso 'i lalo ge'i 'e pa'ū.
DAVID: 'Ā pa'ū, 'ua pa'ū.

(He stands up on the railing. PITO *goes right on working.)*

PITO: Ā gau lou ua, 'o 'oe ā.[2]
DAVID: 'Ioe. . . . Na 'aumai lā'ea 'o au teu, 'e teu ai le tātou falesā lea 'o le'ā fai ai si o'u maliu. Tālofae 'i si tātou uso. . . . 'Ioe. *(He clears his throat elaborately: a rheumy, doddering, toothless old Samoan preacher.)* Le 'au usōe: sā iai sē tasi o tātou na lē fa'alogo 'i ā Pito. Va'ai mai lā 'i lona ī'uga: na pa'ū . . . na gau le pogāua. . . . Taga'i: 'O lea 'ua ta'atia atu i 'outou luma. . . . 'Ua 'āmata 'ona manogi. . . .
PITO: David, sōia! *(She takes the new bowl of flowers to a table below the porch upstage center.)*
DAVID: 'Ua elo. . . . 'Ua pipilo. . . . 'Ioe.

Kneubuhl's original version of this play included only the Samoan language lines. English translations have been added for this publication.

[1]DAVID: Your flowers are pretty, Pito.
PITO: *(Goes right on working.)* Jump down before you fall.
DAVID: If I fall, I fall.

[2]PITO: You will break your neck.
DAVID: Yes. . . . Then you can bring your flowers and decorate our church for my funeral. Poor thing, our brother. . . . Yes. *(He clears his throat elaborately: a rheumy, doddering, toothless old Samoan preacher.)* My brothers: there was one of us who did not listen to Pito. See what happens: he fell and broke his neck, the fool. See him lying there in front of us. . . . He begins to smell . . .
PITO: David, stop it! *(She takes the new bowl of flowers to a table below the porch, upstage center.)*
DAVID: He smells. . . . He stinks. . . . Yes.

(PITO *turns somewhat angrily to* DAVID.)

PITO: *(Sharply.)* David! Sau loa ʻi lalo![3] *(She moves to the steps.)* Koe ikiiki lava oʻu alu aku, makuaʻi mimilo lou ua.

(DAVID *jumps down, comes down the steps into the yard.*)

DAVID: *(Still preaching.)* Toe vaʻai mai, ʻoutou nā e lē talitonu ʻi ā Iēsū lo tātou Faʻaola: ʻUa toe tū ʻi luga lē na maliu, ʻua savali, ʻua namu lelei—pei ʻo Pito. ʻO se fafine ʻe matuaʻi manogi mānaia tele, pei ʻo se laumoli, pei ʻo se suafaʻi, pei ʻo se ʻurosa....[4]

PITO: Pei ʻo se ā?

DAVID: ʻUrosa.

PITO: ʻO le ā lāʻea mea?

DAVID: ʻO se itūʻaigā rosa.

PITO: *(Pleased.)* ʻA ʻea?

DAVID: ʻIoe. ʻE lē matuituia. ʻE anu uliuli, ʻe fulufulua, ʻae ʻo le manogi ia!

PITO: ʻO le ā lāʻea ikūʻaigā losa e fulufulua?

DAVID: ʻO le ʻūrosa, my dear. ʻO le ʻuʻūrosa.

(LUʻISA KREBER *comes onto the porch with a tray of tea things—fine porcelain, Chinese. She is a lovely lady, thirty-nine, copper complexion. The accent is New Zealand.* PITO *goes immediately to her, takes the tray, and brings it to the garden table at center stage.* DAVID *moves to a bench at downstage left and sits there, cross-legged.*)

---

[3] PITO: David! Come down! *(She moves to the steps.)* Pretty soon I'm going there to squeeze your neck.

[4] DAVID: Yes, see here those who believe in Christ, our savior, the dead will stand, they will walk, they smell nice like Pito, a woman who smells very nice, like an orange, like banana soup, like a ʻurosa ...
PITO: Like a what?
DAVID: ʻUrosa.
PITO: What is that?
DAVID: A kind of rose.
PITO: *(Pleased.)* What?
DAVID: Yes. No thorns, black, furry with no smell.
PITO: What is that kind of rose that is furry?
DAVID: The ʻurosa, my dear. The smelly rose.

LU'ISA: David, have you got your lessons all ready for Brother
   Patrick? He should be here any minute.
DAVID: Yes, Mama.
LU'ISA: (*To* PITO.) Tu'u pea nā mea 'i ā a'u, Pito. (*She means the
   flower arranging.*) 'O lelā 'o fa'atali mai le tou ti.[5]
PITO: Fao'afekai.

(PITO *goes into the house.* LU'ISA *moves to the tea table.*)

LU'ISA: Would you like to have some tea with me, Precious? (*She
   sits at the table.*)
DAVID: No, thank you.
LU'ISA: Still, it would be nice to have a little company.
DAVID: Oh. Yes. (*He comes to her side, sits. She pours tea.*)
LU'ISA: Sure you won't have a little? There's real milk, and it's ever
   so good.
DAVID: I had tea already . . . with Veni.
LU'ISA: Oh? Where? . . . Here?
DAVID: No. I—took some in a jar. Cook let me.
LU'ISA: Where'd you go?
DAVID: To the old graves back there, by the swamp. Mama, na fai-
   mai Veni 'e sau i se pō, ma te ō e momoe i luga o . . .[6]
LU'ISA: Dearest, dearest! English! . . . You know how upset Daddy
   gets. . . . Now, Veni said?—
DAVID: Said he would come one night soon and we'd go and sleep
   on the graves. . . .
LU'ISA: (*Laughing.*) Why ever would you want to do such a thing?
DAVID: Because we'll see a ghost that way. Veni says he knows lots
   of ghosts, and he can make them come. . . .
LU'ISA: Oh dear! And if a ghost did come, whatever would you do?
   Bring her for tea?
DAVID: I think I would bring him to meet Cousin Tamasese.
LU'ISA: Oh? And does Veni speak proper chiefly Samoan? We
   don't want to seem rude to our cousin, you know.
DAVID: Oh yes! He's a very high chief's son, Mama. . . . Faimai

---

[5]LU'ISA: . . . Leave that to me, Pito. (*She means the flower arranging.*) Your tea is
   waiting.
PITO: Thank you.

[6]DAVID: . . . Mama, Veni said he'll come some night, we'll go to sleep on . . .

Veni, 'ā maua sau . . .[7] *(Feeling somewhat foolish for the lapse, he scratches his head.)* Veni said, if you catch a ghost, you can make it do anything you want. Even magic things.

LUʻISA: Like?

DAVID: He can make Cousin Tamasese win his war against the New Zealand government.

LUʻISA: It isn't a war, Precious. It's a struggle. . . . Our people's right to govern themselves, run their own affairs.

DAVID: Does that mean us, too? Here?

LUʻISA: Good heavens, no! Our people across the channel, over in Upolu. We here belong to the United States of America! They belong to New Zealand.

DAVID: New Zealand people are bloody awful, aren't they?

LUʻISA: Language, Precious, language! *(A moment.)* Mummy went to school in New Zealand. They're lovely people.

DAVID: Then why did they send Cousin Tamasese into exile?

LUʻISA: The people in New Zealand didn't send him off into exile. Their terrible high commissioner over in Upolu did. . . .

(A pause. DAVID watches his mother sip her tea.)

DAVID: Is he really coming, Mama?

LUʻISA: Mmmm? . . . Oh, of course.

DAVID: Then why didn't he arrive last night, like you said he would?

LUʻISA: It's a long way from New Zealand. Almost two thousand miles.

DAVID: Veni says he isn't coming. . . .

LUʻISA: Veni says, Veni says! I'd like to meet this friend of yours! Why don't you ever bring him?

DAVID: He's *mā*.

LUʻISA: Well, he doesn't seem to be shy about expressing his opinion!

DAVID: He can't speak English.

LUʻISA: Oh? I was beginning to think he knew everything. . . .

(BROTHER PATRICK moves in at the upstage left edge of the backyard. He is in the black cassock of a Marist brother. A thin man, pale, mid-forties, Irish.)

---

[7] DAVID: . . . Veni said, the two of us . . .

LUʻISA: Well, here's someone who does!

(DAVID *rises and moves away a bit.* LUʻISA *holds out her hand as* BROTHER PATRICK *comes close, takes the hand.*)

LUʻISA: Good afternoon, Brother Patrick! And a very Merry Christmas.
PATRICK: Mrs. Kreber. (*A quick nervous bow.*) David. . . . Merry Christmas to all in this blessed home.

(DAVID *nods.*)

LUʻISA: Some tea, Brother. . . . David, you come around here and sit. . . . Brother Pat can have your seat.

(DAVID *does as he's told.*)

PATRICK: No no, thank you very much. Very much indeed, Mrs. Kreber. But I've had a bit of tea before I came. With the sisters. Our little Christmas party.
LUʻISA: But aren't you early for your lessons? It isn't five yet.
PATRICK: Well, I thought perhaps we—that is, Mr. Kreber, if he's in, and you and I—well— (DAVID's *presence makes him ill at ease.*) —there's something I would like to ask—so, I came early, hoping . . .
LUʻISA: But, of course. . . . Frank's having a little nap, I think. . . . (*She rises.*)
PATRICK: Ah, but then, perhaps another time! . . .
LUʻISA: No no, I'll fetch him. (*She is about to go, turns back to him.*) It's nothing serious, is it, Brother? You seem quite—upset.
PATRICK: No . . . oh no. . . . It's . . . (*Again, the awareness of* DAVID.) . . . personal. . . . A small and private matter . . .
LUʻISA: I'll send Pito out with a little Christmas something—
PATRICK: Thank you. Thank you very much.
LUʻISA: (*Heading for the door.*) Mind you take good care of Brother Patrick now, David. . . . And clear the table for Pito, will you?
DAVID: Yes, Mama.
LUʻISA: Oh—and stay for dinner . . . I insist.
PATRICK: Thank you. . . . A great honor, indeed. . . .

(*She is gone.* DAVID *comes to the table for the tea things. He moves them to the table downstage right where Pito was fixing flowers.* PATRICK *watches him very carefully, concerned. When* DAVID *finally turns around to face him,* PATRICK *looks away quickly. He moves to a seat. It takes him a moment or two to compose a casual face and manner.)*

PATRICK: So, well then— *(He sits.)* How are you this fine Saturday, Davey me boy-o?

DAVID: Fine.

PATRICK: Headache gone?

DAVID: Headache?

PATRICK: You were excused early yesterday because . . .

DAVID: *(Cutting in quickly.)* Oh, it's all right now. Thank you.

PATRICK: And did you come straight home, like I told you?

DAVID: Yes.

PATRICK: Well, I'm glad you're better. . . . *(He notices the flowers for the first time.)* Ah, so many beautiful flowers, Davey. Is it a Christmas party you're having tonight?

DAVID: We're decorating the house for my cousin Tamasese.

PATRICK: Tamasese is coming here? To this house?

DAVID: Tonight. It's a secret. His boat isn't going straight to Western Samoa; it's coming here first. So he can talk with Daddy and Uncle Lilo about things. . . . Daddy says it'll be safer for Tamasese to arrive there in the dark. Because of the New Zealand soldiers. . . .

PATRICK: I see. . . .

DAVID: Daddy says ever since the newspapers in Upolu wrote that Tamasese was coming back from his exile, lots more soldiers have arrived from New Zealand. . . .

PATRICK: The exile is over, Davey. He's allowed to come home. *Allowed,* it is. Sure there'll be no trouble now.

DAVID: *(Quietly.)* Daddy's afraid there's going to be lots of trouble.

PATRICK: Pray God he is wrong then.

*(*PITO *comes out of the house with a tray, two decanters of whiskey, a pitcher of water, two tumblers.)*

PITO: David, fai mai Lu'isa e 'aumai mea ia mo le felela.[8]

*(*DAVID *indicates the table center stage where he and* PATRICK *are sitting.)*

---

[8]PITO: David, Lu'isa said to bring this for the priest.

DAVID: 'Aumai 'i 'ī.[9]

(PITO *brings the tray, sets it down.*)

DAVID: Fa'afetai.[10]
PITO: 'Aua ke 'ōgā!

(DAVID *laughs.* PITO *takes the tea things offstage with her.*)

PATRICK: What did she say to make you laugh?
DAVID: She told me not to get drunk.

(PATRICK *is already pouring himself a drink. He smiles at* DAVID*'s answer.* DAVID *watches the pouring carefully; the tumbler is about three-quarters full.*)

DAVID: Tell you what, Brother Pat.
PATRICK: What?
DAVID: You get drunk, then we won't have to have our Latin lesson.
PATRICK: Oh no, me boy, Latin! Latin is what has held the world together since that dark and terrible day on Golgotha! The glue, me boy, binding scholar to scholar, present to past, and all, all the Church, the Rock, *petrus*, the blessed Saint Peter . . .
DAVID: *(Taking the empty tumbler, raising it as in a toast.)* To the glue! And old Pete!
PATRICK: *(Raising his near-full glass.)* To the glue, and to grand old Pete!

(*And then he drinks—a long, steady pull.* DAVID *puts his glass down and watches* PATRICK*'s long swallow in awe.* PATRICK *puts his glass down, a big grin on his face.*)

PATRICK: Ah, Davey, you do have a sweet and thoughtful lady for a mother. Another saint, to be sure.

---

[9]DAVID: Bring it here. . . .

[10]DAVID: Thank you.
PITO: Don't get drunk!

(The porch door opens. LU'ISA'S *husband,* FRANK KREBER, *steps aside and she comes out. They head for the table center stage as* PATRICK *rises. His usual nervousness is upon him at once.* FRANK *is about forty, a stockily built American—blunt, open, friendly. He goes over to* PATRICK.*)*

FRANK: Hello, Brother! Good to see you. Merry Christmas.
PATRICK: Mr. Kreber.

(They shake hands. FRANK *notices* PATRICK'S *glass.)*

FRANK: Good Christ, man! Is that what you call a drink?
LU'ISA: Frank!
FRANK: *(Pouring a drink for himself.)* Now—you're not going to let me drink alone, are you?
PATRICK: Ah—no, no sir . . .

*(*FRANK *refills* PATRICK'S *glass generously.)*

PATRICK: Thank you . . . thank you very much . . .
FRANK: *(Taking his own glass.)* Well, here's mud in your eye, Brother. . . .

(He gestures for PATRICK *to pick up his glass.* PATRICK *does.)*

PATRICK: Yes . . . yes . . . thank you . . .

(They drink, FRANK *taking a big swallow,* PATRICK *taking a big sip. He looks at his glass a thoughtful moment, looks over to* FRANK, *then— after all, what is there left to hide?—he takes another long guzzle.* DAVID *moves to the side bench at stage left humming "Nearer My God to Thee.")*

FRANK: That's better.

(They put down their glasses.)

FRANK: Lu'isa says you— *(*DAVID *continues humming.)* David, can it! . . . *(To* BROTHER PATRICK:*)* Lu'isa says there's something bothering you and— *(*DAVID *has continued humming softly.)* Cut it out, David. Daddy wants to talk with Brother Pat a little, okay?

(DAVID *stops.* LU‘ISA *comes to him.*)

LU‘ISA: Your books, Precious. For your Latin lesson. *(She gently urges* DAVID *to the porch step. She remains there while the boy crosses to the door.)* And please see that the Japanese lanterns have been strung up properly along the front walk. . . . Help the men.

DAVID: Yes, Mama. *(He goes into the house.)*

FRANK: Well, Brother. Lu‘isa says there's something you want to get off your chest.

LU‘ISA: Would you like me to leave the two of you alone?

PATRICK: No, no. You—have to stay, I want you to stay. . . . *(A pause. He obviously doesn't know how to begin.)*

FRANK: Sit down, Brother. Sit down.

(PATRICK *sits.* FRANK *takes his drink. Silence.*)

FRANK: It can't be that hard, Brother.

PATRICK: No—it—it isn't. . . .

FRANK: Then what is it?

PATRICK: It's about little Davey. . . .

(FRANK *and* LU‘ISA *exchange a quick look of concern.*)

LU‘ISA: What is it, Brother?

PATRICK: Have you noticed how he's been behaving lately?

(LU‘ISA *is visibly worried.* FRANK, *calmer, sips at his drink.*)

LU‘ISA: Why, what do you mean, behaving?

PATRICK: I mean, anything—unusual? . . .

FRANK: David is a bright little rascal. *(Chuckles.)* His usual behavior is usually unusual. . . .

PATRICK: *(A weak smile.)* Ah yes, yes, that I know. . . . But—well— you see, for the last day of school, Christmas break, Davey's job during noon recess yesterday was to put all the inkwells in the sink and wash them out . . . then, dry them off and put them back in the desks, in the classrooms.

(A pause.)

FRANK: Go on.

PATRICK: So . . . David was in the classroom, collecting the ink-wells, and—I heard him talking to someone. I thought he was alone, you see, and I wondered who it might be, so I looked in. . . . There was nobody there. Nobody, Mrs. Kreber. Only Davey. And he was talking in the Samoan language to an empty desk as if someone was sitting there, plain as day. . . . Then—it was like he was walking somebody to the side door and he stood there and said, "Tōfā!" . . . and he stood in the doorway for a good while, watching, waving goodbye. . . . Then he went back to the inkwells. . . . And there was a cold chill in every bone of my body. . . . *(The chill seems to have hit him again.)*

LUʻISA: *(Relieved and trying to relieve.)* Brother, Davey's forever making up imaginary friends. . . . That's not uncommon among children. . . . I shouldn't worry. . . .

PATRICK: But I do. . . . You see, when recess was over and we were not ten minutes into our Pacific Geography lesson, he started to complain about a headache. . . . A bad one, he said. . . .

FRANK: And did he have a headache?

PATRICK: I didn't believe him.

LUʻISA: He makes things up, Brother, yes: adventures, imaginary playmates, make-believe escapades—but he doesn't deliberately lie!

PATRICK: He kept insisting he wanted to come home, right away, the headache was going to make him vomit. . . . So I let him go —told him to come straight home.

FRANK: *(To LUʻISA.)* Did he?

LUʻISA: I was over at the dispensary, using their telephone.

FRANK: All afternoon?

LUʻISA: A bit over an hour. . . . David could've come and gone. . . .

PATRICK: *(To LUʻISA.)* I know he didn't. . . . I wanted him to. I wanted him to make a fool of me for thinking him a little liar!

LUʻISA: *(Gently.)* Brother!

PATRICK: I know, I know. . . . *(A bit shame-facedly.)* That's why I called in Brother Leo to take my geography class for me and—I followed him. . . . *(It is an agonizing confession.)*

FRANK: *(Warmly, concerned for the brother.)* And so you followed him? . . .

PATRICK: Through the village, always stayin' at least two huts back. . . . *(He looks at FRANK as if reluctant to continue.)*

FRANK: And—?

PATRICK: Those graves? By the swamp? By the grove of pandanus?

FRANK: Yes?

PATRICK: He stopped there. He sat on one. Just a little rectangle of smooth black stones, filled in with bits of white coral. No gravestone—but a little boy's grave. . . . Davey spoke to it. I was too far away to hear. Then he would listen, sort of. And, of a sudden, he would laugh. Then listen. And speak. And listen. And laugh. And so it went, for almost an hour. . . . Then he came home. . . . *(A longish pause.)* I'm that worried about him.

(FRANK *and* LU'ISA *exchange a look.* LU'ISA *is beginning to smile.*)

LU'ISA: Exactly why, Brother? Because he pretended he had a headache, or because he talked to an imaginary friend?
PATRICK: Ah, but not just an imaginary friend. A dead child. A little boy. His age. . . . A little boy named Veni.

(The smile goes from LU'ISA *instantly.)*

FRANK: How do you know that? You said there was no gravestone.
PATRICK: After David left, I went to the nearest hut and asked about the grave. One of the men spoke a little English, and an old woman there said it was her sister's son's grave. Died very many years ago. Long before David was born.
LU'ISA: Veni's no dark secret, Brother. I know about him.
PATRICK: You do!
LU'ISA: Of course. Davey prattles about him all the time.
PATRICK: *(Almost disappointed.)* You know!
LU'ISA: Why ever not? Davey shares his games with me . . . with both of us.
PATRICK: And you're not worried that his friend is a dead child?
DAVID: *(Stepping out onto the porch.)* Mommy . . .

(A pause from the others. How much has the boy heard?)

LU'ISA: Yes, Dearest?
DAVID: Uncle Lilo is here. . . . He's in the kitchen with cook. He brought some fish for the dinner tonight.
LU'ISA: *(Moving to him.)* How lovely! . . . Excuse me, Brother.
DAVID: And the Japanese lanterns are hanging everywhere in the front porch and the men are stringing them along the road. . . . (LU'ISA *is moving him back into the house.*) Can I help the men light them tonight, when it's time? And it doesn't rain?
LU'ISA: Of course, of course, now come along.

(And they are gone. PATRICK *is staring after them in great concern.* FRANK *moves for his drink.)*

FRANK: Jesus, Brother, it can't be all that bad. You've hardly touched your drink.

PATRICK: He was at the door so suddenly. . . . Did he hear me telling?

FRANK: Of course not! And what if he did! . . . Come on. Down the hatch. *(He has the bottle ready to pour.)*

PATRICK: Yes. *(He empties his glass.* FRANK *pours.)* Thank you. (FRANK *keeps pouring.)* Oh, thank you, thank you very much. Ta. Plenty. *(The glass is brimming.)*

FRANK: *(With a grin.)* It's Christmas! *(He holds up his drink.)* Noel!

PATRICK: Yes, yes. . . . Cheers.

*(*FRANK *drinks.* PATRICK *has put his drink down.* FRANK *finishes, notices that* PATRICK *is deep into himself, staring at the tabletop.)*

FRANK: Hey—hey. . . . Come on. . . . Drink up.

*(*PATRICK *takes a halfhearted sip, puts the glass down.)*

FRANK: Christ, man, Lu'isa and I aren't worried about him. . . . *(He comes to* PATRICK*'s side, sits.)*

PATRICK: When he was sitting on that grave, he wasn't—he wasn't talking and laughing, as I said. . . . I was lying, God forgive me. . . . He leaned his head down against his knees and cried. . . . Sobs. . . . His whole body shook. . . . It was like my own heart would break for him. I wanted to go to him. . . . I couldn't.

FRANK: Why not?

*(*PATRICK *only shakes his head.)*

PATRICK: I—just—couldn't. . . . Something stopped me. . . . I suppose it was just that I didn't want to embarrass him.

(He stops. And now, very slowly, he drinks. FRANK *watches in gathering concern. Then he rises and moves away thoughtfully.* PATRICK *remains pensively intent on his glass.)*

FRANK: Why? Why did you lie?

PATRICK: Mrs. Kreber . . . I did not want to frighten her.

FRANK: Lu'isa doesn't frighten as easy as all that.

PATRICK: *(A moment; softly.)* It isn't normal behavior in a boy.

(FRANK *takes the decanter, refills his glass. As he pours:*)

FRANK: I don't know what upset him yesterday, but a small boy playing on an old grave—laughing—okay, crying, whatever he was doing—is—that isn't so unusual here. . . . Hell, these people bury their dead almost under the eaves of their huts. On moonlight nights, they like to move their sleeping mats outside, beside their dead, on them even, and visit, and sing. . . . I've even seen them make love there. . . . Their dead are family. . . . There's nothing morbid about it, or anything like that. . . . David was raised with all that around him, all his young life. . . . Davey's part of that kind of thing. It can't be avoided, I guess. *(Smiles.)* It's part of the fun of growing up half-savage! . . . So, thank you for your concern, and—uh—let's forget the whole thing. . . . *(He gestures to* PATRICK's *drink.)* Come on, I'm too far ahead of you. . . .

PATRICK: *(Rising.)* No, no . . . I've had enough. Thank you. I'd better get on with our Latin.

FRANK: Must you? It's Christmas Eve. . . .

PATRICK: Yes, yes. Must. . . . You see, *(conspiratorially)* Davey is planning a little surprise for tonight. . . . Shhhh! *(He steps away from his chair and totters. He steadies himself against the table, as* FRANK *reaches for him.)* No no, I'm all right.

(LILO, LU'ISA's *younger brother by four years, comes out from the house. Once a muscular athlete, the years have been rather kind; the fat is a thin patina over the stocky, rugby-player frame. A very likable, boyishly charming man, more Samoan in appearance than his sister. He has a nicely wrapped Christmas present with him—obviously a bottle—and he is speaking as he hurries out the doorway.*)

LILO: Frank—guess what I've just— *(He stops on the porch, noticing* PATRICK.) Oh, hello, Brother Pat. *(He comes off the porch and to the table center stage.)* No one told me you were here. I should've guessed, of course.

PATRICK: *(Vaguely defensive.)* I was invited, you see. . . .

LILO: Delighted, delighted! A Merry Christmas to you, Brother! *(He holds out his hand.)*

PATRICK: And the same—the same to you. . . .

LILO: Am I interrupting?

FRANK: Brother Pat was just going inside.

LILO: Oh, by all means— *(He steps aside with a little deferential gesture.)*

PATRICK: *(Mumbling.)* Latin. . . . Excuse me. . . .

(FRANK watches PATRICK make his unsteady way to the porch door and into the house; he shakes his head slowly in sympathy. LILO watches, too, amused.)

LILO: *(Irish brogue.)* Ah, but it's a heart-warmin' thing to see what solitary masturbation can do to a man! *(Regular voice.)* I brought you a Christmas present. *(He puts the bottle down on the table.)*

FRANK: What is it?

LILO: A Bible! What the hell do you think it is?

FRANK: *(Picking up the present to open it.)* May I?

LILO: If you don't, I will.

(FRANK opens the present. A neat man. It is a bottle of cognac. Meanwhile:)

LILO: Guess what I just heard, in the village: The boat's been sighted, up the coast, above Poloa. . . .

FRANK: Above Poloa? *(LILO nods.)* That much off course! No wonder they're so late. . . .

LILO: Yes.

FRANK: Well—that means they'll be here in—what? A coupla hours?

LILO: At the very most. Ocean's smooth as glass.

(The bottle of cognac is now fully revealed. FRANK holds it in both hands.)

FRANK: Jesus Christ in heaven, man! Where did you get this?

LILO: Radioman First Class Bellini. At the wireless station.

FRANK: You getting friendly with Bellini? *(Begins to fold the wrapping paper neatly.)*

LILO: He has his uses. And I fascinate him.

FRANK: Oh? How?

LILO: Conceiving of an articulate gorilla is quite within the reach of his imagination. . . . But with a cultivated English accent? *(Chuckles.)* I'm a source of infinite wonder to him!

FRANK: Be careful. You might send the poor gink to the hoosegow.

LILO: How?

FRANK: Being so open about who supplies you with liquor. Violation of the Volstead Act—prohibition is prohibition—and that goes for Bellini, too.

LILO: Who'll arrest him? He supplies half the officers on the naval base. . . . And if you're really a good boy, you'll be invited to the Governor's New Year's Cocktail Party, catered by guess who?

(FRANK *has unwrapped the bottle of cognac completely, set it on the table, and is now at the table downstage right looking for something.*)

LILO: What are you looking for?

FRANK: A glass. . . . For you. (*There isn't one on the table. He moves to the steps.*) I'll get you one.

LILO: No, no. I'll use this one. (*He takes* PATRICK'*s.*) Brother Pat's?

FRANK: I'll get you a clean one.

LILO: No, no. I'll just rinse it out with a little germicide here. . . . (*He pours a good slosh of whiskey into the glass, swirls it around.*) Bellini told me something shocking this morning.

FRANK: What?

(LILO *tosses off the whiskey.* FRANK, *who has poured cognac for himself, now pours for* LILO.)

LILO: Do you have any idea how many Western Samoans, half-castes included, have been exiled in the last three years?

FRANK: Twenty or so? . . .

LILO: Almost two hundred!

FRANK: How does Bellini know that?

LILO: Governor's report to Washington. Bellini sent it out. . . . Three New Zealand commissioners in succession, each one more arrogantly tyrannical than the previous one. . . . Why, Frank? I grew up in New Zealand, went to school there. Lovely people. . . . I don't think I've ever been so happy. . . . I've never known such fair-mindedness . . . such simple decency. . . . What changes them, Frank?

FRANK: It's a disease all white men catch when they live away from home.

LILO: And what's that?

FRANK: They get scared.

LILO: Of?

FRANK: They're afraid you might become their equal. . . . It's a funny thing: they can handle your superiority, when you are superior. . . . Talent is talent, brains is brains, and they have to be acknowledged, no matter how reluctantly. . . . Just yesterday I heard a white officer refer to a young Samoan teacher, with some admiration, as "a fuckin' smart nigger." . . . But equality—? Uh-huh. In—oh. Never, not ever, not in a million years . . .

LILO: Frank, is there any truth to the rumor that you're really an albino Samoan?

FRANK: Gospel truth!

LILO: Let's drink to that!

FRANK: Good idea! *(He raises his glass.)* Here's to Senator Volstead. May he be pickled in panther's piss some day.

LILO: Loud cheers!

(They drink.)

FRANK: Lord! This stuff is worth breaking the law for!

LILO: *(Softly.)* Hallelujah!

(They drink again. A silent moment of deep appreciation.)

FRANK: You tell Lu'isa about the boat?

LILO: Hm?

FRANK: Tamasese. The boat. Lu'isa know?

LILO: Oh, I told her. When I gave her the fish. She's almost out of her mind with excitement. *(He shakes his head, amused.)* It's amazing, it really is!

FRANK: What really is?

LILO: She's in the dining room, helping the housegirls set the table, and she's going on and on about her dear, dear cousin, Tamasese.

FRANK: She cares about him. Very much!

LILO: Eight generations ago, maybe nine, we shared a common ancestor, but to hear her in that room, she and Tamasese sucked at the same tit as kids, this morning! . . . Lu'isa's how old?

FRANK: My lips are sealed.

LILO: Thirty-nine! . . . Tamasese is twenty-eight, for God's sake! (FRANK *only smiles.*) But the amazing thing, what makes me almost bonkers, is—well, she has the seating arrangement at table to her satisfaction—Tamasese, of course, to her right—but she's completely forgotten that the man has a wife and three little children! There're no places for them at the table. The children are too little, all right, feed them in the kitchen with Davey. Separately. But Frank, you won't believe it, there's no place at table for Ala, Tamasese's wife! . . . And when I called it to her attention, Lu'isa turned beet red. Blushed! Blushed, mind you. At her age! . . . Like a little girl.

(A moment. LILO *just shakes his head. He drinks.* FRANK *joins him.)*

FRANK: What's she like, the wife?
LILO: Very young. Very beautiful. If she were a man, she would be him.
FRANK: And the kids?
LILO: Two boys. Bit younger than Davey . . . seven . . . eight. . . . Bright. . . . A bit too quiet for my taste. . . . Perfect little gentlemen. . . . The third is a little girl, not yet two, I think.

(Another pause.)

FRANK: Be nice for Davey. The two boys. They do speak English?
LILO: The older one does, a little. After six months in New Zealand, probably quite a lot now.
FRANK: I hope they stay a while. Davey needs the companionship.
LILO: Davey's got a village full of boys to play with.
FRANK: It's not the same thing. I mean, his English. Sometimes you worry about his English. . . . He'll be going away to school, in a couple of years. . . .
LILO: Good Lord, Frank, the boy speaks beautiful English!
FRANK: Still, you worry about his falling behind. . . . *(Quietly.)* I worry sometimes about his running around the village so much, night and day, like any other native kid. . . . I mean, he comes home from school, off go his pants, on goes a lavalava, and he's out of the house. . . .

*(*FRANK *doesn't notice* LILO*'s upraised eyebrows. But this is an old plaint.* LILO *is resigned to it.)*

LILO: *(With a sigh.)* Tamasese's kids are always impeccably dressed: wide-collared little white shirts, English schoolboy jackets, matching pants, knee-length proper stockings, and unscuffed, shined leather boots. Oh . . . and perfectly folded little handkerchiefs, right here . . . *(He points to his left shirt pocket.)*

FRANK: *(A quiet demurrer.)* Christ, I don't mean for the boy to turn into a sissy, Lilo. . . .

LILO: *(Easily.)* Tamasese's kids love football. And scraped shins. And they're not afraid of bloody noses, Frank. . . . *(A moment.)* Davey's taking after his mother more and more every day. . . . He needs games. . . .

FRANK: Oh, he gets enough of that over with the Brothers. . . . Seems to me every time I go by the school, they're either reciting catechism or kicking hell out of a ball. . . .

LILO: *(Quietly.)* He needs *you*, Frank.

(FRANK *is silent. Before he can answer,* DAVID *and* PITO *come out the door. David has a box of matches and he is nicely dressed for dinner.*)

DAVID: Papa, Mommy said we can light the lanterns now. The yardmen are doing the front.

FRANK: Sure, son, go ahead.

(DAVID *crosses to the upstage left corner of the porch. As he goes, followed by* PITO:)

DAVID: And Mommy wants Uncle Lilo to come clean the fish.

LILO: At your service.

(LILO *goes on drinking.* DAVID *climbs up to the railing and, supported and steadied by* PITO, *moves along the line of paper lanterns, lighting them with the matches. Meanwhile:*)

FRANK: What about the Latin?

DAVID: Brother Pat fell asleep.

FRANK: Poor guy must be tired.

DAVID: *(Casually, almost airily.)* No, just squiggly-boo.

FRANK: Squiggly-boo?

DAVID: Blotto!

(FRANK *and* LILO *exchange a grin.* LILO *makes an elaborate, open-armed "Oh, what the hell" gesture with the bottle of cognac. Then he pours for himself and* FRANK.)

LILO: So much for language worries! *(He raises his glass to* FRANK.) Squiggly-boo!

(They drink, emptying their glasses. LILO *rises.)*

LILO: Fish guts, here I come. *(He heads for the steps and the door.)*
FRANK: *(Calling after him.)* I'll check on Brother Pat.
LILO: Right.

(LILO *goes into the house.* FRANK *has gotten up. He places the whiskey decanter, the bottle of cognac, and the two glasses on the tray. Then he watches* DAVID *lighting the paper lanterns.* DAVID *knows he is being watched but pretends not to notice. . . . Deeply thoughtful,* FRANK *picks up the tray and goes into the house. Now, as he goes,* DAVID *watches him, thoughtful himself. Then he moves to finish lighting the lanterns, as* PITO *exits into the house. The stage lights change slowly from late afternoon to dusk. The Japanese lanterns are the garden's main illumination, although now the kerosene lanterns in the house go on as well. . . . Out of the dusk, the* WRITER *moves onstage.)*

WRITER: Night comes swiftly to our island. And in our village, days end in vivid sunsets: russets and pinks, greens and yellows and gold—gold everywhere across our village sky—a brief, breath-wrenching awe in our eyes and in our hearts. Then twilight, when the nesting birds yield their voices to the gathering silence.

(A bird chirp or two.)

WRITER: And then the cicadas.

(Cicadas are heard. The WRITER *listens for a few moments.)*

WRITER: Then there is quiet—except for the distant breaking of the surf near the fringing reef.

(The cicadas fade to silence. From a great distance, the soft, dull, irregular boom of the surf.)

WRITER: In the huts, those villagers who owned mirrors covered them with cloth—especially if there was a moon—for the glitter of glass, especially moon-struck glass, brought the dead out of their graves, searching for their human images—*us*—their children—their grandchildren's children—their otherness which is themselves. . . . In the old days, this was a time for prayer, appeasing them. In my boyhood, we gathered in our thatch-roofed Samoan hut across the road, by the seashore, for vespers. Uncle Lilo, Pito, cook, the housegirls, the men of our native family who helped in the yard, and did the fishing, and worked the taro and banana patches back in the hills behind the village . . . and me. Everybody in our family . . .

(DAVID *has finished lighting the lanterns and has gone into the house; the porch is empty.*)

WRITER: . . . except my father and mother. They sat in the living room, reading by the light of the kerosene lamps with the beautiful shell shades. They did that every night, reading and listening to our prayers and our hymns.

(*A hymn, sung in Samoan, is heard softly in the distance.*)

WRITER: Every night of the year, but one . . . Christmas Eve . . . when, instead of vespers, we gathered in the back garden for our Nativity story. . . . (*He has moved onto the porch.*) At dusk, I lighted the candles on the Christmas tree. . . . (*He takes a box of matches from his pocket, lights some candles on the tree.*) And my mother and father came out, bringing two Bibles with them— one in English, one in Samoan—and Pito and I would bring good things to eat. . . . And Uncle Lilo brought the wine.

(*Out of the house comes* LU'ISA *with the Bibles and a red and green Christmasy tablecloth;* FRANK *is carrying a tray of liquor and tumblers, including the gift cognac. Behind them is* LILO, *carrying another tray with an ice bucket containing a bottle of wine, other bottles of wine, and several wine glasses. Then comes* PITO *with a tray of hors d'oeuvres; then* DAVID *with small glass dishes and forks and napkins.* LU'ISA *comes immediately to the table center stage, sets the Bibles aside, spreads the tablecloth.*)

WRITER: And we got ready for our reading. And my great Christmas surprise that I had been preparing so secretly during Latin lessons . . .

(FRANK *is with* LU'ISA *at the table center stage, setting down his tray. All the others are at the table downstage right with their things.*)

LU'ISA: David, David dear, bring that little vase of flowers, would you, Precious?

(From the table downstage right DAVID *brings a small vase of flowers to her.)*

WRITER: And on that night which we are now remembering, everything was specially wonderful. . . .

LU'ISA: Thank you, dearest. *(She takes the flowers from* DAVID, *puts them on the table center stage with the Bibles.)* Pito! Pito, fa'amole-mole ā. Alu e fesili pe 'ua iloa atu mōlī o le va'a.[11]

PITO: 'Ia. *(Goes into the house.)*

LILO: He should be coming around the point by now.

*(*FRANK *is pouring for* LILO *and himself.)*

LU'ISA: Pito will find out. *(To* DAVID.) Isn't it exciting, dear? In a little while, he'll be here, sitting with us. . . . *(Seeing* FRANK *hand* LILO *his drink.)* Do be careful, Frank. *(To* LILO:) Both of you. For once, try not to drink so much.

*(*BROTHER PATRICK *appears at the door in a kind of post-drunk funk.)*

LU'ISA: Ah, Brother! There you are! Come on, come on. . . . We'll have our Nativity reading the moment Pito comes back; she's gone to see about the boat. I'm sure it won't take much longer. *(She has gone to* PATRICK *and is leading him to a seat.)* Sit—sit down, Brother. Frank, what's come over you? Where is Brother Patrick's drink?

PATRICK: *(Mumbling.)* No, no . . . I think—

*(*FRANK *brings his own untouched drink to* PATRICK.)*

PATRICK: I—don't—think I had—better . . . *(But he takes the drink, submissively and a little disoriented.)* Thank you . . . thank you very much. . . . It's Christmas Mass, you see—early, very early in the morning . . . five-ish.

---

[11]LU'ISA: . . . Pito! Pito, please go and ask if the light of the boat can be seen.
PITO: Okay. *(Goes into the house.)*

(He trails off. FRANK *goes back to pour for himself anew.)*

FRANK: Hair of the dog, Brother. You'll feel better.

LUʻISA: And you mustn't go before Tamasese gets here. You *were* asked for dinner. . . .

PATRICK: *(Faintly.)* Yes. *(Tired, submissive, he sips his drink tentatively. He looks down at it pensively. Then he takes a huge swallow.)*

LILO: Feeling better?

PATRICK: Yes. Very much. Thank you.

LUʻISA: Well, then! Something for—? Ah, David, David, your glass! And Mommy's.

*(*DAVID *takes two glasses from the table.* LILO *takes wine from the table downstage right, pours a glass for* LUʻISA, DAVID *holding.)*

LUʻISA: Good heavens, Frank! The tree! The candles aren't all lighted!

*(*FRANK *takes matches from his pants pocket, goes to the tree, and, during the following, lights the rest of the candles. He has his drink with him.)*

LUʻISA: Davey, Davey, shame on you, Precious! You didn't light all of the candles, like you were supposed to. . . . And Lilo, I meant to ask: Does Tamasese smoke?

LILO: How should I know?

LUʻISA: Well, you do see him for days at a stretch over in Upolu, spend hours talking politics. Don't you notice? *(*DAVID *brings her a glass of wine.)* Ta.

*(*DAVID *goes back for his own glass, which* PITO *is now filling, one-half wine and one-half water from a carafe on the table downstage right. Meanwhile:)*

LILO: Come to think of it, I've never seen him smoke.

LUʻISA: Well, just to be sure: Frank, you will see that there are cigarettes? One of the boys can run to the store.

(But FRANK *has gone around to the upstage side of the Christmas tree and hasn't heard.)*

LUʻISA: Frank . . . Frank!

FRANK: *(Coming around into view.)* Hm? What is it?

LU'ISA: We'll need cigarettes. For Tamasese.

FRANK: Oh? (*To* LILO:) He smokes?

LILO: I rather think he doesn't.

FRANK: I see. Well . . . (*To* LU'ISA:) in that case, I'll send one of the boys to the store. (*She stops, for* PITO *has hurried out from the house.*)

PITO: Lu'isa . . . 'E lē 'o le va'a.[12]

(LU'ISA *hurries to her, concerned.*)

LU'ISA: 'O le ā?[13]

(LILO *too.*)

PITO: 'E lē 'o le va'a e fa'apea e sau ai Tamasese! 'O le va'a a Sitafenē. . . . (LILO *steps to her.*) 'Ua alu sa'o 'i Fagatogo.[14]

(LILO *hurries into the house. Stunned, hurt, in quick-rising anguish,* LU'ISA *stumbles against a porch post.*)

LU'ISA: (*Weakly.*) Frank!

(*From the Christmas tree,* FRANK *rushes to her.*)

FRANK: What is it?

(*But she is fighting tears;* FRANK*'s arms are around her.* FRANK *looks over to* DAVID *for help.*)

DAVID: (*Near tears himself.*) It wasn't Cousin Tamasese's boat. . . . It was old Captain Steffany's copra schooner, and it went right by —going to town . . .

(BROTHER PATRICK *is on his feet, feeling very awkward and out of place.* PITO *takes* LU'ISA *from* FRANK *and brings her to the table center*

---

[12]PITO: Lu'isa . . . The boat is not there.

[13]LU'ISA: What?

[14]PITO: That's not the boat that Tamasese is coming on! That's Steffany's boat. . . . (LILO *steps to her.*) It went straight to Fagatogo.

stage, where LUʻISA *sits, barely able to control her disappointment.* FRANK *hurries into the house. . . . During the following, the stage lights go from twilight to full night.)*

WRITER: We never had our Nativity Story reading that night. . . . The surprise I had worked for so many weeks to perfect was a translation of the Nativity Story into Latin which I had made with Brother Patrick's help. . . . I never got to read it. I never even got to tell my mother and father what the surprise was. . . . And, in fact, at the time, I didn't think of it—not until some time after midnight when everyone was gone . . .

(As PITO *goes back into the house slowly and* BROTHER PATRICK *goes off at stage left,* DAVID *moves to the table center stage and, in silence, gathers the two Bibles up.* LUʻISA *has withdrawn utterly into herself, staring into the nothingness before her.)*

WRITER: . . . and we realized that he had passed us by—and would not come.

*(*DAVID *goes into the house with the Bibles.* LUʻISA *is alone at the table center stage, her face a mask of loss.)*

WRITER: Then, with the passing hours, the awful fear grew that now he would never, never come again. . . . Pito and I watched my mother from behind a window, and it was as if we were both afraid to breathe—as if, on the very night of his coming to us, his Death had come as well, and—faced with the fact of that Death, *our* Death, we had no right to breathe. . . . Pito wept softly as we watched, but I could not cry. . . .

*(*DAVID *comes out and stops on the porch, watching his mother. He has a small tray holding coffee things and a single cup.)*

WRITER: I remember that I wondered what my mother, so pale there in the garden, would look like, if she were dead. . . .

(He moves to the table center stage with the tray, sets it down there. LUʻISA *is hardly aware of his presence. As he goes:)*

WRITER: Well, my mother has been dead now for many years, and when I knelt down beside her coffin to kiss her and whisper goodbye, the face my lips touched was that face in that garden, on that fear-filled night.

(After a moment's silent look at his mother, DAVID *steps close and kisses her gently on the forehead. She lowers her head.)*

DAVID: *(Softly.)* Brother Patrick just drove back from town. . . .
LU'ISA: Then—there's word—?
DAVID: Brother Patrick's coming. . . . Pito thought you would like some coffee. . . . It's after four o'clock. . . . It's almost morning, Mommy.

*(*LU'ISA *numbly registers the fact of the coffee tray.)*

DAVID: Do you want me to pour some for you—?

*(*LU'ISA *reaches out and touches the boy's face with great tenderness.)*

LU'ISA: *(Silently forming the words with her mouth.)* No, thank you . . . Precious. . . .

*(*DAVID *goes to the side, sits, always regarding his mother.)*

WRITER: And I think it was that night, too, that I first began to wonder if, in all of the world, in all of Life, since the beginning and to the end of Time, there were things that were so infinitely fragile that one could never, ever, speak them.

*(*BROTHER PATRICK *comes out of the house. He is no longer drunk, but he is physically and emotionally drained.)*

PATRICK: Mrs. Kreber . . . *(He comes to the table center stage, nodding his head at* DAVID *as he goes by.)* I can't stay but a little . . . Mass is at five . . . but I promised Mr. Kreber I would see how you were.
LU'ISA: Frank didn't come with you?
PATRICK: No, he and your brother are still in town, at the wireless station. . . . Oh, it's a mob there, around the wireless set, all trying to hear the news through that squeaking and wailing and meowing. . . .

(Pause. LU'ISA *and* DAVID *wait intently.)*

PATRICK: Tamasese has arrived in Apia. There are thousands of people lining the shore, welcoming the dear man and his wife and little ones home. . . .
LU'ISA: Was there—trouble?

PATRICK: He and his family were driven away from the wharf by some chiefs, through the crowds. . . . Nothing happened.

LU'ISA: Oh, I'm glad. . . . Will you have some coffee, Brother? *(He gestures vaguely toward the liquor tray.)* Help yourself.

PATRICK: *(Pouring himself a—for him—modest drink.)* Mr. Kreber and your brother will stay in town, at the wireless station, all day, for more news. . . . They let me use the car for the morning. . . . I'll be going back after Mass. . . .

LU'ISA: Yes. Of course.

(He drinks. The glass is quickly emptied.)

LU'ISA: Were there many government soldiers at the wharf? Did they say on the wireless?

PATRICK: No. . . . No, the wireless didn't say. . . . Besides, the wireless called them police, not soldiers.

LU'ISA: Oh. . . . Were there many police, then, anywhere?

PATRICK: The wireless didn't say. *(Helps himself to another drink.)* But even if there were, by the hundreds, I don't think there would've been trouble. . . . Not with the thousands of our people there.

LU'ISA: Our people. . . . You said, Our people!

PATRICK: *(Embarrassed.)* Oh. . . . Well—one comes to identify . . . I meant no impertinence, Mrs. Kreber. . . . It is just that—one is with the village children so much. . . .

LU'ISA: *(Touched.)* What a good and loving man you are, dear Brother Patrick.

PATRICK: Oh . . . *(He raises a protesting hand as if to ward off the compliment.)*

LU'ISA: You love young people. It shows.

PATRICK: *(Softly.)* Thank you. . . . *(He puts his empty glass down carefully—pointedly?—by the whiskey.)*

LU'ISA: Do help yourself, Brother.

PATRICK: Yes. Thank you. *(He pours another drink.)*

LU'ISA: It must've been very colorful. . . . Was there music?

PATRICK: I could hear a brass band in the distance.

LU'ISA: *(With quiet, sentimental joy.)* Oh, that band! That beautiful handsome band with their purple turbans and white shirts and blue lavalavas with the single yellow stripe along the hem. . . . David, they have the most imposing cornet player: a large powerful man, with only one eye and such a proud imperious walk—proud of his cornet playing—and it was *awful*. Loud.

Blaring. Off the beat. Wrong note everywhere. But it isn't funny, David. . . . No one laughs. . . . It is—awesome. . . .

(DAVID *smiles, stifles a yawn, doesn't answer; he is quite sleepy.*)

PATRICK: I know. Mata'utia. . . . Mata'utia Karaune. . . . He's the Secretary of the Mau, David . . . a brave man.

LU'ISA: *(Impressed.)* You know him, Brother?

PATRICK: Everyone in Apia—in all of Upolu, everywhere—knows him. . . . *(A chuckle.)* You cannot play the cornet so much like a bleating goat and be so proud of it—and not be famous, Mrs. Kreber. . . .

LU'ISA: You—you've lived in Western Samoa, then?

PATRICK: Yes . . . in Apia . . . I taught at the Brothers School there. . . .

LU'ISA: For how long, Brother?

PATRICK: Until I came here last year. . . . Ten years. . . . Since 1918.

LU'ISA: *(Even more impressed.)* Since 1918! . . . Then you were there during that frightening epidemic?

PATRICK: The influenza. Yes. I was assigned to Vaimoso. We all helped. With the dying.

LU'ISA: David, David—a New Zealand High Commissioner—the first one—knowingly allowed a ship with sick people on it to come to Apia from Auckland. . . . They made a few other people sick and the sickness spread and David, David, one out of every five people in Western Samoa died as a result. . . . Every High Commissioner has been heartless, David, heartless!

(*This is the most animated she has become since* DAVID *entered with the coffee. But it drives her to the edge of tears again, and her voice breaks, and she has to stop. She averts her face, hand to her mouth, pushing the threat of sobs back.* DAVID *goes to her immediately, reaches for her.*)

DAVID: Mommy—!

LU'ISA: *(Taking his hand in hers.)* No, no, I'm all right. *(She struggles to be all right; but the fear keeps rising.)*

DAVID: Mommy—please, don't . . . *(And rising.)* Please, don't, Mommy . . . Brother!

(BROTHER PATRICK *moves to her.*)

LU'ISA: They're going to kill him, Brother. . . . I know it . . .

PATRICK: No no . . .

LU'ISA: I know it. . . . They are awful, they are awful people. . . .

PATRICK: No . . . no . . .

(And she fights it out. BROTHER PATRICK *lets her, signaling* DAVID *away.* DAVID *backs off, sits on the bench at stage left. Then* BROTHER PATRICK *himself moves away. He finishes the last swallow from his drink.* LU'ISA *is calmer.)*

PATRICK: Are you all right, then? *(She nods.)* Are you sure?

LU'ISA: Yes yes. . . . It'll be time for your Mass soon. . . . *(A moment longer and she is calm.)* Pray for us, Father.

PATRICK: *(A slight smile.)* Brother.

LU'ISA: Brother and Father . . . and friend. . . . Good, good, dear friend.

PATRICK: Well then . . . I'd better be off. *(He puts his glass down.)* I'll drop in again in the morning—before I take the car back to Mr. Kreber.

LU'ISA: All right.

PATRICK: Well then, goodnight. . . . Goodnight, David.

LU'ISA: Goodnight.

DAVID: *(Together.)* Goodnight, Brother.

(BROTHER PATRICK *is almost off at left when he is stopped by:)*

LU'ISA: Brother . . . (PATRICK *looks back.)* Thank you for taking the time.

PATRICK: God bless and keep you both, Mrs. Kreber.

(He goes off. DAVID *moves to watch him go. The lanterns begin to die out, singly and randomly. In the distance, the church bells begin to ring.* DAVID *moves back to the bench at downstage left and sits. He is lost in his own thoughts. Finally he looks over at his mother. The* WRITER *moves in by* DAVID.)

WRITER: Then the bells in the Catholic church began to ring for early Christmas Mass. . . .

DAVID: *(Quietly, at a loss for what else to say.)* Merry Christmas, Mommy . . .

(LU'ISA *is fast withdrawing into herself again.)*

LU'ISA: *(Very softly.)* Merry Christmas, my precious.

(And they are silent and still, as the lanterns continue to die out.)

WRITER: And so we sat, the bells ringing throughout the remaining hour of darkness, and the lanterns dying out in the pre-dawn chill.

(The lanterns keep dying out. Then the stage lighting fades. And we are in darkness.)

Scene Two

(It is early morning. The table center stage and the table downstage right have been cleared. Flower arrangements are now neatly placed every-where. LU'ISA is removing candles and ornaments from the tree, cartons beside her. The WRITER enters from downstage left, watches LU'ISA a moment or two, then addresses the audience.)

WRITER: Such was the sameness of our village days that most of us, without clocks or calendars, seldom knew the hour of day, or sometimes the day itself. . . . There were the nights, with their differing moons; and the days, with the sun's arcing move from sunrise to sunset. That was Time—a concept for which we had no word in our language. We named the days by their events, and as they receded from memory, the events were forgotten, and the days became nameless again.

But sometimes, after Christmas, in the early weeks of the new year, violent, twisting winds would move down upon us from the northwest. Hurricanes. The tearing and smashing would last a day, two, three; there would be the ugly wounds everywhere. Then root and seed and human hands would do their healing work, and all would be well again. But we knew that they would return, those violences. That was the surest certainty in our living: sooner or later, the raging winds would come.

And so, very often, in the last days of the dying year, it was as if each hour held its breath and clung to what it could hold of sunshine, and gentle breezes, and a calm that seemed to fall from the sky over land and sea.

Such a day was the twenty-seventh of December, the last Saturday of the year, 1929.

(He sits on the bench downstage left and watches PITO come out of the house and go to LU'ISA.)

PITO: E 'aumai se kofe po 'o sau kī?[1]

LU'ISA: Leai, fa'afetai. 'A e fa'apēfea 'outou? 'Ua fai se tou mea'ai o le tāeao?

PITO: 'Ua 'uma.

LU'ISA: 'A e ā David?

PITO: Ga 'a'ai fa'akasi ma Lilo. 'O lelā 'e sui o lā 'ofu 'e ō ai e fāgogoka ma le felela. (She has moved over beside LU'ISA.)

LU'ISA: Sau. Sau 'i le itū lea. Fesoasoani mai.

PITO: 'Ia. (She goes around to the side of the tree opposite LU'ISA and helps with the dismantling.)

LU'ISA: 'O fai i fea le lātou faiva?

PITO: I gakai o Sogi . . . le mea fo'i lea e keu ai le va'a a Lilo.

LU'ISA: 'Ua sāuni se lātou mea'ai e 'ave?

PITO: 'O saguisi ma le sālaki pakeka, ma le fagu vai kīpolo. . . . Ga sau le felela ma lana ia lava fagu. . . . 'O le igu ia o lea kamāloa. . . . 'Aiseā?

LU'ISA: (Preoccupied.) Pau ā.

PITO: Pei 'ua pala le fai'ai.

(LILO comes out of the house. He wears a tattered old shirt, old lavalava, slippers, and a frayed coconut leaf hat. He has an old pair of dungarees over one shoulder and is holding a needle and thread.)

LU'ISA: Good morning, Sleepyhead!

LILO: Morning . . . Frank up yet? (He is crossing over in the rear to the porch corner where PITO sits.)

---

[1] PITO: Should I bring some coffee or tea?

LU'ISA: No, thank you. What about all of you? Have you had breakfast?

PITO: We're done.

LU'ISA: What about David?

PITO: He ate with Lilo. Then he changed his clothes to go fishing with the priest. (She has moved over beside LU'ISA.)

LU'ISA: Come, come to this side. Help me.

PITO: Okay. (She goes around to the side of the tree oppsite LU'ISA and helps with the dismantling.)

LU'ISA: Where did they go fishing?

PITO: To the ocean at Sogi . . . that's where Lilo's boat is kept.

LU'ISA: Did they take some food?

PITO: Some sandwiches, potato salad, and a bottle of lime juice. The priest came with his bottle. He drinks too much. Why?

LU'ISA: (Preoccupied.) That's the way it is.

PITO: His brain must be rotten.

LU'ISA: Good heavens, he's been in town since dawn. . . . Aren't you interested?

LILO: Of course I am. . . . Piko, fa'amolemole ā, sio'u kigā, su'i le muli o lo'u 'ofuvae.[2] *(He hands* PITO *trousers, needle, and thread across the porch rail.)*

PITO: Makua'i makagā lou guku.

LILO: When's he coming back?

LU'ISA: Midmorning, he said.

PITO: Va'ai 'oe, 'ua 'ou makua. 'E vaivai o'u maka. *(She hands needle and thread back to him.)* Kui e 'oe le filo. 'E lē 'o a'u sau kāvigi.[3]

*(*LILO *takes the needle and thread. He smiles pointedly, sweetly, at her.)*

LILO: *(Syrup.)* You are a mean-hearted, nasty-minded, foul-breathed, fart-faced old witch!

PITO: *(Absolutely delighted.)* Fao'afekai![4]

*(*LILO *tries to thread the needle.)*

LILO: I live in dire fear that one of these days we'll discover that Pito has understood English all these years, ever since we were children.

LU'ISA: She would have murdered you before you were twelve. . . . You were perfectly awful to her as a little boy. Do you know that?

LILO: I was a model child. *(He is busy trying to thread the needle.)*

LU'ISA: It's good of you to give up your Saturday morning like this, Lilo.

LILO: I like fishing, you may know that. And David needs to get out. He's bored silly.

*(*PITO *reaches over, across the rail, and grabs his wrist.)*

---

[2]LILO: . . . Pito, please bring me tea, sew the back of my pants. *(He hands* PITO *trousers, needle, and thread across the porch rail.)*
PITO: What an ugly mouth.

[3]PITO: See here, can't you see I'm old. My eyes are weak. *(She hands needle and thread back to him.)* Thread the needle. I'm not your slave.

[4]PITO: Thank you!

PITO: 'Aumai! *(She takes the needle and thread from him.)* 'E 'uma lo'u ōlaga 'o fa'akali 'oe.[5]

LILO: 'Aua ke popole, 'o lelā 'o fa'akali mai Ieova 'iā 'oe.

PITO: Guku guku guku. . . . Koe ikiiki lava o'u alu aku e su'i fa'amau.

(She threads the needle with the greatest ease, sews the trousers. DAVID *comes out of the house. He is dressed in an American Indian suit, complete with feather headdress and moccasins.)*

LU'ISA: Ah, good morning, Precious!

DAVID: Good morning.

LILO: *(The Indian war-whoop.)* Whowhowhowhowho . . .

*(*DAVID *comes to* LILO*'s side.)*

LU'ISA: Are you going fishing, or on the warpath?

LILO: Both. We are going to start with Pito's flea-bitten scalp.

PITO: Salapu lou guku! 'Aua le ka'u fua lo'u igoa.[6]

LU'ISA: Are you sure Brother Patrick won't be peeved at you, wearing his lovely Christmas gift to go fishing?

DAVID: He said it should be a—what?—a—?

LILO: —memorable—

DAVID: —memorable thing to do.

LILO: *(Raising his right hand, oath-taking.)* Honest Injun! I heard him say so. . . . Fa'avave, Piko.[7]

PITO: Lea 'ua koe ikiiki 'uma.

DAVID: I'm going to catch a dozen mackerel for lunch. Will Papa be back?

LU'ISA: He'll be back. Don't worry.

*(*PITO *continues sewing;* LILO *and* DAVID *wait.* LU'ISA *packs the Christmas things away. The* WRITER *faces the audience from the bench.)*

---

[5]PITO: Bring! *(She takes the needle and thread from him.)* I'll die if I wait for you.
LILO: Don't worry, Jehovah is waiting for you.
PITO: Mouth, mouth, mouth. . . . Pretty soon I will sew it shut.

[6]PITO: Shut up your mouth! Don't talk freely with my name.

[7]LILO: . . . Hurry up, Pito.
PITO: I'm almost done.

WRITER: Breakfast was over, and it was a good day for fishing. Mackerel were running, and the sea lay flat and still. A few girls searched along the reef for shellfood and octopus. . . . The village men were already in their hillside plantations, the older women in their huts, plaiting mats from dried pandanus leaves. Little boys went about their morning chores. Everywhere, copra was spread out to dry in the morning sun. . . . It was a morning, like every other morning, for hundreds and hundreds of years.

(PITO *hands the trousers over to* LILO, *who takes them and throws them over his shoulder. His other hand has caught and held* PITO*'s wrist.*)

LILO: Fa'afekai.[8]

(*And he kisses the old lady's hand. She touches his head affectionately. It is obvious that there is deep love between them.*)

PITO: 'E lē āfāiga.[9]

(LILO *puts an arm around* DAVID*'s shoulders and they go out at left.*)

WRITER: On such days, my Uncle Lilo would often take me up to the hills where we would look down on our village with its brown huts like mushrooms growing out of the brown sand, the palm trees waving, the big Catholic Church and even bigger Protestant Church blazing white in the sunshine, and the blue ocean stretching away, meeting the blue sky at the horizon, blue and blue. . . . And, as we looked down, my Uncle Lilo would say, "Well, David, it all goes to show what God can do when he sets his mind to it."

We did not know that two hours earlier, over in Upolu, along the beachfront road in Apia, the sharp crack of a rifle shot had singled this day out forever in our lives and in the lives of those who would come after us.

(*The tree is completely dismantled, the ornaments packed away.*)

---

[8]LILO: Thanks

[9]PITO: No problem.

LU'ISA: 'Ave loa tā pusa ia, Pito, fa'amolemole.[10]
PITO: 'Aumai.

(As LU'ISA *piles the boxes of ornaments onto* PITO*'s outstretched arms,* FRANK *comes out of the house. The strain shows. He steps aside to let* PITO *go in with the boxes. The* WRITER *exits at left.)*

LU'ISA: You're back sooner than you said.
FRANK: *(Tiredly.)* The Apia radio shut down, right after the early morning report. *(He comes tiredly to the table center stage, sits, rubs his face with both palms slowly, keeping awake.)*
LU'ISA: Would you like some coffee?
FRANK: Not right now. I'll take a cup upstairs with me in a minute.

(LU'ISA *has come off the porch, sits in the yard.)*

LU'ISA: Well, what did the report say?
FRANK: There's some kind of parade going on in Apia . . . marching down Beach Road to the wharf to meet someone returning from exile in New Zealand on the *Lady Roberts.*
LU'ISA: Who?
FRANK: I don't know. Our radio reception in town was very bad. . . . Over a thousand marchers.
LU'ISA: Tamasese among them?
FRANK: Towards the rear. Faumuinā and Tuimaleali'ifano are in the lead. A peaceful parade. Official government okay. Music—bands—people cheering—and then the radio went on the blink. Or so the Apia announcer said. Transmission difficulties, he said. . . . Bellini thinks it's a lot of hooey.
LU'ISA: Why?
FRANK: He said he heard a coupla days ago about 85 percent of the people over in Upolu now belong to the Mau. Last thing the New Zealand Commissioner, Allen, wants to do right now is to give them so much publicity. . . . I think Allen just ordered the wireless station in Apia to shut down until the parade is over.
LU'ISA: And when will that be?
FRANK: Oh, another hour at the most.
LU'ISA: Will you be going back to town then?

---

[10]LU'ISA: Take this box, Pito, please.
PITO: Bring.

FRANK: No. They'll spend the rest of the day and weekend celebrating—feasting and church. . . . *(He tries to stifle a yawn.)*
LU'ISA: You should be upstairs. In bed.
FRANK: Yeah. *(A pause, another yawn.)* You want to come up?

(She stiffens, almost imperceptibly.)

FRANK: I need you.
LU'ISA: *(A quiet fact.)* I have things to do, Frank.

(Pause.)

FRANK: You can't go on fretting about his not showing up forever.
LU'ISA: *(As quietly as before.)* I really do have things to do. *(She rises.)* I'll see to your coffee. If there's anything else you need, I'll send Pito up.

(FRANK bursts into laughter.)

LU'ISA: What is so funny?
FRANK: What you just said. Sending Pito up for what I need.
LU'ISA: Oh! . . . *(Not a trace of humor.)* That isn't funny.
FRANK: *(Deflated.)* No. It isn't. . . . It is absolutely *not* funny, Lu'isa. *(He sighs, heads for the steps.)* Don't bother about the coffee. . . . I've changed my mind. I think I *will* go back to town, after all.
LU'ISA: David is bringing you a fish for lunch.

(FRANK stops.)

FRANK: What fish?
LU'ISA: He's gone fishing. The least you can do is share his catch at lunch. Besides, how do you know the wireless will be on again?
FRANK: I don't.
LU'ISA: Then, why go in—and run the risk of disappointing David also?
FRANK: Okay . . . you win. *(He sits.)*
LU'ISA: *(A little laugh.)* Good heavens, Frank! I don't want to win! It isn't a contest! *(She sits too, some distance away.)*
FRANK: *(Softly.)* No.

(There is a pause. PITO comes out for the last ornament boxes by the tree.)

FRANK: Lilo take David fishing?

LU'ISA: And Brother Pat.

FRANK: Oh? (*A moment.*) I wish there was some kid his age he could play with. . . .

LU'ISA: Davey has a whole villageful of boys his age to play with.

FRANK: I mean—in the house.

LU'ISA: (*Amused.*) In the house! . . . Good heavens, they'd be into everything like inquisitive little monkeys! What an idea!

FRANK: (*As if to himself.*) That isn't what I meant.

(*He yawns, obviously very sleepy.* PITO *looks at him.*)

PITO: Lu'isa! 'O le'a oki Falagi 'i le fia moe.[11]

LU'ISA: 'E ā lā?

PITO: Ō ia 'i lugā 'i le lua poku e fa'amoe si kamāloa.

(LU'ISA *is smiling.*)

FRANK: So, why the smile?

LU'ISA: (*Beginning to chuckle.*) Pito. . . . What she said.

(FRANK *can't suppress the beginning of a smile at her growing amusement.*)

FRANK: Well, what did she say?

LU'ISA: I won't tell.

(*He is now beginning to laugh along with her.*)

FRANK: Come on.

(*She shakes her head, getting somewhat coy.*)

FRANK: Why not?

LU'ISA: Because.

FRANK: Because why?

LU'ISA: Because you hate so to do anything she says.

---

[11] PITO: Lu'isa! Frank wants to go to bed.

LU'ISA: So what?

PITO: Go upstairs to your room and put him to sleep.

FRANK: Okay. So I promise I won't do it—whatever it is she said.

LUʻISA: *(Big, mock-serious relief.)* Oh good! Such a relief! Now we don't have to go upstairs to the bedroom and—

FRANK: She said that?

(She nods, then laughs briefly. He too. A pause.)

LUʻISA: She's getting very naughty.

(FRANK gets up, holds his hand out to her.)

FRANK: Come on.

(She rises, still smiling. She goes a few steps past him for the door.)

FRANK: Hey.

(She turns to face him, even as he is moving to her. He kisses her tenderly, a long kiss.)

LILO: *(Offstage.)* Pito! Pito!

(LUʻISA and FRANK break from their kiss and turn to left, where LILO's voice is heard again, closer.)

LILO: *(Offstage.)* Pito!

(And LILO runs in, agitated, from left. He is wearing the trousers. LUʻISA goes to him quickly.)

LUʻISA: Lilo, what is it?

LILO: Davey. He's been hurt! *(He goes past LUʻISA and FRANK for the door.)*

LUʻISA: Oh God!

FRANK: Hurt how?

LILO: Not badly. *(At the door, he calls inside—loudly.)* Pito! Sau! Faʻa-vave![12] *(He turns back to FRANK and LUʻISA.)* Well—badly—but not seriously.

FRANK: What happened?

---

[12]LILO: . . . Pito! Come! Quickly!

LU'ISA: (*Together with* FRANK.) How badly?
LILO: He's been hit by a rock. Here. (*He touches the left side of his head.*) He's bleeding a lot, but I don't think he's seriously hurt. . . . Brother Pat is bringing him.

(PITO *appears in the doorway.*)

PITO: 'O le ā?[13]

(*And before she is answered,* BROTHER PATRICK, *in old faded clothes, brings* DAVID *on from stage left. He uses* LILO's *lavalava, now quite bloody, to stem the flow of blood from the left side of* DAVID's *head.* DAVID *is still crying, not loudly, and more out of shock and confusion than hurt.*)

PITO: 'Oi, ka fēfē![14]

(*She hurries to* DAVID. LU'ISA *beats her to him. She grabs him.*)

LU'ISA: Oh, Precious . . . Precious.
PITO: (*To* LILO.) Ga lavea fa'afefea?[15]

(LU'ISA *keeps holding* DAVID *close. The fuss makes the boy cry more.*)

LILO: Ma'a.[16]
FRANK: (*To* BROTHER PATRICK.) What happened? (*He reaches for* DAVID.) Let go, Lu'isa. (*She keeps hanging on.*) Lu'isa!

(*He takes the boy from her, looking at the wound.* LU'ISA *looks anxiously to* BROTHER PATRICK *for an answer.*)

FRANK: Hush, David. (*Sharply.*) Hold still!
LU'ISA: Brother—?
PATRICK: A stone. . . . He got hit by a stone.

---

[13] PITO: What?

[14] PITO: Oh, my goodness!

[15] PITO: (*To* LILO.) How did he get hurt?

[16] LILO: A rock.

FRANK: *(Angry.)* Goddamn it, David, hold still.

(DAVID *cries even more.*)

LU'ISA: Frank, you're hurting him.

FRANK: *(Angrier.)* It isn't that bad! *(He straightens up.)* Pito! *(He hands the boy over to* PITO. *To* LU'ISA:*)* Get it cleaned. He just needs a bandage. I'll drive him over to the dispensary. . . . *(This doesn't sit well with* DAVID.) Oh, for Christ's sake, David, it isn't going to kill you! *(To* LU'ISA:*)* Hurry up!

(He gestures to PITO *to take the boy.* LU'ISA *reaches for* DAVID; *he burrows his head deeper against* PITO.)

PITO: *(Consolingly.)* Sau. . . . Kā ō. . . . 'Ua lava, 'ua lava. . . . 'O 'oe 'o le koa 'Igikia. . . . Sau loa. . . .[17]

(She takes the clinging boy into the house, LU'ISA *following and trying to hold* DAVID *by the shoulders; she is in the way.*)

PITO: *(Irritated.)* Ku'u 'ese ou lima![18]

(LU'ISA *withdraws as if slapped.* PITO *leads them inside.*)

FRANK: *(To* LILO, *seething.)* Well, what happened?
LILO: A lot of kids followed us. Two or three men.
PATRICK: It was the Indian suit, you see.
LILO: They were teasing. When we got to the boat shed, I went inside for the outboard . . .
PATRICK: . . . and the fishing rods. But I don't think it was—
FRANK: Brother, will you shut up and let him finish!

(Instant silence. Moments pass.)

LILO: *(Quietly.)* I don't know what happened, Frank.
FRANK: What the hell do you mean, "I don't know." You took the boy out; you're responsible. *(To* PATRICK:*)* Both of you.

---

[17]PITO: Come. . . . Let's go. . . . That's enough. . . . You are the brave Indian . . .

[18]PITO: Come now. . . . Take your hands away!

LILO: I was in the boat shed. I didn't see. Evidently some kid threw a stone, probably out of envy. But I don't know.

FRANK: Didn't you ask? Didn't you try to find out?

LILO: *(Exploding.)* Stop yelling at me, Frank. *I* didn't hurt Davey.

(Another pause. FRANK *turns from* LILO *to* BROTHER PATRICK.*)*

FRANK: *(Softly.)* I'm sorry. *(He turns upstage, collecting himself.)* Why —why the hell would another kid want to hurt little Davey? *(He turns back to* LILO.*)* Surely someone saw which kid threw the stone?

LILO: Our first reaction was to the blood running down Davey's face. We brought him away immediately. . . . I'll investigate later.

FRANK: *(Swallowing his returning rage.)* Damned savages!

LILO: *(Chiding softly.)* Frank!

FRANK: Well, what else? What else would you call them? Their goddamn parents are barely out of the Stone Age. . . . That's all they know. Stones. Settle everything with stones. That's the level of their mentality. *(He turns away again, as if to conceal his deeper feelings which are surfacing.)*

(Another pause.)

PATRICK: But, you see, it wasn't a little boy who threw the stone. It was a man.

FRANK: A man! A man threw a stone at Davey?

PATRICK: No. A man threw a stone—at me I think. It hit Davey instead.

LILO: Oh, Brother, no. I don't think so.

PATRICK: I saw him aim the stone at me.

FRANK: Why would anybody want to hurt you, of all people?

PATRICK: Some people don't really know the difference between a brother and a priest.

FRANK: What the hell does that mean?

PATRICK: Not every man in the village is a Catholic, Mr. Kreber. . . . Or likes us.

*(*LILO *and* FRANK *exchange a look. They need a moment to digest this.)*

LILO: You saw the man?

PATRICK: Yes.

LILO: Who was it? Do you know his name?

PATRICK: No.

LILO: Would you recognize him again?

PATRICK: I—don't think so. It happened so fast. He stepped out from behind a *milo* tree, by the water's edge, threw, and Davey was hit . . . and you were running from the shed . . . the confusion . . . and when I looked again he was gone.

LILO: One of the kids will know who it was.

PATRICK: I don't want to put in a complaint, Lilo.

FRANK: (*Shocked.*) You—*what*—?

PATRICK: I don't want to cause trouble, Mr. Kreber.

FRANK: Damn it, man, my kid's head's busted open . . .

PATRICK: It was an accident. (*To* LILO:) Trouble spreads . . . grows . . .

FRANK: (*Dumbfounded.*) I can't believe it. (*He gets up, shaking his head, his anger returning in redoubled force. He points a finger at* BROTHER PATRICK.) Okay, you listen to me. We're going to find that son of a bitch. And when we do, you are going to identify him for the police, and tell them what you've just told us. . . . (*A moment.*) Now, is that understood?

(BROTHER PATRICK *is silent;* LILO *turns away in embarrassment.*)

FRANK: Is that understood, Brother?

PATRICK: (*Very softly.*) Yes. But I really don't—

FRANK: (*Interrupting hard.*) And no buts about it. . . .

(*In the distance a sound of wailing is heard faintly. The men listen. As the sound grows—more people are joining in—and spreads, the* WRITER *enters from behind the plants and foliage at upstage left. He is very subdued.*)

FRANK: Now what the hell is that?

(*A moment. Listening. The* WRITER *is moving to downstage left.*)

LILO: Wailing. . . . Down by the dispensary. . . . Trouble. . . . Sounds bad. I'll go see. (*He goes out at left. The wailing grows.*)

PATRICK: Keening. . .

(*They listen as the wailing keeps growing. It is quite loud now.*)

WRITER: It was like Death moving through the whole village and to our house. . . . A runner came from the dispensary where the

radio operator in town had telephoned a message for my father.
. . . My mother was in the kitchen with Pito and the housegirls,
washing and bandaging my head. She met the young man at the
back door. He spoke through the screen. . . . "Lu'isa!" he cried.
" 'Ua momotu le 'ulā fala!" . . . "The princely garland of pandanus corms has been broken." . . . We knew immediately what
that meant. . . . Even I.

*(There is a scream—*LU'ISA*'s—from the far end of the house, followed
immediately by* PITO*'s and the* HOUSEGIRLS*' loud crying and wailing:
a hysteria of grief-stricken voices.)*

FRANK: What the hell—?

(He rushes into the house. BROTHER PATRICK *follows more slowly.)*

WRITER: Three hours earlier—at about 6:30 that morning—
Tamasese was shot.

*(*BROTHER PATRICK *hesitates at the door. He doesn't want to intrude.
He moves to leave, vaguely, stops, goes back to the door, looks in, listens.
The hysteria from the kitchen seems to overwhelm everything. Then it
begins to die down slowly.* BROTHER PATRICK *goes into the house very
slowly.)*

WRITER: In those days, our people expressed their grief with their
blood. When a loved one died, they would take a piece of coral
or a sharp stone and, using it for a knife, gash their faces, fore-
heads, arms, chests, until their blood streamed freely. The ulti-
mate gift of love. . . . And so, even as I cried out when my mother
screamed and fell against the sink, I knew what she was going to
do when she grabbed a green bottle and smashed it and held the
jagged neck in her hand. Even before her hand moved, I foresaw
that ravenous shark-toothed mouth rip at my mother's face, over
and over, and Love, red and red and red, everywhere, spilled all
over the walls and me. And then it was my father's hand, lifting
my mother's by the wrist, and when he had forced the bottle
fragment out of her hand, she started to scream and flail at him
with her fists, and I started to scream, and then it was Brother
Patrick holding me tight so that I couldn't run to her, and my
father was shaking and yelling, "Lu'isa! Lu'isa!" all the time. . . .
And then she was limp and crying in his arms, and he carried her
upstairs, and I was still crying in Brother Pat's arms. . . . It was

not until I was allowed to see her for a minute the next day, that I realized no harm had come to my mother's face.

(He goes to a seat downstage right, watching DAVID, *head bandaged, come out of the house, followed by* PITO *with a cardboard box containing wooden soldiers, Danish, with black busbies, red coats, white crossed straps over the coat, and white trousers.)*

WRITER: I was gotten out of the way that afternoon. And every afternoon after that. Outside. I was not to make a noise in the house. My mother was to be kept very quiet. Doctors came out from the hospital in town. Naval officers. They gave her medicine to quiet her. Everybody hovered around her. Brother Patrick thought it tactful to stay away.

(During the preceding, PITO *has set the box down at the table center stage and taken the wooden soldiers out.* DAVID *sits at the table, watching her without much interest.)*

PITO: 'O au meaka'alo ia . . . se'i va'ai fo'i 'i le māgaia.[19] *(She smoothes back his hair lovingly.)* 'E 'aumai sau vaikīpolo?
DAVID: *(Very softly.)* Leai, fa'afetai.
PITO: Ka'alo fa'alelei. 'Aua ke pisa, 'o Mama lā e moe.
DAVID: 'Ia.

(She smiles at him, goes into the house. DAVID *plays diffidently with the soldiers.)*

WRITER: The next day, the New Zealand High Commissioner in Apia, Colonel Stephen Allen, reported briefly on what had happened: A procession of Mau members, going down Beach Road for the Tivoli Wharf where the *Lady Roberts* from New Zealand was docking, was stopped by the police. They arrested one of the men in the band for failure to pay his annual poll tax. The man protested. There was a skirmish, and suddenly the Samoans

---

[19]PITO: These toys, see how nice. *(She smoothes back his hair lovingly.)* Shall I bring some lemon juice?
DAVID: *(Very softly.)* No, thanks.
PITO: Play nicely. Don't make noise, Mama is sleeping.
DAVID: Okay.

closed in. They clubbed the arresting policeman, someone struck him in the head with an axe. The police who were in the open escaped into the police building nearby. The riot frenzy spread, Tamasese leading the rioters. More clubs, more axes, appeared everywhere. From their building, the police opened fire with rifles. A machine gun, up on the second floor porch, was fired seaward, over the rioters' heads, in the hope of dispersing them.

(DAVID *accidentally knocks a soldier off the table.*)

WRITER: A single, accidental rifle shot brought Tamasese down. In the confusion, other Samoans were hit, a few fatally.

(DAVID *gets down by the fallen soldier, sets it standing up, just stares at it.*)

WRITER: And when the Samoans saw their leader and comrades fall, the rioting stopped. The Samoans fled with their wounded, their dying, and their dead. The whole thing had lasted about five minutes. . . . No one believed the official story. Least of all, my father. And so, to learn the truth, my father took the boat to Apia that very night. Early the next morning, Sunday, in hospital, Tamasese died. . . .

(DAVID *stands up with the toy soldier, packs it and the others into their boxes, then sits, staring at the bench downstage left. The* WRITER *remains downstage right. During the following scene,* DAVID *plays exclusively to the bench downstage left as if there were, indeed, someone there. And the* WRITER *faces front throughout.*)

WRITER: *(Always quietly.)* . . . I wanted to cry out loud for Veni, but I knew I couldn't. Pito had said, "No loud noises; no friends from the village." . . . So every afternoon, I called for Veni in my mind. . . . But he would not come. Then, on the afternoon of the last day of the year, he came. *(Always looking to the bench area downstage left,* DAVID *rises slowly.)* I mean, not in my mind, as he had always come before . . . I mean, I saw him. He was there, smiling at me. I really saw him.

DAVID: *(Softly, awed.)* Sole . . . *(He approaches the bench at downstage left.)* 'Ua 'e sau?[20]

---

[20]DAVID: You've come?

(DAVID *stops, partway to the bench, looking intently with rising joy at his "friend," who has evidently "entered" from downstage left.*)

WRITER: He wore a short piece of tapa for a loincloth. . . . Nothing else. . . . Now that he was really and truly there, I saw how very wrong I had been about how he would look. His hair wasn't like mine at all. His head was almost bald, except for a small bump of hair, like a coxcomb, here . . . (*He touches the front of his head, just above the forehead.*) And his eyes were like cats' eyes.

DAVID: (*Holding out a hand slowly.*) Toe itiiti ā 'ou fiu e fa'atali 'oe.[21]

WRITER: I took his offered hand. And it was firm and warm.

DAVID: Fa'apea ā a'u 'e te lē toe sau.[22]

WRITER: 'Aiseā?

DAVID: 'Ua mālaia le mātou 'āiga.

WRITER: 'Oi, tālofa e. 'O le ā le mala?

DAVID: 'Ua maliu Tamasese.

WRITER: Tālofa e.

(*A pause.* DAVID *slowly sits on the ground.*)

WRITER: He sat on the ground instead of the bench. I sat beside him.

DAVID: Veni . . .

WRITER: (*Always softly.*) 'O a'u.[23]

DAVID: 'E mafai 'ona tā ō?

WRITER: 'I fea?

DAVID: 'I le mea na 'ē sau ai.

---

[21] DAVID: Soon I'm going to tire waiting for you.

[22] DAVID: I thought you weren't coming.
WRITER: Why?
DAVID: Something happened to our family.
WRITER: Poor thing. What's the problem?
DAVID: Tamasese died.
WRITER: Poor thing.

[23] WRITER: It is me!
DAVID: Can we go?
WRITER: Where?
DAVID: From where you came.

WRITER: 'Aiseā?
DAVID: 'Ua 'ou fia va'ai 'iā Tamasese. . . . 'E mamao?
WRITER: 'E mamao mamao lava, 'a e pu'upu'u le ala.
DAVID: 'Ua 'ou fia alu, Veni.
WRITER: 'E lē mafai.
DAVID: 'Aiseā?
WRITER: 'E le'i 'uma tā ta'aloga.
DAVID: 'Ia . . . fa'a'uma lā.
WRITER: Muamua 'oe.

(DAVID *gets up, sits on the bench downstage left.*)

DAVID: 'Ia . . . mate mai po 'o fea na 'ou eva ai.[24] (*He sticks out a foot.*) Sogisogi. (*His mood changes; he begins to smile.*)
WRITER: 'Ese ā a 'oe ta'aloga.
DAVID: (*Wriggling his toes.*) 'Aumai loa lou isu, ma mate mai!
WRITER: 'Ia . . . (*Uncertainly.*) Na 'ē eva—eva—tafatafa o—le—tafa-tafa o . . . (*Triumphant success!*) . . . sai pua'a!
DAVID: (*His face falls.*) Na 'ē iloa a'u. Na 'ē lafi i tua o se lā'au ma tilotilo atu 'i ā a'u. Pei 'o se sipai.
WRITER: Leai. 'E matua'i leai leai leai leai lava.

(DAVID *thinks it over. Then he sticks his foot out.*)

WRITER: Why?
DAVID: I want to see Tamasese. . . . Is it far?
WRITER: It is very far, but the road is short.
DAVID: I want to go, Veni.
WRITER: You can't.
DAVID: Why?
WRITER: Our game is not finished.
DAVID: Let's finish it.
WRITER: You first.

[24]DAVID: Okay, guess where I've gone to. (*He sticks out a foot.*) Smell me. (*His mood changes; he begins to smile.*)
WRITER: What a different way to play.
DAVID: (*Wriggling his toes.*) Bring your nose and guess!
WRITER: You (*Uncertainly.*) have been to the side of the . . . (*Triumphant success!*) . . . pig pen!
DAVID: (*His face falls.*) You know where I've been. You hid in back of me and looked at me. Just like a spy.
WRITER: No. No no no no.

DAVID: Okay, fia poto! Ta'u mai lā![25] *(Pause. The acid test.)* 'O le sai pua'a a ai?

WRITER: Fa'afefea na 'ou iloa lā'ea mea? E tutusa 'uma lava tae pua'a. . . . Va'ai 'oe. Na solia tae pua'a 'i ou vae; 'e lē 'o ni tae tagata.

DAVID: *(Crowing.)* 'Ua 'ē pala'ai, 'ua 'ē pala'ai!

WRITER: 'Ana 'ou fai atu fo'i 'o ni tae tagata, 'e te fesili mai po 'o ni tae papālagi po 'o ni tae Sāmoa.

DAVID: 'Aua ne'i 'ē faitio mai fua! 'Ua 'ē pala'ai.

WRITER: 'Ia . . . 'ua lelei.

DAVID: *(Rising.)* Sau loa 'oe. Fai lau turn. *(He and Writer change places,* DAVID *kneeling and facing the bench.)* Tu'u mai loa lou vae.

(He takes the "foot" in both his hands, bends forward, sniffs, keeps sniffing. LILO *comes from upstage left. He is in work clothes, and he brings papaya and ripe bananas in a basket. He is headed for the porch door when he sees* DAVID. *He is amused at first by what he sees:* DAVID *kissing the air above his cupped hands. But then he becomes concerned. Perhaps it is the intensity with which the boy is caught up in his smelling and soft mumbling.)*

DAVID: Na 'ē eva i luga o tu'ugamau.[26]

WRITER: Tu'ugamau a ai?

DAVID: Tagata oti . . . elo . . . 'o le elo o le tino maliu . . . pala . . . 'ua pala . . .

*(*LILO *puts the fruit on the table and moves slowly with rising concern toward* DAVID.)*

---

[25]DAVID: Okay, smarty! Tell me now! *(Pause. The acid test.)*

WRITER: How would I know? It was like pig shit . . . you see. You stepped in pig shit, that's not people shit.

DAVID: *(Crowing.)* You lost, you lost!

WRITER: If I told you it was people shit, you will ask if it's a white man's or a Samoan's.

DAVID: Don't try and get out of it. You lost.

WRITER: Okay . . . that's good.

DAVID: *(Rising.)* You come. Your turn. *(He and Veni change places,* DAVID *kneeling and facing the bench.)* Bring your foot.

[26]DAVID: You were on a grave.

WRITER: Whose grave?

DAVID: Dead people . . . stink . . . the stink of dead bodies . . . rotten . . . rotten.

LILO: David—? (*He hesitates. Something tells him to proceed carefully.*)

WRITER: My Uncle Lilo told me years later that I was mumbling things about walking on the bodies of the dead.

(*And the first little sound, like an animal's soft yip, comes from* DAVID.)

LILO: David! (*He moves quickly to the boy, kneels beside him.*)

WRITER: Even today I remember the smell—the rot—the stink of Death that was growing in my lungs . . .

LILO: (*Terribly worried.*) David, David, what is it?

(DAVID *is looking straight at him, scared, and the sounds come continuously now; he is trembling badly.*)

WRITER: . . . and filling my whole body until I burst!

(DAVID *screams.*)

LILO: David!

(*He grabs the boy, pulling him close.* DAVID, *with the scream, breaks into body-wracking sobbing.* LILO *holds him very close, rocking slightly.*)

LILO: Shhh . . . shhh . . . no more . . . no more . . .

(LILO, *worried, goes on comforting* DAVID. *The* WRITER *continues to look straight ahead.*)

WRITER: And it was then that I felt the slash of the broken bottle across my face, and heard the rifle shot.

(*The lights fade quickly to black.*)

Scene Three

(A week or so has passed, and all signs of Christmas are gone. It is late of an afternoon. The WRITER *enters, sits at the table center stage. He addresses the audience.)*

WRITER: During the week that followed, I was kept to my room. I was allowed no visitors. So no one came, except Pito with my food and good things to drink, and Uncle Lilo, who sometimes slept beside me. But after midnight I would wake up, and he'd be gone, and I would lie there alone, thinking of Veni. And then, just before morning when it was still dark but you could see a little and the little winds would come, so small you could barely feel them on your cheeks, the curtains at my garden windows would move. . . . And I would fall asleep at last, knowing he was there. *(He gets up and moves to his usual place downstage left.)* I never told anybody. Not even Uncle Lilo when he kept asking me what had frightened me in the garden. Because in my room, he became beautiful again, the way he always was in my mind. . . . I was alone with Veni. . . . I didn't want to see anybody.

*(*BROTHER PATRICK, *once again in his cassock, comes in from the left. The* WRITER *watches him go to the door, look in, then, somewhat hesitantly, knock. He waits, knocks again, waits, looks in. He steps back from the door, then decides to call.)*

PATRICK: *(Calling, but rather weakly.)* Mrs. Kreber—? *(A wait.)* Lilo? . . . Hello?

(Silence. PATRICK *gives up. He comes off the porch in disappointment, starts to go slowly. But then he stops, for* PITO *has come to the door.)*

PATRICK: Tālofa . . .[1]

PITO: Kālofa lava.

PATRICK: David. . . . Fa'amolemole. Lu'isa . . .

PITO: *(Shaking her head.)* 'O lelā e ma'i. . . . Koe sau 'i se isi aso. . . . *(With patient emphasis.)* Ma'i! Ma'i!

PATRICK: But I must talk to them. . . . David, Lu'isa . . .

PITO: 'O lo 'o ma'i David. Fa'apea ma Lu'isa.[2]

(She gestures for him to go. And he does so, reluctantly, exiting at left. PITO *watches him go, sympathetically, then returns into the house.)*

WRITER: When Pito brought my meals on a tray, she would sit beside my bed while I ate, and she would tell me stories about the great men and women in our people's past: Nāfanua and Salamāsina, Tuna and Fata and their brother Savea, the first Mālietoa, and Māui and Tigilau, whom Sina brought back from the dead. . . . And one night, Pito explained to me why my mother had tried to cut herself like that. . . . "White people killed Tamasese," Pito said. "And Lu'isa was ashamed of her white blood and white skin. She was trying to cut it away in grief and disgust." Then Pito would hug me and say over and over, "Promise me, promise me that you will always remember who you truly are." And I would hug her more tightly than she hugged me, and cry out, "Oh, I promise, I promise, Pito!"

Towards the end of the week, I saw my mother from my window when she left her rooms for the first time since that frightening day in the kitchen. I could see; I could not hear.

(LU'ISA comes out with LILO, her hand on his arm. She has a light silk shawl around her shoulders. They move for the table center stage. As they go:)

LILO: It's a lovely warm sun this afternoon. . . . You need it after being cooped up in that room all week. . . .

---

[1]PATRICK: Hello.

PITO: Hello.

PATRICK: David. Please. Lu'isa . . .

PITO: *(Shaking her head.)* He's sick. . . . Come another day. . . . *(With patient emphasis.)* Sick! Sick!

[2]PITO: David is sick. So is Lu'isa.

LU'ISA: It *is* lovely.

(He seats her at the table center stage. She is smiling as she looks around and then, somewhat turned in on herself, she lets out a little laugh.)

LILO: Feeling better?

LU'ISA: The sun. It made me think of Mama, when we were very small.

LILO: Oh? What?

LU'ISA: Remember how she forbade us to sit out in the sun without a parasol? She would get so cross!

LILO: With you. Never with me. Aristocratic young Samoan ladies were supposed to grow up fair and comely. She didn't care if I burnt myself black.

LU'ISA: She was very proud of you, Lilo!

LILO: Except for my nose! Proud of my Samoan skin, ashamed of my flat Samoan nose.

LU'ISA: *(Laughing.)* She was not!

LILO: She was, she was! Remember how she used to massage it, pulling it forward so that it would grow straight down like a white man's nose.

LU'ISA: *(Merrily.)* Well, it worked, she succeeded! You have a lovely nose! . . . And your toes! How she massaged them. "I will not have splayed toes," she said, "like a common villager!"

(The laughter fades; they are silent. He rises.)

LU'ISA: Some tea would be nice.

LILO: Pito is bringing it. *(A pause.)* How are you feeling? Really?

LU'ISA: All right. . . . I keep thinking more and more of Mama the last few days. . . .

(The WRITER turns to go off, but turns back on:)

LU'ISA: Someone with David?

LILO: He's all right. Reading, I think. I'll go up in a bit.

(A pause again. The WRITER goes out at left.)

LU'ISA: Is he feeling better?

LILO: He's become a little too—quiet, for my taste. . . . I wish I could find out what frightened him so much. He won't tell.

LU'ISA: Being stoned like that. . . . That's enough to terrify any child.

LILO: He wasn't stoned, for heaven's sake, Lu'isa. It was one man, throwing one stone. And evidently not a very big one.

LU'ISA: Animals.

LILO: Brother Pat thinks the stone was aimed at him. A case of anti-Catholicism.

LU'ISA: How do you know?

LILO: I'm just saying what Brother Pat thinks. . . . I've asked around the village.

LU'ISA: And?

LILO: They're not very talkative.

LU'ISA: Have you tried the authorities in town?

LILO: No.

LU'ISA: No! . . . Lilo, Davey's been hurt. . . . And from what Pito says, hurt deeply. Deeply, Lilo. . . . Why haven't you had the man arrested?

LILO: Because he's gone. Evidently when he heard I was asking questions around the village, he got into his fishing canoe and— vanished!

LU'ISA: To?

LILO: I don't know. *(At her unbelieving look:)* I really don't know.

(A couple of moments.)

LU'ISA: What's his name? I can make the family *bring* him back to me. *(For all her frailness, there is a sharp edge to her steely anger.)*

LILO: I don't know his name, Lu'isa!

LU'ISA: Surely the children said . . .

LILO: They didn't.

LU'ISA: Didn't you ask them?

LILO: *(Almost losing his temper.)* Damn it, of course I asked them.

LU'ISA: Then they're lying.

LILO: They obviously don't want us to know.

LU'ISA: Why?

LILO: *(Irritated.)* If I knew, I'd tell you . . . *(He sees PITO coming out of the house with tea.)* Here's tea.

(LU'ISA is too preoccupied with her thoughts to respond. PITO comes to the table, puts down the tray.)

LU'ISA: Are you sure you wouldn't rather have something other than tea?

LILO: Now that you mention it, much rather. Thank you. (*To* PITO:) 'Aumai le kā fagu, Piko.[3]

PITO: (*Grumbling.*) Igu, igu, igu, koe ikiiki pala lou fai'ai. Pe'ā iai se fai'ai.

(*Only* LILO *smiles at her grousing;* LU'ISA *is into herself again.* PITO *goes back to the house.*)

LILO: Any word from Frank yet?

LU'ISA: No. It isn't like him.

LILO: He must be terribly busy.

LU'ISA: Yes.

LILO: Worried?

LU'ISA: No. Not really. (*She takes one of the two teacups from the tray, pours tea for herself.*)

LU'ISA: That man—the New Zealand High Commissioner—

LILO: Allen.

LU'ISA: Yes. Allen. . . . Do you believe what he said? His official report?

LILO: The part about Tamasese leading an attack with armed men? Clubs and axes and God knows what else?

LU'ISA: Yes.

LILO: It's not like Tamasese.

LU'ISA: Still, pushed far enough—? He's not wishy-washy, you know.

LILO: (*A gentle correction.*) Was not wishy-washy, Lu'isa.

(LU'ISA *puts down the pitcher of milk she was about to use, averts her face.*)

LU'ISA: Oh, Lilo, I wish that—things—had gone differently.

LILO: So do we all.

LU'ISA: So much—so very much—had depended on him. A people's freedom. Our dignity and pride in being ourselves. (*Suddenly she is fighting back a surge of intense feeling.*) He must have been provoked. . . . I cannot, simply cannot, believe he would start—instigate—such ugly violence.

---

[3]LILO: . . . (*To* PITO:) Bring the bottle, Pito.

PITO: (*Grumbling.*) Drink, drink, drink, pretty soon your brains will rot. If you have brains.

LILO: It's preposterous.

LU'ISA: That man, Allen—he lied. Lilo, the man lied.

LILO: Of course he lied.

LU'ISA: And I can't see how anyone in government, in Wellington, would believe such lies.

LILO: Allen's their only source of information. They really have no reason not to believe him.

LU'ISA: *(Firmly.)* Then you must tell them the truth!

LILO: Who?

LU'ISA: When Frank comes back, and we finally know the truth, you must go to New Zealand. Both of you. Tell them.

LILO: I'm hardly in a position to be of—

LU'ISA: Frank knows everybody of importance in government there. . . .

LILO: Then why should I have to go with—?

LU'ISA: Because you are still remembered there. People still worship you. Especially the young fellows. They still talk about your remarkable achievements as a drop-kicker. *(Laughs.)* The Toe, they called you! . . . *(Sentimentally.)* Mama's wonderful Toe.

LILO: Lu'isa, that was years ago!

(Their laughing banter dies down.)

LU'ISA: The decent people, outside of government, will all listen to you.

LILO: Well, perhaps a few chaps still remember. . . . But—

LU'ISA: Then, there you are! . . . We can't just sit back.

LILO: I'm just one man. What can one man do in the face of so much—?

LU'ISA: *(Intensely.)* One man can die for his fellow man. That's what one man can do, and one man did. For us. . . . He cannot have died in vain, Lilo.

LILO: *(Somewhat taken aback by her intensity.)* Did he mean so much to you then?

LU'ISA: *(Averting her eyes downward; the intensity is seeping away fast.)* Doesn't he—to you? He should. He should to all of us. *(Quietly, firmly.)* He must be avenged, Lilo!

(PITO comes out of the house with a decanter and tumbler on a tray. LILO turns away as PITO puts decanter and glass on the table. BROTHER PATRICK comes on, rather shyly, from the left.)

LILO: Well, well, look who's here!

(PITO *goes back in the house.*)

LILO: Come, Brother, come, come and sit down.

(BROTHER PATRICK *approaches the table center stage but does not sit.*)

PATRICK: Good afternoon to you, Mrs. Kreber.
LUʻISA: Good afternoon, Brother. (*She fusses with milk and sugar.*)
LILO: Where have you been keeping yourself?
PATRICK: Well, with school started—busy. I came by yesterday, but Pito said David was feelin' poorly. . . .
LILO: I didn't know. She never told me.
LUʻISA: (*Quietly, stiffly.*) She told me.
LILO: Well, we were going to have a little tea. Sit down, Brother, sit down. (*He offers the seat facing* LUʻISA.)
PATRICK: Thank you. Thank you very much. (*He sits.* LILO *takes the upstage seat between* PATRICK *and* LUʻISA.) I hope David is feeling better.
LILO: Oh, he'll be himself in another two or three days. . . .
PATRICK: Ah, that is good to hear. Very good, indeed. And—whatever was wrong with the dear lad? (*He notices that the question seems to irk* LUʻISA *a little.*) I ask because—well—school has started and Headmaster has asked after David and will want to know. All the boys in his classroom are asking as well.
LILO: He complains about having—headaches.
PATRICK: (*Alerted.*) Headaches!
LUʻISA: Real headaches, Brother. Nothing very dramatic this time, I'm afraid. (*She starts to pour tea for* PATRICK.)
LILO: Nothing dramatic! . . . Luʻisa, that boy was frightened by something—
LUʻISA: (*Cutting through.*) Lilo, you're spoiling our nice tea, and I—
LILO: (*Going right through her interruption.*) . . . down there—something he was talking to, and it frightened—
LUʻISA: (*A little interrupting laugh.*) Here we are, Brother Pat! (*She gives* PATRICK *his tea.*) I just don't see why you should turn Davey's innocent play into something dark and—and unnatural.
LILO: I never said it was unnatural, Luʻisa.
LUʻISA: (*Teasing, as with a child.*) Such a long face. (*She offers the milk pitcher to* PATRICK.) A little milk, Brother?

PATRICK: No, no. Just—like this, thank you.

(LU'ISA *is busy with sugar for her own tea.*)

LILO: *(A little glumly.)* You needn't drink that tea, Brother. *(He pushes the decanter toward* PATRICK.*)* Here's something more to your liking.

LU'ISA: *(To* Lilo:) I wish you wouldn't force Brother.

LILO: I'm sure Brother Pat would prefer a drink.

PATRICK: No, no, really, tea is fine, really.

LILO: But if you want a—

LU'ISA: *(Firmly.)* He wants *tea*, Lilo. How clearly must the dear man say it? . . . Could we make a little room?

(She gestures to the decanter. LU'ISA *gets up, takes the decanter and glass to the table downstage right. He immediately pours a drink for himself.* PATRICK *covers his acute embarrassment by concentrating on sipping his tea.)*

LU'ISA: I've been thinking, Brother Pat.

PATRICK: Yes?

(Throughout the following, LU'ISA *maintains a pleasant tone and manner.)*

LU'ISA: I've been thinking, what with things as they are, perhaps it would be best if David continues his schooling here . . . I mean, at home.

(There is a marked reaction from LILO. *Unsure what to think,* PATRICK *looks over to him in silent questioning.)*

LU'ISA: What do you think, Brother?

PATRICK: I don't know—I don't know what to think.

LILO: I think it's a lousy idea!

LU'ISA: What a dreadful word! You're beginning to sound like Frank! Anyway, I wasn't asking you, dear. You're not a teacher. Like Brother.

(She looks directly at BROTHER PATRICK, *smiling, waiting for his answer. He is acutely uncomfortable.)*

PATRICK: Well, it would take arranging with Headmaster for someone to help with my classes at school. We are shorthanded this year.

LUʻISA: (Gently.) No no. I wouldn't put such a burden on the school, Brother. I won't hear of it. . . . I mean—with a new teacher, not from the school. . . .

(There is a shocked, hurt reaction from BROTHER PATRICK. LILO drinks moodily, suppressing rage.)

PATRICK: (Aspirately.) Why——?

LUʻISA: (Carefully.) It's something I've wanted to discuss with you for a long time. We—are not Catholics, as you know, of course.

PATRICK: But there are many boys at school who are not of the faith. Like Davey.

LUʻISA: David needs to find himself, be himself, live in his own world.

PATRICK: But I agree!

LUʻISA: (Hasn't heard.) And so, perhaps it's time he began to see things from the point of view of his own religion. I'm sure you'll agree that's very important to any growing youngster.

PATRICK: Yes, of course. But we've never forced our faith on Davey.

LUʻISA: But then, neither have you ever actively taught him *his* faith, have you? (Nicely.) Not, of course, that you were ever supposed to.

PATRICK: (Utterly defeated.) No . . .

LUʻISA: And, after all, David's great-great-grandfather and great-grandfather—between the two of them—virtually Christianized the South Seas.

PATRICK: Yes.

LUʻISA: Well, there we are then, aren't we?

(BROTHER PATRICK cannot bring himself to look at LUʻISA, and he sits in dejection. LILO stares at PATRICK in heartbreak and anger.)

LUʻISA: So, I've made arrangements with the Reverend Mister Barton for David's lessons. It's for the best.

PATRICK: (Softly.) Do as you wish, Mrs. Kreber.

LUʻISA: I knew you would understand.

LILO: Well, I don't!

LUʻISA: (Ignoring him.) Thank you for understanding, Brother. . . . I will see to your final payments in the morning.

PATRICK: Davey is dear to me, Mrs. Kreber.

LU'ISA: He's dear to all of us. Including his silly doting mother.

LILO: *(Loud, emphatic.)* Oh—shit! Shit shit shit shit. *(All but screaming.)* Shit!

(BROTHER PATRICK *is more shocked than* LU'ISA, *who stiffens visibly in an effort—a successful one—at control.*)

LILO: Brother Pat deserves an explanation.

LU'ISA: I've given a perfectly reasonable explanation.

LILO: But not the truth.

LU'ISA: Which, of course, you know. Only you.

LILO: Which, of course, I can find out. Here and now.

(LU'ISA's *patronizing niceness is disappearing fast. A defensiveness takes its place and, soon, rage.*)

LU'ISA: Do I need to remind you, Lilo, that I am Davey's mother and I may do with my child's life as I think best?

LILO: Brother Pat, when that man threw that stone, how far from Davey were you?

LU'ISA: This is absolutely insupportable!

LILO: *(To* BROTHER PATRICK.*)* How far? *(No answer.)* The village children told me. *(No answer.)* My sister's been told the man threw the stone at you, for anti-Catholic reasons, as you've said yourself. And that's really why she wants to separate David from you and anything Catholic. . . . Better run away from intolerance than stand and face it.

LU'ISA: *(Rising in anger.)* I will not stay and listen . . .

LILO: *(Together with* LU'ISA.*)* Because she would be facing herself!

LU'ISA: *(Direct continuation.)* . . . to this irresponsible ranting! You're drunk!

(*She starts for the door.* LILO *moves with her, all but shouting in her ear.*)

LILO: The man is himself a Catholic, Lu'isa!

(*This slows, then stops her. She is suddenly uncertain: go or stay?*)

LILO: And Davey was at least twenty feet from Brother Pat. *(To* PATRICK:*)* Right?

PATRICK: *(Almost softly.)* Yes.

LILO: *(A more normal tone.)* Until very recently, our people fought with stones. And they have, since the beginning of their history, three thousand years ago. They never, never, miss a target by more than inches.... *(Flat, quiet emphasis.)* Brother Pat wasn't the target, Lu'isa. Davey was. God prove me wrong, but I think he meant to kill Davey.

(Stunned by this, LU'ISA *sits by the table downstage right, speechless, shaking her head slowly in dazed disbelief.* LILO *turns back to* PATRICK, *quieter now.)*

LILO: Am I wrong, Brother? I think you know more than you've told us. *(No response.)* Am I wrong?
PATRICK: *(Finally, softly.)* No. You're not wrong.
LILO: *(More statement than question.)* And you do know ... ?
PATRICK: Yes.

(Now that it has come to the crucial question, LILO *himself suddenly seems unsure, reluctant to ask it. He leans against the upstage center rail for a moment. Then:)*

LILO: Why did he want to kill Davey?
PATRICK: *(With difficulty.)* I think he still does.
LU'ISA: *(An agonized cry.)* Why?

*(*BROTHER PATRICK *takes his time before answering. His tone and manner are almost apologetic.)*

PATRICK: For the last four or five weeks, David has had a friend, his age, named Veni. *(He stops.)*
LILO: So—?
PATRICK: Veni is not a—real—little boy.
LU'ISA: *(To* LILO.*)* An imaginary playmate. Frank and I know about him.

*(*BROTHER PATRICK *is reluctant to continue.)*

LILO: Well—?
PATRICK: Mrs. Kreber—? *(As if asking her permission to continue.)*
LU'ISA: *(Softly; despite herself.)* Go on.

(A moment.)

PATRICK: Not imaginary, really.

LILO: What then—?

PATRICK: There was a little boy named Veni. He died a few years before you were born. David visits his grave often, and they talk, play together. . . .

LILO: They—talk—?

PATRICK: So Davey thinks. Veni is very real to him. I think, if we do not do something, he will take complete possession of Davey's mind, very soon. . . . And own him.

(LILO *has moved over toward the bench downstage left, looking at it intently, realizing.*)

LILO: You say, they talk together—play together?

LU'ISA: What are you doing, Lilo?

(LILO *ignores her, perhaps hasn't heard. He turns back to* BROTHER PATRICK.)

LILO: Go on, Brother.

PATRICK: Many of the villagers say Veni's ghost is now walking the village at night. They have seen a stranger—a fifty-year-old man —that's how old Veni would have been had he lived. . . . They have seen Davey, sitting on Veni's grave, talking to him. . . . Davey has told them he has visits from Veni. . . . They are very frightened. And they blame Davey for disturbing their dead.

LU'ISA: *(Heartbreak now, not anger.)* How stupid!

LILO: And so the man that threw that stone . . . ?

PATRICK: Yes. . . . Veni was his older brother. He was two when Veni died at the age of eleven.

(*There is another pause.* LILO *sits, spent, saddened.*)

LILO: How do you know all this, Brother?

PATRICK: The villagers told me.

LU'ISA: Who is this man? . . . He'll be dealt with, of course.

PATRICK: It doesn't matter now. He's gone. I think to Upolu.

LU'ISA: *(Shocked.)* Doesn't matter? Doesn't Davey matter?

LILO: *(Sharply.)* And why didn't you tell us all this at once?

PATRICK: I tried to. Yesterday. Pito sent me away.

LILO: I've asked the villagers, and they wouldn't tell me. Why not?

LU'ISA: We have always seen to their needs—cared for them—cared about them. . . . They have always looked to our family for guidance. . . . Why not now?

PATRICK: *(Evasively.)* I—told—I don't know.

LU'ISA: You were about to say something else, Brother. You told—? . . . Please tell the truth.

PATRICK: I told—one of the—older men—to come to you. . . .

LU'ISA: Why didn't he?

PATRICK: I think it is because—they—no longer— *(He shakes his head, finding it too difficult to go on.)*

LU'ISA: No longer—? (PATRICK *looks at her helplessly.)* Please!

PATRICK: They—no longer think of you—as Samoan. Your mother, yes. But not you. Perhaps they never have. . . . The man said. . . . And so, they are afraid of you a little, many of them. . . . You have become like a white person, he said.

LU'ISA: *(Quietly.)* But they are not afraid of you, and so they come to you . . . ? *(Head low,* PATRICK *does not respond.)* So now, I am a white person, and you have become—a Samoan. *(She rises, deeply offended and hurt, but trying to pull her pride and dignity together. Her voice is quiet but the sarcasm is a snarl.)* I—bow—to my better, Brother. *(She holds out her hand.)* Goodbye. . . .

(BROTHER PATRICK is embarrassed, looks to LILO, wishing to be anywhere but here.)

LILO: *(Grumbling very softly.)* Oh, for Christ's sake, Lu'isa.

(But he too remains seated, deflated. LU'ISA *remains standing with outstretched hand.)*

LU'ISA: Will you not—demean—yourself, Brother?

(This hurts BROTHER PATRICK even more. He gets up, confused, and then tries to escape. He starts to the left, but this won't do, so he stops, turns uncertainly to look back at LU'ISA, who lowers her hand.)

LU'ISA: I'll say goodbye to David for you.

PATRICK: *(Softly.)* Yes . . .

(And he goes out at left, very near tears of hurt and embarrassment. LU'ISA stands for a while, stock still, then sits at her tea, overcomposed to a breakable rigidity.)

LU'ISA: There are times I feel out of sorts with that man. . . . He can be quite, quite tiresome.

(She pours her tea, takes sugar, adds milk, all with methodical care. LILO *regards her with something like disdain.)*

LILO: *(Trying to control his feelings.)* Does Frank know?
LU'ISA: Know what?
LILO: About David.
LU'ISA: Frank's known all along about Davey's imaginary—
LILO: I don't mean his playmate. *(He gets up, paces: more of a sulk than anger. He doesn't quite look at her.)*
LU'ISA: What then—?
LILO: Your taking him out of school.
LU'ISA: *(Taking her time, gathering.)* Do you know what they teach in their catechism class?
LILO: Answer my question, please.
LU'ISA: *(Goes right on.)* They teach that only their beliefs are truly Christian, and that all nonbelievers are doomed to eternal flames in hell. . . . And their obsession with Satan and possession and speaking with saints! It's medieval!
LILO: *(Flares.)* Goddamn it, Lu'isa, a straight answer! Answer me. . . . Does Frank know you've taken David out of the Marist school, and practically cut Brother Pat out of his life? *(No answer.)* Does he? Yes or no.
LU'ISA: *(A moment.)* He's due back any day now. Tomorrow or the day after, probably. I'll tell him then. . . . He'll agree I've done the right thing.
LILO: *(Carefully.)* Oh sure!

*(*LU'ISA *regards him a moment. That "reasonable" tone has returned.)*

LU'ISA: I have acted in the best interests of my child. Ever since Brother Pat started tutoring him over the long holiday, he has become—fretful. No wonder, considering what is going into his little head. . . .
LILO: David is on the verge of a nervous breakdown, Lu'isa.
LU'ISA: Oh, what drivel!
LILO: He may be going mad!
LU'ISA: Rot! . . . That's—that's exactly what I mean . . . this kind of talk. You say it often enough, Davey will start to believe it himself. . . . Possibly Brother Pat wants him to believe it!

LILO: Why should the man—?

LUʻISA: To keep him in thrall. They do that to young minds.

(LILO *points downstage left at the bench; the anger is beginning to boil.*)

LILO: I saw, Luʻisa! I saw!

LUʻISA: *(Firmly.)* I forbid this kind of talk in my house.

LILO: It's my house, too! You conveniently keep forgetting that Papa left it to both of us. To share, if you still know what that word means.

LUʻISA: A pile of rotting timber was what he left us! At my urging, Frank has restored it. . . . Without me, there'd be no roof over your head.

LILO: Me! Me! Me! Me! Me! . . . Can't you think of someone else for a change? . . . *(Strongly.)* Think of David!

(LILO *is getting to her—for she has grown tense again, and now there's a sudden catch in her voice.*)

LUʻISA: I am thinking of Davey—

LILO: Then if you've ever cared, pay attention now, Luʻisa. *(He again points downstage left.)* I know now what happened there. . . . Davey was insane, for a minute or two!

LUʻISA: Stop it!

LILO: His eyes rolled back in his head, his body twitched, out of control, and he whimpered—like a little animal.

LUʻISA: *(Now on her feet.)* I said stop it, Lilo! I won't have this!

LILO: And later, he didn't remember a thing. . . . He still doesn't remember. (LUʻISA *turns to go.*) Why won't you listen?

LUʻISA: There is nothing to listen to. There is absolutely nothing wrong with David. . . . He simply needs to be with his own kind!

LILO: Why don't you hear? Oh, why don't you see? *(She stops, faces him.)* Don't you care about him?

(*An upsweep of rage;* LUʻISA *raises her hand to strike blindly.*)

LUʻISA: Damn you! *(But her blow is arrested by:)*

LILO: We may lose him, Luʻisa. . . . And if that happens, I will never forgive you. The sister I've loved all my life. . . . But I've become afraid of you, Luʻisa. Like the villagers. I, too. . . . You've lived for so long in your own world—apart . . .

(LUʻISA has come back to the table center stage, sits. LILO sits facing her.)

LILO: Oh, Luʻisa, why have we always been so afraid of the truth? Why have we always lied to ourselves?

(There is a long pause. Now, as if contrite, LILO sits with lowered eyes. LUʻISA gathers herself.)

LUʻISA: I will not be intimidated by the alcoholic fears of a drunken little schoolteacher. Or by the superstitions of ignorant savages!

LILO: Luʻisa, our own mother was one of these sava—

LUʻISA: *(Interrupting strongly.)* Our mother was in the royal line—!

LILO: *(Almost pitying; chiding.)* Luʻisa!

LUʻISA: *(Emotionally.)* High, high aristocratic men and women of royal ancestry, for a thousand years back . . .

LILO: *(Softly.)* Oh, what does it matter?

LUʻISA: That blood flows in you! . . . I'm surprised at you! . . . When our grandmother moved here with her husband as a young bride, from Upolu, these people worshiped her with pride, and gratitude for the majesty her presence, just her being here, gave them. . . . Even their chiefs knelt down and bowed before her, when she was carried past. . . .

(Elbow on table, forehead to hand, LILO is about to give up.)

LUʻISA: And Mama. Mama, too. Mama was always carried by strong men wherever she wanted to go. Her feet were not allowed to touch the ground. . . .

LILO: Luʻisa, Luʻisa . . .

LUʻISA: Well, it's true, isn't it?

LILO: Those people died years ago. No one remembers.

LUʻISA: But we dare not forget! And we dare not let them forget. . . . It is our Past, it is the pride that inspires us—men like our beloved Tamasese—it is what will inform Davey's future. Our future. And even if they don't know *(she means the villagers, of course)* or seem to care, Davey is their future too. (LILO *has been silenced. Chin set, defiant,* LUʻISA *is yet on the verge of tears.)* And I will not let ignorance cheapen that! *(She rises.)* I admit no blemish, Lilo. None!

(*Spoken quietly in an attempt at voicing an assured fact, the last word, nevertheless, breaks her voice. She turns quickly to hide her true feelings. She is about to go back in the house, her shawl forgotten on the seat. As she turns,* FRANK *appears in the doorway. He is torn, dirty, exhausted.* LU'ISA *is halfway to the door when she sees him.*)

LU'ISA: Frank! (*She rushes into his arms, weeping in relief.*) Oh, Frank!

(FRANK *holds her close, almost desperately.* LILO *moves partway to them, does not want to intrude.* LU'ISA *looks at* FRANK, *touching his shoulders and face.*)

LU'ISA: Look at you. . . . Oh, look at my precious. . . . What happened—?
FRANK: Come . . . come . . . sit down . . .

(*He brings her back to the table center stage; she sits. He turns to* LILO, *and the two men embrace with great affection.* FRANK *turns back to the table, sits by* LU'ISA, *who takes his hand in both of hers.* LILO *goes downstage right to pour a drink for* FRANK.)

LU'ISA: You look so tired. Are you all right?
FRANK: (*Nodding.*) I'm okay.
LU'ISA: Have you eaten? I'll call Pito. (*She starts to rise; he stops her.*)
FRANK: No, no. Later. . . . I think Lilo's got the right idea. . . . You look so lovely. . . . You've been okay? Everything?
LU'ISA: Yes. Everything.
FRANK: David all right?
LU'ISA: Couldn't be better.

(LILO *gives* FRANK *his drink; the tumbler is half full.*)

FRANK: Boy, do I need this! (*To* LU'ISA:) Where is he?

(*A quick exchange of looks between* LILO *and* LU'ISA.)

LILO: In his room . . .
LU'ISA: . . . taking his nap.
FRANK: (*Amused.*) Nap! David?
LU'ISA: It's—something new. He seems to like it.

FRANK: *(Raising his drink.)* Well! *(He drinks, clears his throat, shakes his head appreciatively.)* This sure hits the spot! *(Another swallow.)*

LU'ISA: *(Despite herself.)* Careful, Frank!

(He nods, takes another swallow.)

LILO: What did you find out in Upolu?

LU'ISA: *(Together.)* What happened to you?

(FRANK puts his drink down. He waits a moment.)

FRANK: It's hard—sorting it all out. . . . Seems like it happened to —somebody else. . . . *(He hands his tumbler—not quite empty—to LILO.)* Mind, Lilo? . . . *(To LU'ISA:)* I'm tired. Bone tired.

(LILO is headed to the decanter downstage right with the tumbler.)

LU'ISA: You look just awful.

FRANK: *(Looking around the yard.)* God, it's good to be here.

(A longish pause. FRANK is still putting himself back together.)

LU'ISA: If you'd rather rest first—? Before you tell us—?

FRANK: No. I'm okay. . . . Anyway, I'd like to see little Davey. Just a few days away from him and—Christ, how I missed him! . . . I never realized how much I loved that little face!

LU'ISA: You—finish your drink. . . . Take a rest. . . . And when Davey wakes up, I'll tell him you're home. And—you'll see him at dinner.

(LILO is back with his drink—the glass is three-quarters full.)

LU'ISA: Lilo went into the Naval Station every day; to the wireless place, expecting your messages. . . . Why the silence?

(A thoughtful moment. FRANK puts his drink down before him without drinking.)

FRANK: I couldn't get into their radio station . . . shut up tighter than a drum. Commissioner Allen's got Upolu completely cut off from the rest of the world, except for New Zealand.

(A longish pause.)

LILO: *(Quietly.)* So—we're still waiting to hear from you, Frank.

(FRANK *looks at him in silence, then at* LU'ISA. *Finally:*)

FRANK: Commissioner Allen's official report was one big fat bunch of lies.
LILO: We thought so.
FRANK: Tamasese was deliberately lured into the right spot, then killed by a sharpshooter. Murdered. In cold blood.

(LU'ISA *gasps. Her hand comes to her mouth, pushing back a surge of feeling.* LILO *puts his hand on her shoulder comfortingly.* FRANK *drinks.*)

LILO: Lured how?
FRANK: You know there was a procession of Mau people headed for the Tivoli Wharf, along Beach Road . . .
LILO: Yes.
FRANK: Well—there was a marching band. . . . Tamasese was a little distance behind it. Just in front of the police station, the New Zealand Police moved in on the band, to arrest the cornet player . . . the one-eyed fellow . . .
LU'ISA: Mata'utia—?
FRANK: Yes.
LILO: What for? He's a gentle, quiet sort!
FRANK: Some trumped-up charge: failure to pay his poll tax. . . . The man had been seen in Apia all week, walking around every damn day. They could've arrested him then. Any time. . . . Why didn't they? . . . Even the morning of the murder: they could've arrested him long before the band got to the front of the police station—which is where most of the police were waiting and, upstairs, three sharpshooters and an expert machine gunner. They had been brought in specially from New Zealand a few days before. . . . A goddamn machine gun, for Christ's sake!
LU'ISA: *(Fighting back tears.)* It's incredible. . . . I just can't believe it!
LILO: *(Patting her shoulder.)* So—they waited . . .
FRANK: Yuh. They waited. . . . And when the band got to where they wanted it, in front of the police station, they moved in for the arrest. . . . The one-eyed fellow resisted. . . . He insisted his family had paid his poll tax days before. . . . Anyway, there was a

ruckus, more policemen rushed out of the station. . . . It spread. . . . Tamasese ran up from the back. You can bet your bottom dollar they were counting on that. . . . He ran to where the trouble was starting. . . . He held up his arms and shouted out, "Samoa! Peace! Peace! Keep the peace!" And almost imme-diately—everybody I talked to insisted it was so—almost imme-diately there was quiet. . . . Then—in the quiet—as he—*(He has to stop. He takes a deep breath. It isn't enough. He has to move around. He gets up, paces a bit. Then he stops, continues, huskily.)*—as he stood there, his arms raised—(FRANK's *own arms are raised.)*—calling for peace—one shot—rifle shot—from the police station . . . upstairs . . . *(His arms come down.)* . . . second floor. . . . He went down, lay there . . . just lay there.

(LU'ISA *is sobbing.* LILO *leaves her, near tears himself; he moves away.* FRANK *sits.)*

FRANK: Then—then down on the road, the police opened fire. Revolvers. Just firing wildly into the crowd. . . . And then the machine gun started. . . . The machine gunner was sitting in a chair, up there on the porch—a goddamn chair!—holding the machine gun in his arms, having the time of his life. . . . *(He gets up and walks back to the table for his drink. As he goes:)* The next day, Allen said he had given orders to fire over the people's heads, to scare them. . . . But three young men ran, one after the other, to shield Tamasese with their own bodies. . . . All three—all three were machine-gunned. Bodies riddled . . .

LILO: *(Weeping.)* Oh, God . . .

FRANK: Slaughtered. . . . In ten minutes—less—it was all over. . . . Eight Samoans dead, fifty wounded. . . . Every eyewitness—and there were many, including tourists, other white people—every one of them insisted it was an obvious ambush. . . . Next morn-ing, in the hospital, Tamasese died. I'm told his last words were to answer violence with nonviolence, that to do otherwise would make a mockery of his death. . . . I didn't get there in time for the funeral. . . .

(He finishes his drink. Then, during the following, he returns downstage right with the glass, pours himself another drink.)

FRANK: I got to Vaimoso that night. Hundreds of young men had gathered in the villages outside Apia, crying for revenge. They were forming into armed groups—guns, knives, clubs, axes, stones.... Some were going to storm Commissioner Allen's house, drag him out, cut his head off, parade it down Beach Road.... Others were going to find and decapitate every New Zealand official, including the police.... They could have done it easily. There were as many as four hundred of them.... I don't think there are fifty New Zealanders in the Administration, including the police.... And there's tens of thousands of Mau members now, on the sidelines, waiting to move in.

LUʻISA: *(Blurting out in rage.)* Then why didn't they do it? *(She moves away from the table.)* All of them together aren't worth one drop of his dear blood!

FRANK: Because the chiefs spoke to them and kept repeating Tamasese's dying wish: violence was not to be answered with violence. *(He sits downstage right.)* The young men went away, back to their villages, put away their weapons . . .

LUʻISA: And I suppose they were proud of themselves!

LILO: Luʻisa, it was Tamasese's wish!

LUʻISA: Frank himself said it, just now: three young men were brave enough to try to protect him with their bodies.... *(To* FRANK:*)* And suddenly there's no hand raised to protect him in death?

FRANK: Not a one . . . *(*LUʻISA *turns away in disgust.)* The next day, the government retaliated.... Police went from village to village, looking for Mau people, especially the leaders.... It was a remarkable thing: here were a few New Zealanders, moving into a village with their guns, and all around them, looking on quietly from their huts, were the village people—in some villages, dozens; in others, hundreds.... Not a hand raised in protest when the police realized the Mau leaders and followers had run away and the police got angry and frustrated and set their huts on fire.... Even when the police beat the hell out of the younger people, trying to find out where the leaders had gone, not one fist, not one hand, struck back.... They just sat there . . .

LUʻISA: And you—? You just sat there?

LILO: *(Furious.)* Oh, will you shut up, Luʻisa!

(A pause. She glares at LILO. FRANK *is not quite drunk, but his mind is almost numb from exhaustion anyway.)*

FRANK: *(Quietly.)* Do you think I didn't want to?

LU'ISA: *(An angry sulk.)* Wanting isn't enough!

(FRANK is silent. He looks at LILO, rather helpless and forlorn. LILO relents his anger, moves over to LU'ISA, who has sat again at the table center stage, a hand over her eyes, trying to calm her furious heart.)

LILO: *(Quietly.)* Sister, I'm sorry. But you're not being fair to—

(His hand has gone to her shoulder; she pulls herself away from his hand.)

LU'ISA: Leave me alone. Both of you.
LILO: Lu'isa—Frank's been through—
LU'ISA: *(Strongly, without turning.)* Both of you!

(LILO looks over to FRANK, hurt—for FRANK's sake.)

LILO: I'll go up to David's room. See how he is.
FRANK: *(Very quietly.)* No. . . . Not yet. . . . *(He is looking at LU'ISA, who has "withdrawn" completely.)* I need to tell you something . . . something important.

(LILO comes closer, sits, quiet, attentive. . . . FRANK sets his drink aside.)

FRANK: In some of the villages, almost all of the men were gone. Especially in Vaimoso. . . . I had a small hut there, to myself. . . . Then—it was two nights after the funeral—some police arrived. In a truck. Kids. One of them came over to me, stuck a revolver to my head . . .

(This brings LU'ISA "back"; she stares at FRANK, shocked.)

LILO: *(Softly, unbelievingly.)* Why—? Why you?
FRANK: They thought I was a part-Samoan sympathizer. Like a lot of the merchants there—
LU'ISA: But you didn't tell them who you are?
FRANK: No.
LU'ISA: Why—why not?
FRANK: *(Always quietly.)* Something in me said: Speak, save yourself, get out of this mess—and spend the rest of your life a coward and a refugee from everything that's decent and good. . . . Speak, and deny that you are a human being. . . .

(A pause.)

LILO: *(Very softly.)* So—?

(He cannot bring himself to look at FRANK: his head is lowered, as if in humble acceptance of the answer.)

FRANK: And so—I remained silent . . .

(With a little impatient sound of disapproval, LU'ISA moves away from her table.)

FRANK: The young policeman kept yelling at me. He threatened to shoot me in the head if I didn't tell where the leaders were hiding. . . . Then a young villager ran up to help me; some other men with him. . . . The policeman—kid, for Christ's sake—shot him. . . .

LILO: *(Aspirately.)* God!

(LU'ISA spins around in silent rage, looking at FRANK in angry disbelief.)

FRANK: The villagers gathered around quickly. Over a hundred of them. . . . Maybe there were six or seven policemen. . . .

LU'ISA: *(Unbelievingly.)* And they did nothing?

FRANK: *(Always quietly.)* We all just stood there, staring at this white kid. . . . He didn't seem to realize what he had done. . . . The other policemen hustled him back to the truck. . . . They drove away. . . . *(A moment.)* That night, some more of the village men went into hiding, in the forest and mountains behind Vaimoso. . . . I went with them. I chose to, Lu'isa. . . . Freely.

LILO: *(Softly, brokenly.)* God bless you, Frank . . .

FRANK: We were hunted like animals. . . . Sometimes at night we could hear them, small groups of searchers, thrashing through the forest. . . . It would've been so easy to kill them. . . . And I would pray, "Please God, please don't let them see us and force us to kill them." . . . And they would go on, and we would huddle there, close to each other and, as the night passed, even closer—closer than our bodies were close. . . . *(He has gone back to the table, taking his drink with him. Now he sits.)* After so many years, I've found—my people, Lu'isa, and, through them, maybe myself. . . . Yesterday the authorities called off the manhunt. . . .

All around, in the forests, women and young people went looking for us, to tell us. . . . We could hear them shouting, "It is
over! Tamasese has won! He lives again! Samoa lives!" . . . We
came down from the mountains, out of the forests. . . . Late yesterday afternoon, I went to see Commissioner Allen. He didn't
know what had happened to me, probably didn't care. . . . He
was smiling, even laughing a little, the way you do when the
other guy has won the game and you're a good sport about
it. . . . (*To* LILO:) Do you know what he said to me? . . . He said,
"This infatuation with democracy will die down. . . . Any movement that is supposed to be democratic is bound to get some
sympathy at first. . . . It is attractive, on the surface, . . . but it
doesn't last. Thinking people realize soon enough that it is one
of the greatest evils of the world. . . . " Then he laughed that
good sport laugh of his, "Dashedly difficult to suppress, however. But, of course, we must. It's the only way these blighters
can be taught to get ahead. . . . Respect . . . "

LILO: (*Looking at* LU'ISA, *although he speaks to* FRANK.) . . . for their
betters.

FRANK: Yes.

LILO: I can just hear him.

(*Silence.* FRANK *drinks.*)

FRANK: I'm—tired . . . I'd like to rest now. . . . The boat I came
over on, it goes back a little after midnight tonight. . . . I want to
be on it.

LU'ISA: (*Can't believe her ears.*) You're going back?

FRANK: Yes . . . I want to see David now. Explain to him.

LU'ISA: He's sleeping, resting. . . . He hasn't been well. . . .

FRANK: Oh? (*Too tired to worry.*) What's the matter?

LILO: I'll bring him. (*He heads for the door.*)

LU'ISA: Lilo, I don't want him disturbed!

LILO: (*From the porch,* quietly defiant.) I'm bringing the boy to his
father, Lu'isa. . . .

(*He goes into the house. She is, for the moment, more frustrated than*
angry.)

LU'ISA: He—really needs to rest. . . .

FRANK: I won't upset him. . . .

(*A moment. She sits, some distance from* FRANK.)

LU'ISA: I'm glad you're home safe, Frank.... And—you really should think of us—Davey and me—before you go risking your life like that....

FRANK: (*Always quietly.*) I *was* thinking of you and Davey... thinking of us.

LU'ISA: Rushing off again like this—? That's thinking of us ...?

FRANK: Will you come with me, Lu'isa?

LU'ISA: And leave Davey?

FRANK: Of course not. He'll come too.... You've always loved Upolu, Lu'isa. Sometimes I've thought you prefer it to here....

LU'ISA: This is my home, Frank. You know that. How can you ask such a thing?

(*There is another pause.*)

FRANK: An investigating committee is coming to Upolu from New Zealand.... I want to be there when they hold those hearings....

LU'ISA: What can you do?

FRANK: Insist on the truth... you've always said I was a good lawyer....

LU'ISA: There are lawyers in Upolu.

FRANK: I can't turn my back, Lu'isa. Not after what has happened.

LU'ISA: Well... if you insist. You go on, do what you can, and hurry back.... Get it out of your system.

(*There is another pause.*)

FRANK: We've grown apart in recent years, Lu'isa. Maybe too far apart for us to have the kind of life we had once.... It seems so long ago now... I'm sorry. I'm profoundly sorry to have failed you.... But please don't think of me, ever again, as a stranger. ... On the boat coming back, I lay there on deck, watching the night and the stars disappear and seeing a new day come, I thought about you all the time.... And now, after what has happened, I caught myself thinking that—perhaps—in many ways —it is you who is the stranger....

LU'ISA: (*Very softly.*) Nonsense ...

FRANK: Maybe ...

(Another pause.)

LU'ISA: Are you—trying to say that—you don't want to come back after your meeting?

FRANK: I don't know, Lu'isa . . . I wish I could say, but I really don't know now.

LU'ISA: We'll talk more about it, after you've had a rest. . . . *(She rises to go.)* It would help matters if you didn't drink any more. . . .

(She turns and goes. But she is only halfway to the porch steps when LILO *appears in the doorway. She stops.)*

LILO: *(Very concerned.)* Lu'isa . . . *(She takes a step or two toward the steps.)* No, no, Lu'isa. Sit down. . . . Sit down!

*(*LU'ISA, *with a backward look at* FRANK, *moves aside.* FRANK *has risen.)*

FRANK: What is it, Lilo?

(For an answer, LILO *reaches back into the house and brings* DAVID *out to the porch; he steps aside. There is a gasp of shock from* LU'ISA.*)*

FRANK: What the hell—?

(For this is a pathetically altered DAVID. *He is naked but for a tapa lava-lava around his waist. He has tried to change the color of his skin to brown with some kind of paint; it is a clumsy job, funny were it not so pathetic.* LU'ISA *hurries to the boy.)*

LU'ISA: Davey! . . . What is the meaning of this? *(Her rising anger turns quickly to dismay.)* Oh, what have you done to yourself? *(She takes him to the side quickly.)*

LILO: It's only paint. *(He comes down to the yard, off the porch.)*

FRANK: What's he up to, Lilo?

LILO: *(Looking at* LU'ISA.*)* He's trying to change the color of his skin, that's all.

LU'ISA: You get that filthy stuff off, right away! *(She uses her shawl to scrub at his arm. It doesn't work. Her anger returns as she scrubs.* DAVID *submits uncomfortably.)* What a ridiculous thing to do! What got into you! *(Her ineffectual scrubbing makes her angrier and is beginning to get to* DAVID. *He is starting to whimper.)* Oh, shut up! *(She wets her shawl from the teapot.)*

LUʻISA: *(To* LILO.) Call Pito! *(He doesn't budge.)* At once!

LILO: Call her yourself. I'm not your servant!

LUʻISA: Of all the cheek! *(But she hurries to the door; her anger is now quite open. Calling into the house:)* Pito! . . . Pito! Sau! . . .

PITO: *(Offstage from deep in the house, faintly.)* ʻIa!

LUʻISA: Vave! *(She hurries back to* DAVID.) Now, young man . . . I'm ashamed of you. . . . Thoroughly ashamed of you!

*(*FRANK *has come over, nearer to* DAVID, *who now whimpers openly, his feelings hurt—but also hurt by the almost violent scrubbing.)*

FRANK: You're hurting him!

LUʻISA: *(Grabbing* DAVID*'s hair to keep his head still.)* Hold still! *(She scrubs at a cheek hard.)*

FRANK: Stop that!

LUʻISA: You ought to be thrashed! *(Another pull, and* DAVID *cries out in pain.)*

DAVID: I hate you! I hate you!

LUʻISA: *(She raises her hand, crying and yelling.)* Wicked! Wicked child!

FRANK: Luʻisa!

(He reaches to stop her hand—too late. It comes down across DAVID*'s face hard. He screams.)*

LILO: *(Together.)* Luʻisa!

(She strikes the boy again, then again, and, from behind, LILO *grabs* LUʻISA*'s upraised hand. He yanks her away from the boy.* FRANK *gathers his hysterical son into his arms.* LILO, *in his almost irrational rage, strikes* LUʻISA.)

LILO: Damn you!

(Then he shoves her hard into a chair. She tries to get up, he shoves her back again. FRANK *rushes to stop him.)*

FRANK: Lilo! . . . Stop it! . . . For God's sake, stop!

*(*PITO *appears in the doorway, sees, is aghast, rushes to* DAVID.)

PITO: 'Oi, ka fēfē! Ka fēfē! *(Trying to comfort.)* 'Aua, 'Aua![4]

(LILO *keeps struggling to get at* LU'ISA. FRANK *tries to hold him back.*)

LILO: *(In direct continuation of his previous speech, over everyone and everything else.)* Bitch. . . . You goddamned pretentious—mean—arrogant—damn you . . . damn you—you half-caste bitch!
FRANK: *(Throughout the preceding.)* Lilo, for Christ's sake. . . . Stop. . . . Stop, Lilo. . . . I said stop!

(DAVID *frees himself from* PITO, *rushes to pound his little fists on* LILO, *just as* FRANK *succeeds in forcing* LILO *away.* LU'ISA *falls against the steps, sobbing, and* DAVID *is weeping beside her.* PITO *moves to* LU'ISA, *even as* FRANK *takes* DAVID *into his arms.* LILO *is weeping against the porch rail by the steps.*

PITO *helps* LU'ISA *to her feet.* FRANK *takes her into the house,* PITO *following with* DAVID. *But at the door* DAVID *stops, looks back at* LILO, *who has now slid down onto the steps, sits there dejectedly, dazed, head lowered.*

DAVID's *crying dies down. He moves slowly, tentatively, unsure of himself, over to* LILO, *sits as close as possible to him. Without turning to him,* LILO *slowly wraps one arm around the boy, pulls him even closer.* DAVID *cries softly now against his uncle. The lights are fading to night. The* WRITER *moves in at left. He sits on the bench downstage left, and the stage is gradually dark, except for the small pool of light that illuminates him on the bench.*)

WRITER: *(Very quietly.)* A night of recriminations, tears, apologies, hurt. . . . It was decided that I be sent away to school, two years before I was supposed to go. . . . They all agreed I would be happier. . . . My life in the garden with Veni was coming to an end. Now only the goodbyes were left. . . . And the first goodbye was from my father, that night. . . . He came to my room.

(*A pool of light fades in at downstage right, and* FRANK *moves into it. He speaks facing the audience but down—at the imagined* DAVID *in his bed. He stands very still.*)

FRANK: *(Very softly, calling.)* Davey . . . Davey . . .

---

[4]PITO: Oh, my goodness! My goodness! *(Trying to comfort.)* Don't, don't!

WRITER: *(Softly.)* In my shame, I pretended to be fast asleep, beyond hearing. . . . But I can remake his words—the love that was in them—even today. . . .

FRANK: *(Always softly.)* Davey. . . . Well . . . *(A pause. He decides to continue, even though the child is asleep.)* Sometimes, son, you have to speak, even to the unhearing silence around you. . . . I'm leaving you, my precious . . . and I don't want to do that without leaving something with you—something against the silence that is going to grow around you more and more. . . . For that is the true enemy—and as you lie in your forests in the future, in your dark nights, reach out across that silence—touch—touch your father who left you . . . touch your mother who loves you, really—touch all who are so much in need of you as they wait at the other end of the darkness . . . reach out, my precious son, and touch us all. . . . *(He reaches forward and down, touches.)* Goodnight, my darling . . . goodbye. . . .

(The lights at downstage right fade out to black.)

WRITER: I would not see him again for many long years. . . . And so, my long dark night began. . . .

(The lights at downstage left fade out. The stage is in darkness.)

Scene Four

(The stage is dark. A pool of light comes up at the downstage left bench area. The WRITER *is seated on the bench. He looks at the audience for a few moments before he speaks.)*

WRITER: All my father's attempts to speak for the Mau before the New Zealand Investigating Committee failed. He was not allowed a hearing. He wasn't allowed to question witnesses. Despite the clustered bullet holes in the bodies of the Samoan dead, the committee chairman insisted the machine gun was fired over the people's heads, and the bullets fell harmlessly out at sea. . . . They refused to call the man who fired the machine gun, and they refused to call the two riflemen who were on the second floor porch—one of whom was surely Tamasese's murderer. Defeated in Upolu, my father went on to Geneva to plead Western Samoa's rights before the League of Nations. . . . Another week passed, then another, and yet another, and then it was time for me to go away to school.

(The lights now rise on stage to a predawn grayness, and BROTHER PATRICK *comes on. He is dressed in his tattered old fishing clothes, and he is very, very drunk.)*

WRITER: My last day was a bright one, although it had rained heavily the previous night. It stopped just before dawn, and I lay in bed, listening to the dripping off the roof until my garden window turned slowly from a black square to a gray one. . . .

*(*BROTHER PATRICK *picks up a handful of pebbles from the ground and throws them up at the window; he stumbles, rights himself, grinning like a mischievous boy.)*

WRITER: And then a handful of small pebbles hit my window lightly, and I went to it and raised it and looked down. It was Brother Pat.

(The gray dawn around BROTHER PATRICK *turns almost imperceptibly brighter—the spill from* DAVID'*s window.)*

WRITER: These are the words he spoke that I can no longer remember:

PATRICK: Top o' the mornin' to you, Davey... I'm on my way to a bit of fishin' this fine Saturday morning ending a splendid Friday evening. . . . Oh, splendid, just splendid. . . . It was like a fine old wake, Davey, for your goin' from us. The Sisters wouldn't come and Father Belwald couldn't, so it was just splendid! *(A kind of giggle.)* Brother Pius threw a pie in Brother Michael's face, like in the movies, and they had a fine old fight, and Brother Leo sang naughty old songs in Gaelic, shame on him, but I was the only one understood what he was sayin', shame on me, and then Headmaster did a fine jig while I played the accordion, and me not knowing at all how to play a single note. . . . Headmaster said it was lovely, Davey, and oh, it was, so lovely, everyone happy and lovin'. . . . *(His euphoria and the cascade of words fade. Instant sadness, guilt.)* I'm drunk, Davey, I've had a wee bit, but it was splendid, and the fishin' will be lovely. . . . Remember how I brought you mackerel from the bay for your breakfast, and your mother would ask me to stay and enjoy the fish with you, and the buttered toast, and wee bits of lemon. . . . She liked me. . . . Splendid lady. . . . *(His voice is fading.)* I will miss you so. . . . *(He is silent. He looks around as if suddenly remembering something. Then he goes to the table downstage right.)*

WRITER: He moved about a little, looking for the whiskey that was always there.

(BROTHER PATRICK *finds the decanter, removes the stopper, then changes his mind, remembering something else. He takes keys, coins, out of his right pants pocket. He searches among them for something with his index finger.)*

PATRICK: Something ... I came to give you something—to remember the good times—something ... *(He returns the keys and coins to his pocket, pats his left pants pocket: nothing. He finds what he is looking for, after more fumbling, in a shirt pocket—a St. Christopher medal.)* Ah! *(He holds it up for* DAVID *to see.)* A Saint Christopher. . . . To guard over you, whichever road you take. . . . *(He looks around, then goes to the downstage corner post of the porch at left.)* I'll just leave it here, then. . . . Right behind this post here . . . *(He does so.)* There. . . . Safe. . . . *(He looks back up to* DAVID's *window.)* Find it there in the morning, Davey, then wear it, wear it always. . . . *(Suddenly dejected.)* Ah, David, the Church has said he never lived: Saint Christopher. . . . Bad show. . . . *(Shakes his head.)* Denying her own saints, them that have seen the face of God and have felt his hand upon them . . . denying them, turning them away from the door, saying they lied . . . they themselves were lies that God needed. . . . As if God dealt in lies, Davey. . . . *(Protesting, near tears.)* Only liars deal in lies . . . and all liars become lies themselves, sooner or later. . . . We have gone mad, Davey. . . . *(He sits at the table center stage, disoriented, on the verge of maudlin tears.)* Find it, wear it, wear it always. . . . He was my hero, when I was a wee lad, like you, and they can't kill him, Davey, not him. . . . Not even the Church. . . . *(He has to cover his eyes with one hand, for the tears come slowly and unstoppably now.)* Oh, I'm sorry, I'm so sorry. I wanted to say goodbye nicely, after such a splendid evening . . . but it's been hard, it's been so hard, Father. . . .

WRITER: I was confused and embarrassed and I think even frightened to see my friend like that . . . so alone. . . . And I didn't want him to see that I was crying too, at my window. . . . So I blew out my lamp and moved back into the darkness. . . .

(The light on BROTHER PATRICK *below in the garden goes out.* BROTHER PATRICK *looks up at the window.)*

PATRICK: Oh? *(Then, crestfallen:)* Goodnight then, little Davey. *(He gets up to go, stumbles, has to use the back of a chair to right himself. He needs a few moments.)* Pray, Davey, pray for us sinners in the darkness of our fears. . . . But never commit the heartbreaking mistake of my life, thinking our prayers are answered, one day I would see his face and feel the comfort of his hand upon me. . . . God doesn't answer prayers, Davey. That is the truth you will come to find one day, and that is my gift to you: God doesn't answer prayers. . . . No matter. . . . Only—love him. Across the limitless vastness of your own darkness, love him. . . . With all the power in your heart through all the days of your life, love him, wanting nothing but to love him, as surely as we are born to live. . . . Goodbye, my little friend. *(He turns and starts off left very unsteadily. He stops, looks back up to* DAVID's *window without turning.)* Oh, how I love you.

(And he goes out. The WRITER *rises, moves to center stage, watching* BROTHER PATRICK *go for a few moments longer. Now, as he stands there, the lights rise to morning. He moves downstage a little, facing the audience.)*

WRITER: And then it was morning, and as the light fell everywhere out of the sky, a hush spread through our house, a hush that would last all day, and we avoided each other's eyes and were gentle with each other all day. Everyone pretended that although something important was happening, the day was really not all that different from any other day, for the family, despite all shocks, was still intact . . . the way people often are when someone in the family has died, and the services are over, and they have come back to the silent house after the last good-byes at the graveside and the silences in the empty rooms say "It is not over; it will never be over."

(He has moved over to downstage right, sits there. DAVID, *in pajamas, comes out of the house, looks around, then goes to the post for the St. Christopher medal. He picks it up, examines it, then puts it back quickly as* PITO *comes out of the house. She brings a tray with morning tea for two and a small fruitcake. She goes to the table center stage, sets two places.)*

PITO: 'O le ā le mea 'ua 'ē usupō ai? . . . 'E ā, 'ua koe susū fo'i lou 'aluga?[1]
DAVID: Susū fa'afefea?
PITO: Ka'ilo. 'E 'ese ā 'oe. 'E susū le 'aluga 'a e mago le moega.

*(*LU'ISA *comes out of the house before* PITO *has quite finished speaking. She wears a modish dressing gown over her night clothes and brocade bedroom slippers. She heads for the table center stage.)*

LU'ISA: Good morning, Precious!
DAVID: Morning.
LU'ISA: You're early. I thought you'd be. Excited?
DAVID: *(Very softly.)* No.

---

[1]PITO: Why did you wake so early? . . . Why, is your pillow wet again?
DAVID: What do you mean, "wet"?
PITO: I don't know. You are different. Your pillow is wet but the bed is dry.

LU'ISA: *(Mock surprise.)* No? . . . Well, in that case, come along and have some of this exciting fruitcake Pito's brought us.

DAVID: No, thank you. I'm not hungry.

LU'ISA: Even so! Come and sit with me while I have some with my morning tea. . . . You might change your mind.

DAVID: I have to go to the bathroom.

LU'ISA: Oh? Well, come along and give Mummy a good morning kiss before you go. *(He comes forward, eyes lowered, makes no move to kiss her. She kisses his forehead.)* Thank you, Precious. . . . Run along! (DAVID *goes into the house.* LU'ISA *sits.*) Pei 'o le'ā tagi.[2]

PITO: Masalo ga kagi i le pō 'ākoa. . . . 'Ua susū leaga lava loga 'aluga.

LU'ISA: 'E a 'ea? (PITO *takes up the empty tray.*) 'Ave lana fasi keke lea 'i lona potu.

PITO: 'Ia.

(LU'ISA *slices a piece of fruitcake, puts it on a plate, then on the tray that* PITO *holds in readiness.*)

PITO: Fa'afekai.[3]

(She goes into the house with the tray and slice of cake. LU'ISA *pours tea for herself. During the following,* LU'ISA *drinks and nibbles fruitcake— she eats with her fingers; raised pinkie; great delicacy. Despite the precisely maintained poise, a slight upsurge of grief hits her. A brief, pensive moment, a dab at an eye with the inevitable lace handkerchief, and she is her controlled patrician self again. Meanwhile:)*

WRITER: *(Rising and moving to center stage.)* Four years after I left, I came home for the holidays for the first time, diverted from my hurts by rugby, cricket, and the kind disinterest of new chums. Rooms that I had known to be high and spacious had shrunk, and I was surprised to find that I had imagined the flowers in my garden and that it took only a few steps to go its length and be

---

[2] LU'ISA: . . . Looks like he's going to cry.
PITO: Maybe he cried the whole night. . . . His pillow is very badly wet.
LU'ISA: What? . . . (PITO *takes up the empty tray.*) Take this piece of cake to his room.
PITO: Okay. . . .

[3] PITO: Thanks.

out of it again. *(He moves to the bench downstage left.)* But she had not changed. Her day started in the same way it always had: tea and her almost-too-sweet fruitcake, listening to the morning birds, concealing her confusion and her heartbreak. *(He sits.)* Her little finger, right hand—when she sipped her tea or picked at her fruitcake—was always unfailingly raised in that delicate, patrician way she had. Even as a very small child, I knew that it was a sure sign of her breeding, like her headaches that sometimes kept her on the chaise in her bedroom when she was feeling, as she put it, bilious. *(He smiles sadly, remembering.)* Fruitcake and nausea, in a world of goodbyes.

(LILO comes out of the house dressed for travel—a fine pongee silk suit, although he doesn't have the coat on yet. He carries it and now drapes it over the porch rail, by the steps, on his way to LU'ISA.)

LU'ISA: Ah, good morning! I was beginning to feel rather neglected.

LILO: Davey's pigskin trunk—

LU'ISA: The one from Hong Kong?

LILO: Yes.

LU'ISA: Not trouble, I hope. We haven't the time . . .

(LILO sits facing her.)

LILO: No. No. I just didn't understand how those Chinese locks worked. . . . It's all right; all solved. David got the hang of it in a matter of seconds. . . . *(A pause.)* He's awfully quick.

LU'ISA: Yes.

LILO: He'll be all right.

LU'ISA: Pray God. *(She is pouring his tea.)* And what about yourself? All packed?

LILO: All done. The men are bringing everything down from upstairs. *(He takes his tea from her.)* Ta. *(He helps himself to milk and sugar. Then:)* Many of the village people are coming to say goodbye.

LU'ISA: I know. . . . Pito and the girls have been in the kitchen since dawn, making doughnuts and scones and heaven only knows what else. . . .

(She sets a slice of fruitcake before him. He eats it, rather diffidently, throughout the following.)

LU'ISA: I've done the necessary banking arrangements for you in Auckland.

LILO: Thank you.

LU'ISA: When do you think you'll be coming back? You'll see to it that Davey is well settled first, of course.

LILO: Of course.

LU'ISA: But then, after that—?

LILO: Don't know. . . . What with the luck Frank's been having in Geneva, I thought I'd stay on a bit—down in Wellington. See what I can do.

LU'ISA: Well, you'll probably do more than Frank will ever accomplish with that silly League of Nations. . . . I just don't know what's come over that man. Can't he see the handwriting on the wall? Of course they won't give him a hearing. He has no official credentials, and he won't be recognized. The New Zealand delegation will see to that. It's Upolu all over again. . . . *(Ruefully.)* And Frank really isn't a fighter.

LILO: *(Softly.)* He's doing his best.

LU'ISA: But he's his own worst enemy. . . . Always thinking the best of people, even when they don't deserve it. . . .

(A pause.)

LILO: Well, I do know a few chaps in Wellington. Old school chums. They'll help, I'm sure. . . . Decent lot.

LU'ISA: Yes. . . . Take all the time you need. You'll not want for funds.

LILO: Thank you.

LU'ISA: It's the least I can do. . . . And Frank would want it, I know.

LILO: Yes. Yes, he would.

LU'ISA: Only—for heaven's sake, put up a good fight! Don't turn soft on me!

LILO: No. *(He pushes his plate away.)* Lu'isa . . .

LU'ISA: *(Preoccupied with her tea and thoughts.)* Mmm?

LILO: I've not apologized enough for what I—

LU'ISA: Don't! Don't!

LILO: But I want—

LU'ISA: *(Firmly.)* You mustn't think of it!

LILO: I was really striking myself, destroying what I loathe in myself. . . .

LU'ISA: *(Urgently.)* Please stop it, Lilo! Don't make me feel worse than I do this morning. . . .

LILO: *(Very softly; brokenly.)* I'm so sorry. And ashamed.

(She reaches over, pats his hand. Then, taking it in both of hers, she raises it, kisses it, holds it against her cheek. He does not look at her.)

LUʻISA: *(Quietly always.)* Be strong, Lilo. Always. Have the assurance that you are in the right and that human decency is on your side. Like your chums in Wellington. . . . *(She lowers his hand to the tabletop, holds it.)* And they aren't just in Wellington, you know. We have friends everywhere.

(He withdraws his hand. They sit in silence, their tea neglected. She lays her hand over his again.)

LUʻISA: Build us our country, Lilo. . . . We make our world with our own hands, stained with the blood of our courageous dead. . . . *(With strong emphasis on each word:)* We—make—it. *(She raises his closed hand again, still in hers—both of hers now.)* This is our mana, Lilo. *This* is our future!

(DAVID appears in the doorway. He is dressed up for travel: a proper little English schoolboy. PITO, a little teary, stands behind him. LUʻISA rises on seeing them.)

LUʻISA: Well, now, aren't we handsome! *(She goes to him.)* Isn't he *just*, Uncle Lilo?
LILO: *(Softly.)* Yes. Quite.

(He remains seated, not looking at DAVID, preoccupied with his hand. LUʻISA is by DAVID's side on the porch.)

LUʻISA: We'll be saying our goodbyes inside. Don't rush your tea.
LILO: No.
LUʻISA: Come along, Precious.

(They go into the house. LILO sits very still. Then he gets up, sees the decanter downstage right, goes to it with his teacup. He pours a little whiskey into the cup. Meanwhile:)

WRITER: He was thirty-five. He never returned home. Defeated at every turn, abandoned by old friends, he died four years later, at the age of thirty-nine. . . . He is buried in Auckland, and on his gray marble gravestone—it is very small—my mother had this inscribed:

(With his cup of whiskey, LILO has gone over to stage left for a last look off.)

WRITER: "Albert Lilomaiava Griffith, beloved only brother of Lu'isa Seumanutafa Griffith-Kreber, born Upolu, Western Samoa, January 2, 1896—died Auckland, New Zealand, May 17, 1934. A fighter for human dignity and freedom."

(On his way back to the table center stage, he stops for a moment at the post where the St. Christopher medal is hidden. He puts his cup down on the porch edge, takes a pack of cigarettes out of his pocket, is selecting one when he sees the medal. He returns the cigarettes to his pocket, picks up the medal, studies it with interest, then brings it with him to the table center stage and sits. He puts the medal in his pocket, pours more tea into his whiskey.)

WRITER: He died, slowly and painfully, of a broken heart and alcohol . . . and, abruptly and mercifully, from the blast of a 12-gauge shotgun pointed into his mouth and up. His right toe pushed the trigger.

(He sits, sipping tea pensively, then he just sits.)

WRITER: Alone in Auckland, I left to be with my father in America. It would be easier that way, he said. I was, after all, his son, and America was, after all, my country. . . . They never divorced; they lived separate lives and died separate deaths. . . . I did not see my mother again, or my garden, until, my father gone, I was called home for her last days and to bury her. . . . She died in the same bed upstairs, where her own mother had given birth to her and, twenty-six years later, I was born. . . . I held her hand, as she breathed her last, and saw, for the first time, that little finger of her right hand which she raised so delicately was not the result of breeding or affectation. She couldn't help it. Her little finger was permanently deformed that way—a birth defect.

(DAVID comes out of the house alone. He hesitates, thinking LILO has dozed off. He hasn't. He raises his head.)

LILO: Come, come and sit. *(DAVID does, more subdued than ever.)* There's a lot of fruitcake . . .
DAVID: No, thank you. Pito gave me cookies.

LILO: Is that what you've been up to all this while? Munching cookies in the kitchen with Pito?

DAVID: No. Mummy and I went about, saying goodbye to everyone: girls in the kitchen: men in the yard and over in the copra shed. And everything.

LILO: Everything?

DAVID: In the house . . . pictures of Grandpa and Grandma and things in my room and—everything. *(He is obviously about to cry.)*

LILO: Hey, hey, I think you'd better have some fruitcake. *(He offers a slice, DAVID takes it, nibbles it, head bowed.)* You'll like Auckland, I promise. And I'll be there, so you won't be lonely; and you'll be there, so I won't be lonely. . . . We'll see each other every weekend; we'll have good times. *(A moment.)* You'll like my old school. You'll make new friends, friends for life. . . . They know how to make a chap feel at home. . . .

DAVID: I don't want to make new friends.

(He stops eating. LILO watches carefully. In a moment, DAVID nibbles some more.)

LILO: I used to have a very special friend when I was your age. His name was Tifa-ma-tio-o-gatai-fale-i-le-tai-tu'i-ma-le-gaalu-lanu-toto.

(DAVID stops eating, looks at him, impressed.)

LILO: There's more to his name, but I've forgotten.

DAVID: Gosh!

LILO: But it did make for all sorts of trouble, a name like that. Imagine if somebody was drowning and I called him for help: "Help! Help! Tifamatioogataifaleiletaitutu'imalegaalulanutoto!" By the time I got his name out, the poor chap'd be a goner. *(DAVID laughs a little.)* Or if his house was on fire! . . . Or he didn't see that a great big coconut was about to fall down on his head!

DAVID: Or he didn't realize his pants were falling down!

LILO: Imagine!

(They laugh.)

DAVID: Didn't he have a short name?

LILO: Of course he did! Tio!

DAVID: Well, that's a nice name. And he'd catch his pants in time.

LILO: Wouldn't have mattered. He never wore pants; didn't own a pair. He always wore a lavalava.

DAVID: Tapa?

LILO: Of course.

DAVID: *(Turning serious.)* What did he look like?

LILO: Something like you. Except he was brown. And his head was shaved almost bald, except for a lock of hair . . . *(He pulls at DAVID's hair gently, over his forehead.)* . . . over here. Very like you.

(A pause.)

DAVID: What happened to him?

LILO: Nothing. Was something supposed to happen?

DAVID: I mean, you went away to school.

LILO: *(Gently.)* He came with me.

DAVID: But village people aren't like us, Mommy said: They don't have advantages. . . .

LILO: He didn't need money. He wanted to come so badly that he crawled inside my head and we went. . . .

DAVID: *(Disappointed.)* Oh, fiddle—

LILO: Really!

DAVID: —faddle!

LILO: No, no. I know he did, because he's still here. (DAVID *looks at him.* LILO *holds the look. He smiles a little.)* Refuses to go away. . . . He'll never leave me, David. *(Pause.)* You know what I mean, don't you?

DAVID: Yes, sir. . . . If he really wanted to be with you, he'd go along, wouldn't he?

LILO: No doubt about it. *(A moment.)* Oh. I almost forgot. *(He takes the St. Christopher medal out of his pocket.)* Is this yours? I found it over there. *(He gestures at the post.)*

DAVID: Yes. It's from Brother Pat. *(He pockets the medal.)*

LILO: Saint Christopher is a good friend to have along on a trip. He'll take care of us. Always.

DAVID: *(Softly.)* Brother Pat said he wasn't true.

WRITER: Then, too soon, time was over and the time had come. A life was over, and a life was to begin. . . .

(LU'ISA comes out of the house, PITO behind her.)

LU'ISA: Lilo, you'd better bring the car around to the front. . . . The men have put your things in the truck. They'll follow you in. One of them will bring the car back afterwards.

LILO: All right. . . . *(He takes his coat from the railing, crosses with her to the door, then, at the door, turns back.)* You *will* be out front?

(She shakes her head; emotion suddenly threatens to overwhelm her.)

LU'ISA: I—think I'll go to my room. After I bring little Davey as far as the front door. . . . I don't want to make a fool of myself in front of the villagers. . . .

LILO: Well then . . . tōfā![4] *(He folds her to him with his free arm, and she hugs him dearly.)*

LU'ISA: La'u pele!

(They are both weeping. PITO *moves away a bit, fussing with a handkerchief to her eyes.* DAVID *removes himself some distance stage left.* LILO *tears himself away, goes into the house. Leaning against the side of the doorway,* LU'ISA *fights to regain control. Finally she turns, moves a little way to* DAVID. PITO *waits on the porch by the door.)*

LU'ISA: The boys from the Brother's school are in front, dearest. To sing a goodbye song. . . . All your friends. *(She holds out her hand.)* Come along. *(He hangs back.)* Come along, dear. We mustn't keep them waiting. . . .

DAVID: I want to say goodbye. To Veni. Alone.

LU'ISA: Oh, do come, David.

PITO: Fai mai e ā?[5]

LU'ISA: Fai mai e fia fa'atōfā to'atasi 'i ā Veni.

PITO: Alu e fa'akali mai i lou poku. Mā ke ō aku.

(Hesitation from LU'ISA.*)*

---

[4]LILO: . . . goodbye! *(He folds her to him with his free arm, and she hugs him dearly.)*
LU'ISA: My dear!

[5]PITO: What did he say?
LU'ISA: He says he wants to say goodbye to Veni.
PITO: Go and wait in your room. We will come later.

PITO: Ku'u pea le kama 'iā a'u.[6]
LU'ISA: (*To* DAVID.) Don't take too long, then.

(*She goes into the house. A moment.* PITO *turns from the door.*)

PITO: (*To* DAVID.) Fai loa le lua māvaega.[7]

(*She goes in.* DAVID *stands very still. Then he faces offstage left.*)

DAVID: (*A half-call.*) Veni! . . . Veni! 'O le'ā 'ou alu. . . .[8] (*He moves upstage left a bit.*) 'Ailoga 'ou te toe va'ai 'iā 'oe. (*He waits. Louder:*) Veni, sau! . . . Sau, fa'amolemole, Veni! (*He is crying in fear now.*) Sau e tā fa'atōfā! (*Louder.*) Veni! Fa'amolemole! . . . 'Ou te lē fia alu to'atasi. (*Louder, lost, heartbroken.*) Sau loa. . . . Sau e tā ō! (*He is overwhelmed. He sobs to himself, repeating over and over to himself:*) O, Veni . . . Veni, sau. . . . Tā ō . . . Veni . . . Veni, fa'amolemole . . .

(PITO *is out of the house and to him. She holds him close.*)

PITO: (*Tenderly.*) Sōia! Sōia! . . . 'Ua lava. . . . Sau, sau pea 'oe, tā ō. . . . 'E lē fia sau lau uō. . . . Sōia, sōia![9]

(*She comforts* DAVID, *stroking his hair back, wiping his tears away with her thumb, the way old Samoan women do.*)

WRITER: The song my friends from school had chosen was a hymn with which their parents sang farewell at graveside. . . . For, as

---

[6]PITO: Leave the boy to me.

[7]PITO: Say your farewell.

[8]DAVID: Veni! . . . Veni! . . . I am going. . . . (*He moves upstage left.*) Will I see you? (*He waits. Louder.*) Veni, come! . . . Come, please, Veni! . . . (*He is crying in fear now.*) Come say good bye! . . . (*Louder.*) Veni! Please! . . . Let's go together. . . . (*Louder, lost, heartbroken.*) Come now. . . . Come let's go! . . . (*He is overwhelmed. He sobs to himself, repeating over and over to himself:*) Oh, Veni . . . Veni, come. . . . Let's go . . . Veni . . . Veni, please . . .

[9]PITO: Stop! Stop! . . . That's enough. . . . Come, come you. He doesn't want to come with you. . . . Stop, stop!

the Brothers had said, my going was a dying away from them and the village.

(Now the hymn—"Tōfāina 'oe"—starts from the front of the house, soft-ened by distance. Holding DAVID *close to her side, weeping now into her apron,* PITO *leads* DAVID *to the door. He buries his face in her side as they go.)*

WRITER: Now, years later, remembering that evening, I keep repeating my goodbyes to that little boy and to his garden. . . . "Never be far from me, little one. Lodge yourself in me, some-where in the words I will seek all my life, and there, cry out your hurt, and cry until the words become a brown and shining young man raising his hands high and calling above the clamor-ing pain around us, 'Peace! Peace!' and only the blessed silence answers, that bright silence beyond which new mornings dawn for all of us. Go, Precious, go. Stay with me always."

(On his last words, PITO *and* DAVID *have disappeared into the house. The hymn has swelled and then died into silence. And the lights, which have faded to spots on him, fade into darkness.)*

Mele Kanikau

A PAGEANT

CAST

Martha	Ginger Lei
The Author	Ululani
Lynette	The Voice
Charles Kelsoe	Jimmy
Bill	Maile
Pageant Court	Clement Iloa
Keoki Random	Joseph Poloke
Arthur Lin	Lokalia
Carl Alama	Lydia Jenkins
Freddie	Noa Napoʻoanaakalā
Frances Corrington	Kamuela
Pokipala	Kaleo
Hiʻiaka	Piʻilani
Malia	Keaka Ching
Girl I	

Place: A Honolulu stage
Time: Mid to late twentieth century

ACT ONE

(The stage of a theater somewhere in Honolulu. It is being readied for a Hawaiian pageant. So far the set—it will be a Throne Room—is far from finished: at stage right there is a dais, backed by a wall, upon which are rehearsal chairs; along the back, a low platform runs parallel to the foot-lights; rising up from this platform are thick rectangular pillars, some painted a coral and rock effect. A sky cyclorama. Benches. At upstage left, a cardboard box for trash.

Many minutes before the start: two hula dancers—girls—enter. They are MARTHA *and* GINGER LEI, *both very pretty in a slick, professional way.* GINGER LEI *is being taught the finishing touches to a hula by* MARTHA. *It is the hula we will later see them perform. After a while, things going well,* MARTHA *exits.* GINGER LEI *goes on practicing. Finally, a man walks on to address the audience. He is in his thirties, mild-mannered. This is the* AUTHOR.)

AUTHOR: Ladies and gentlemen, I am the author of the play you are about to see. Well, that isn't quite true, of course. The real author is a man named John Kneubuhl. I don't look like him, not in the slightest; I don't sound like him. Besides, he's a much older man than I am. About the only thing we have in common is—well, we're both hapa-haole. He's part Samoan; I'm part Hawaiian. Anyway, he made me up. I don't know why. I've asked him why, but he only shrugged and said I just happened to show up one day, when he was sitting around not thinking of anything in particular—in fact, thinking of nothing, nothing at all. It was, he says, a very rainy afternoon. . . . Well, so here I am, an act of the imagination, created out of nothing in particular on a rainy day so that other acts of the imagination—this play, these char-acters—might come into existence: an unreality bringing forth, into the world of reality, other unrealities. Does that seem so strange to you? It isn't, you know. Not really. Without these other characters, I have no reason for being here, and, without us, the real author really has no reason for existing; in fact, has no existence. . . . Oh, it's true enough that without the poet there is no poem; that's so obvious it seems almost silly to say it. But what isn't so obvious, what's even truer, is that, without the poem, there is no poet. Poets don't merely create; they, too, are created by their creations. They don't just write; they are themselves written. So, you see, I have as much right as he to say I am the author—the real author—of this play. Even to use his name as mine. . . . Ladies and gentlemen, here and now I create him. And, in that creation, create myself. *(He smiles, pleased with himself.)* Now that you understand, let me begin again. . . . Friends, dear friends, my name is John Kneubuhl. I am the author of the play you are about to see. As I've explained, I *am* the play . . . them.

(GINGER LEI moves downstage where her shoebox of cosmetics has been left. She takes out a little bottle of nail polish, begins to do her toes. With her move, three other hula dancers—ULULANI, MARTHA, and LYNETTE—walk on from either side, costumed like GINGER LEI; they seem like clones of each other. They all sit on benches and primp. Meanwhile:)

AUTHOR: We present our fiction, our *mele kanikau:* the lament that is ourselves, the grief that is mine.

(A very melodious male voice comes over the PA system. The DANCERS pay no attention to it.)

VOICE: A-l-o-o-o-ha! Welcome to the golden shores of Paradise! Welcome to the golden days of Hawai'i-nei when the *ali'i* reigned in their regal splendor over their loyal and carefree subjects. . . . Welcome to an Eden of perfumed flowers and dew-spangled days that reflect rainbows across azure skies. . . . Welcome to the land of true aloha, Hawai'i, the land of Love and Music and the Hula. . . .

(CHARLES, the stage manager, has entered, listening to the VOICE. He, too, is part-Hawaiian, in his late twenties.)

CHARLES: *(Calling offstage.)* Jimmy! Hey, Jimmy! That's good! Set your reading at that!
JIMMY: *(Off.)* Right!
ULULANI: Ginger Lei.

GINGER LEI: Hm?

CHARLES: *(Calling off.)* Bill! Hey, Bill!

ULULANI: You *pau* with your polish?

GINGER LEI: Sure. *(She recaps the bottle.)*

CHARLES: *(Calling off.)* Bill, you there?

BILL: *(Off.)* Yeah.

CHARLES: *(Calling.)* I want to check the lights for the opening. Okay?

BILL: *(Off.)* Go ahead. I'm ready.

(GINGER LEI brings the bottle of polish to ULULANI, sits with her.)

CHARLES: Never mind about the projections—the rainbows and all that stuff. I just want the lights.

(Another hula dancer, MAILE, enters.)

DANCERS: *(Variously.)* Hey, hiya, Maile. . . . Hello, Maile. . . . Hey, you're late.

BILL: *(Off.)* What did you say, Charlie?

MAILE: Hi.

CHARLES: I said, Lights! I just want the lights!

AUTHOR: Lights! To probe the darkest mysteries of the human heart. A stage. A handful of actors. . . . Listen:

(The DANCERS speak standard, non-Island English.)

MARTHA: *(To MAILE.)* Where's your sister?

MAILE: Helen's not coming.

MARTHA: Why not?

MAILE: You know very well why not. . . . The abortion. Remember?

MARTHA: Good heavens, I forgot.

(ULULANI, preoccupied with her toe polishing, has paid no attention.)

LYNETTE: Ululani . . . *(No response.)* Ululani!

ULULANI: Mmm? What?

LYNETTE: Did you hear? Maile's sister Helen is getting a scrape job.

ULULANI: *(Preoccupied.)* That's nice.

GINGER LEI: Doesn't she want the baby?

MAILE: You know how she is. Young. She doesn't see any sense in getting tied down so young.

LYNETTE: She's got a point.

MARTHA: Don't you have anybody who could—uh—you know—what's that word, Lynette?

LYNETTE: *Hānai?*

MARTHA: Yes, *hānai.* Isn't there someone?

MAILE: If my mother and her sisters ever found out that Helen was knocked up by a Hawaiian elementary school dropout, they'd throw a fit.

ULULANI: *(Preoccupied.)* Oh well—babies are hell on the figure anyway.

(During the preceding, the work lights have changed to the show lights. CHARLES, *intent on the lights, has been oblivious to the* DANCERS *throughout.)*

CHARLES: *(Calling.)* Bill. . . . Bring Number Three up a little more.

(As Number Three light comes up, more of the PAGEANT CAST *move on. A few are in costume: white, crepe paper "feather" capes and so forth.)*

AUTHOR: Not only the mysteries of the human heart, but we search for and find and celebrate the sanctity of all created things. . . . Like this:

(Now the DANCERS *speak with marked Island accents.)*

GINGER LEI: E, Martha.

*(*MARTHA *is now making repairs on a floral coronet.* GINGER LEI *wanders over to look.)*

GINGER LEI: Where you get that orchid?

MARTHA: From Nakaguchi's Authentic Hawaiian Novelty Shop.

(Number Three light is set.)

GINGER LEI: Gee, jes' like real, yeh?

MARTHA: More. An' 'you oughta see the lehua and *'ilima* those guys got in that store. You can almos' smell 'em they look so real.

CHARLES: *(Calling.)* No. . . . You don't have to bring Ten down so far. Take it up a little. . . .

(More of the cast are coming on: Kāhili bearers, ATTENDANTS, *the* COURT. *Among the men are* CLEMENT ILOA, KEOKI RANDOM, JOSEPH POLOKE, ARTHUR LIN. *Among the women is* LOKALIA. *They are not yet fully costumed.)*

CHARLES: That's it. Set it right there, Bill. . . . Okay. I think that'll do it. Mahalo!
BILL: *(Off.)* Roger!

(CHARLES *turns to check the assembled cast as slowly the show lights fade.)*

AUTHOR: Beloved, this is the story of a man who, although living, was dead. The son of a long line of *ali'i.* This is the story of how two lovers came to him in his kingdom where he ruled over the dead and the dying and offered him the gift of Life. This is a story of Love, the mysteries of the human heart, the sanctity of all created things. . . .

(The show lights have all but gone out as he steps offstage. Now the work lights bump in with the entrance of CARL ALAMA, *the* mō'ī *of the pageant. He is a handsome Hawaiian in his mid-fifties: a charmer. He is in costume but for his cape and helmet.)*

CHARLES: All ready, Carl?
CARL: Yes. Lydia's coming.
CHARLES: *(To the* COURT.) Everybody else here?
COURT: Yeah. . . . I think so. . . . Sure. . . . *(And so forth.)*

(Two or three stragglers hurry on in the background. Then, from downstage right, the queen, LYDIA JENKINS, *enters in full costume—* holokū, *flowers, hairdo, makeup, pendant earrings, the works! A big, handsome, statuesque woman.)*

LYDIA: Has he come already, Charles?
CHARLES: *(Glancing at his wristwatch.)* He ought to be here any minute. . . . Freddie, go to the back, in the parking area. . . . When you see his car coming, run back here and tell us.

(FREDDIE, *a boy at the back in a T-shirt and* malo, *runs off to upstage left.)*

LYDIA: (*To* CARL.) I don't understand why we need this man. What's wrong with Charles? He's the stage manager.

JOSEPH: Yeah, he knows what to do.

KEOKI: Sure. He can do it fine.

CARL: It's a big pageant, Keoki. Charlie can't do everything.

LYDIA: But why Napo'o? This is supposed to be dignified—to show our people's dignity. And they get a man like that!

ARTHUR: Sounds like you know him, Lydia.

LYDIA: I don't want to know him. But I've heard the talk. All through the years. (*A moment.*) Anybody here know him?

(*A general ripple of denials from the cast.*)

CARL: I do. I mean, I did. Years ago, long time. He used to work for me, when I was just starting my travel agency. I haven't seen him since. . . . You ready to start, Charlie?

CHARLES: Sure. But don't you want to explain first?

CARL: No, no. You go ahead. On stage, you're the boss.

LYDIA: Then, if he's the boss, why don't you let him be the boss?

CARL: Go on, Charlie.

CHARLES: (*To the* CAST.) All right. . . . You all know that Mrs. Pakalimu got a hurry-up call last Friday to go to Las Vegas. It's a big break for her, really big time. . . . So the Board of Directors for our Festival Week got together and they picked a new director to help us out during our dress rehearsals. . . . (*He has to refer to a slip of paper to get the name right.*) His name is Napo'o-ana-a-ka-lā—

LYDIA: We know all that, Charles.

CHARLES: Well—then, that's all. I don't know anything more about him. But—according to Carl, here—he really knows about putting on a show.

CARL: He's—very good.

LYDIA: (*A flat fact.*) He's a *māhū*. (*She pronounces it* "MA-hu," *the accent on the first syllable. There is an awkward, somewhat embarrassed silence.*)

KEOKI: Well—how come we never heard of him, Charlie?

CHARLES: I guess—well—I don't know.

CARL: He's a—kind of recluse.

KEOKI: Oh, I see. (*Pause.*) What's that?

CARL: What?

KEOKI: Recluse.

CARL: Oh, you know—a loner. He sticks to himself, stays away from people. He lives in a valley, north shore, way in the back, in a little Hawaiian settlement he built.

CLEMENT: Settlement? You mean, grass huts and like that?

CARL: Yes. He runs a kind of hula school there. With his wife.

LYDIA: *(A derisive hoot.)* Wife!

LOKALIA: What, Lydia?

LYDIA: She's no wife, Lokalia. That's his haole mistress.

LOKALIA: You know her?

LYDIA: *(Shakes her head.)* You know the old Corrington family over on Kaua'i?

LOKALIA: Sure, of course.

LYDIA: She's a Corrington. You're too young to remember, but when it happened, everybody talked about it.

LOKALIA: When what happened?

LYDIA: She ran away with him. To live in a grass hut. Was a big scandal.

LOKALIA: Yeah. How come they have to live like that? The Corringtons, they're rich. She *pupule* or what?

LYDIA: The family told her, Come back. She refused. So, they kicked her out. Not one cent.

JOSEPH: Gee! Must be quite a guy, though, to have a wahine lose her head like that over him.

CLEMENT: What kind of a guy is he, Carl?

CARL: Oh, like I said, I knew him a long time ago—before he went off on this Hawaiian kick. This is a different person altogether from the Noa Napo'o I knew. . . . Anyway, he's become a great *kumu hula*. . . . And, look, when he comes— (LOKALIA *is busily whispering with a* PRINCESS.) Lokalia . . . Lokalia, please pay attention. . . . What I have to say is very important. *(He gets undivided attention.)* When he comes, I want you—the Board of Directors wants you—to treat him with professional respect. After all, what we want to do is put on the best kind of pageant we can in the tradition of Hawai'i-nei. . . . Another person's private life is none of our business. We don't go around sticking our noses into each other's private lives, so why should we bother our heads about his? Our one job here, the only thing that is our business here, is to pull together and *kōkua*—to make sure—that . . .

(He becomes aware that they are no longer paying attention to him. Their attention has wandered to the front of the house. CARL *turns to the front.*

Coming up into the light and onto the stage are NOA NAPO'O, FRANCES CORRINGTON, KAMUELA, *and* POKIPALA. NOA *is a Hawaiian in his late fifties: a deceptively unprepossessing man sloppily dressed in dark, faded trousers, faded shirt, and an old army jacket that is too large for him; a strand of maile is draped around his shoulders.* FRANCES *is his age, quiet spoken, a born patrician. She wears an old-fashioned* mu'umu'u *that began to fade years ago. She carries an old cloth bag.* KAMUELA *and* POKIPALA *are Hawaiian boys, very poorly dressed; they are rare combinations of humility and power, tenderness and virility, child-men.* CARL *is somewhat embarrassed at the sight of them.* FRANCES *leading, they stop before him.)*

FRANCES: Hello, Carl.
CARL: Good Lord . . . Frances . . . Frances! How are you?

*(*FRANCES *smiles a little, nods "all right," as they shake hands.* CARL, *his affability scarcely masking his embarrassment, moves to* NOA, *holding out his hand.)*

CARL: Noa—it's—good to see you.

(Instead of shaking hands, NOA *kisses him in the old Hawaiian way, cheek to cheek, breathing in.)*

NOA: *(Quietly.)* Hello, Carl. Hau'oli nō au e 'ike hou iā 'oe ma hope o nā makahiki lō'ihi loa.[1]
CARL: *(Gesturing to the back, behind the theater.)* We expected you to arrive in the parking lot back there, so—we—
NOA: *(Always quietly.)* No. We parked in the front. We didn't want to interrupt, so—we— *(He gestures to the front of the house.)* —just came in and sat down.

*(*CARL *looks nervously, involuntarily perhaps, over at* LYDIA, *turns back to* NOA.*)*

CARL: You been sitting out there long?

Kneubuhl's original typescript included the stage direction "(in Hawaiian)" along with the English lines. The Hawaiian has been added for this publication.

[1]NOA: . . . It's very good to see you again after so many years.

NOA: A few minutes.

CARL: Well—let me introduce—This is Charles Kelsoe, our stage manager. . . . Noa Napo'o.

(CHARLES *and* NOA *shake hands.*)

NOA: *(A gentle correction.)* Noa Napo'oanaakalā.

CHARLES: *(Almost inaudibly.)* Aloha.

CARL: And Noa—Noa, this is Lydia Jenkins. She's our queen.

(NOA *bows slightly. Not a move from* LYDIA.)

CARL: And Frances Corrington.

FRANCES: *(In flawless Hawaiian.)* Ua hau'oli nō kēia hui 'ana o kāua. Nui ko'u hau'oli e launa pū me 'oe.[2]

(A very dignified small nod from LYDIA, *utterly expressionless.)*

NOA: *(Politely.)* He pili koko 'oe i ka 'ohana Kaleihulumamo i male i kekahi lālā 'ohana Jenkins no Kaua'i?[3]

LYDIA: *(Stiffly.)* How do you do.

NOA: *(Politely.)* No. I asked if you're a part of the Kaleihulumamo family that married into the Jenkins family on Kaua'i.

LYDIA: Yes.

NOA: You were famous *ali'i*. Maybe not as famous as Carl's family, but well known.

LYDIA: We are still as high as any *ali'i* family.

NOA: Of course you are. *(He turns away, but then he turns back remembering something. He is always pleasant.)* Oh, if I may: It's pronounced ma-HU. Hoo—hoo, like an owl. Mahu *(with the short syllables)* means to nibble, to eat a little snack. You know, so you can keep your mouth busy, until there's something you can really sink your teeth into.

CARL: *(Interrupting somewhat nervously.)* And Noa—this—let me introduce you to Clement Iloa . . . Joseph Poloke . . . Keoki Random . . . Arthur Lin . . . *(Handshakes, mumbled greetings.)* And over here is Lokalia, with the other princesses and—

---

[2] FRANCES: It's a great pleasure to meet you.

[3] NOA: Are you related to the Kaleihulumamo family that married into the Jenkins family on Kaua'i?

NOA: Later, Carl. Later. . . . Names just mix me up. (*To the* CAST:) We're all going to be good friends, as we work. (*To* CHARLES:) Maybe we better start?

CHARLES: Sure. You—want to see the whole pageant from start to finish?

NOA: Of course.

CHARLES: Okay. . . . Listen, people. We'll run through the pageant in a few minutes. The folks whose costumes are all ready, please wear 'em. . . . We'll go through the whole thing like a performance. If you make mistakes, don't stop, keep it moving. . . . (*To* NOA:) Would you like to say something?

NOA: Yes. Where's the *lua?* I would like to pee.

(*Consternation from the cast. Some stifled snickers, hidden smiles. Appalled,* LYDIA *rises with great dignity and walks off.*)

CHARLES: (*To the nearest man.*) Would you show him? (*To* NOA:) He'll show you.

NOA: Thank you. E Kamuela, e hele mai, pono 'oe e kōkua ia'u.[4]

FRANCES: E hele me lāua, e Pokipala.

(POKIPALA *goes offstage after them.*)

CHARLES: All right, people. . . . Ten minutes.

(*The cast goes off, all talking softly at once.* CHARLES *moves downstage left, calling up and off.*)

CHARLES: Bill—Bill?

BILL: (*Off.*) Yeah?

CHARLES: (*Calling.*) Can I see you down here? Bring your cue sheet.

(*He goes off. Alone on stage are* CARL *and* FRANCES. *She moves to a bench and sits.* CARL *is looking in the direction of* NOA's *exit.* FRANCES *looks at him, smiling a little.*)

FRANCES: You seem—worried.

---

[4]NOA: . . . Kamuela, come, I'll need you.
FRANCES: Go with them, Pokipala.

CARL: *(Too quickly.)* No. *(He sees that she is smiling. He smiles too, shrugs.)* It's none of my business.

FRANCES: When a *kumu hula* sullies himself, there are rites of purification. He needs the two boys to assist him.

CARL: I'll explain to the others.

FRANCES: Still the same circumspect Carl.

CARL: Oh, it's just that—I think it's better if we don't start off with any—misunderstandings.

FRANCES: Much better.

(A pause. It's obvious he wants to talk but doesn't know how to begin.)

CARL: It's—been a long time.

FRANCES: Yes. *(Another pause.)* I read about you in the newspapers from time to time. Your successes.

CARL: *(A shrug.)* Oh—I package tours. You know—tourists. . . . Put shows together . . . still do a little public relations work. . . .

FRANCES: A little? . . . Official greeter—your picture in the magazine advertisements—your Mainland trips for the Visitor's Bureau. . . . You've become the successor to Duke Kahanamoku, they say. . . .

CARL: Big deal.

FRANCES: Success has made you modest. Treasurer, Hawaiian People's Association . . . Vice-President, the Hawaiian Foundation . . . President, the Society of Ali'i . . . Chairman, the Jubilee Festival Week . . . and so much more.

CARL: I do what I can to help my people.

FRANCES: Like being the *mō'ī* for the pageant.

CARL: It isn't just—for the tourists, you know. It's good for our own people to see—especially the young people.

FRANCES: Yes. I must say, you make a very handsome—a very striking—*mō'ī*. *(There's another pause.)* Have you forgiven us?

CARL: For something that happened so many many years ago? I can't even remember that evening very well now.

FRANCES: Then it wasn't really such a hurt. I'm glad.

(Another pause.)

CARL: Have you been happy, Fran?

FRANCES: Happiness has had little to do with it. Very little. I don't think I've thought about it much.

CARL: Then you can't have been unhappy . . .

FRANCES: No.

CARL: No regrets?

FRANCES: I regret not a moment of it, Carl.

CARL: Then I'm glad. *(Another pause.)* Maybe I'd better get ready for the run-through. *(A pause.)* It's a very good pageant. I'm sure you and Noa will like it.

FRANCES: Yes. I'm sure.

CARL: Well . . . *(He starts to go.)*

FRANCES: Carl . . . *(He turns back.)* Was it you who got Noa this job?

CARL: It was a committee decision. The Jubilee Festival Board of Directors.

FRANCES: How do they know about Noa?

CARL: Noa is a great artist.

FRANCES: His own people have neglected him for years. Too many years to remember. . . . We hardly ever come out of the valley; we see nobody. And suddenly a man drives up in a jeep yesterday, all the way up those hills, and he asks Noa if he would oversee this pageant. . . .

CARL: Yes, I know. Tom Bruner, the committee's lawyer.

FRANCES: They talked for a long time.

CARL: Tom was impressed by Noa's interest in everybody connected with the show. The careful detailed questions . . .

FRANCES: Noa wanted to be sure.

CARL: Of?

FRANCES: Integrity.

CARL: That's why we picked him—his demand for integrity.

FRANCES: But—after all these years . . . ?

(CHARLES comes in from left.)

CHARLES: You ready, Carl? It's about time.

CARL: Okay.

(CHARLES exits.)

CARL: I'd better get ready.

FRANCES: Yes.

CARL: It's—nice to see you again.

(He goes off at right. FRANCES remains seated, quickly lost in thought. The AUTHOR steps in, addresses the audience.)

AUTHOR: Well—does she seem *pupule* to you? Does she look or speak like a woman who would turn her back on a heritage of wealth, of cultivated tastes, of Christian rectitude and rush off to live in a thatch hut, plant taro, pound poi, make *kapa*, weave baskets, pray to forest gods, and spend one week out of every month in a menstrual hut? If you say that it isn't reasonable, that it isn't true to life, then you are very, very mistaken. . . . (*He gestures to* FRANCES.) Because, you see, there actually was a woman I patterned Frances after. A woman I knew when I was a small boy. Well, I never really knew her, I never even saw her. Not that I can remember. I was told about her. What I wasn't told, I imagined, pieced together out of odds and ends of the imagination—as one pieces together a character for a play. . . . (*He again indicates* FRANCES.) Anyway, she was real, and she was my parents' dear friend. Her name was Georgina. She came from a very good haole family, and she was going to marry a successful merchant, also haole, of course. It was all arranged. Not just by the families. It was like the entire community agreed: this was the proper joining of families who represented the best that anyone could wish for, not only for themselves but for the community. And proper Georgina knew all that, accepted all that gladly as her duty. People even remarked how increasingly radiant she looked as her wedding day approached. . . . And then, suddenly, one day, she walked out, leaving family and friends and betrothed to live with a Samoan man in an old tent in the foothills, away from everybody. She had met him just once—the day before she disappeared. He was a man of no education, not even by native standards, an ignorant savage, my mother said. And Georgina had been educated in a private seminary for proper young ladies in New Zealand. She could paint water colors, play Chopin and Mendelssohn on the piano, and she pressed little flowers between the pages of a diary she kept. Of course. And she had been to Sydney . . . many, many times. And why did she go off like that? The haole community was shocked and mystified. Our servants whispered about native magic herbs. . . . But what was it really?

(FRANCES *stirs out of her silent reverie as* NOA *comes on.*)

NOA: One *'opihi* for your thoughts.
FRANCES: Only one?

(He touches her face tenderly.)

NOA: What were you thinking? You looked sad.

(She shakes her head, not wanting to talk about it. Emotionally, she crushes his hand against her mouth, very near tears.)

AUTHOR: Why did she go off like that? I don't know. . . . And so, I wrote this play, in an effort to find the answer to that question.

(He steps off. NOA *sits beside* FRANCES.*)*

NOA: You're still frightened. . . . Mai makaʻu.[5]
FRANCES: It's the other children. Where are they, why aren't they here?
NOA: I don't know. We have to be patient.
FRANCES: And if they don't come . . . ?
NOA: Then—they've been held back. They won't go with us. . . . But they'll come. I'm sure of it.

(Pause.)

FRANCES: Kamuela and Pokipala don't know. I can tell. Why is it being kept from them?
NOA: Maybe they just need more time.
FRANCES: But how much more? . . . Time is over now, it's ended; *pau.* . . . They're bound to find out very soon. (NOA *remains silent.)* Why can't we tell them?
NOA: Because they must listen and hear it themselves. And each of them must say, "I know this song. I heard it before. Only one time before. At the moment when I was born." And each must say, for himself, "I accept my song." *(Pause.)* We cannot sing their *mele kanikau* for them. No one can. . . . *(Pause.)* Say with me. I accept.
FRANCES: *(Softly.)* I accept.
NOA: *(In all tenderness.)* Look at me, *kuʻu ipo.*

(She does.)

---

[5] NOA: . . . Don't be afraid.

FRANCES: *(The fear returning.)* I can accept anything—forever ... heaven or hell, anything—if you are there beside me. . . .

NOA: Say only, I accept . . .

FRANCES: *(Against the fear.)* I accept . . .

NOA: *(Whispering.)* I love you.

FRANCES: *(The same.)* I love you.

(He kisses her gently with great love. He holds her close, her head against his chest.)

FRANCES: Free me, Noa . . . free me from my fears.

NOA: Soon. Soon we shall be free. . . . Don't be afraid.

(NOA chants in Hawaiian. It is almost a wailing. In the background, attracted by his voice, KAMUELA appears, unseen by them. He hears, listens in rising grief, and he dances, dances out his fear, grief, and finally acceptance. He moves off into the darkness, as the chant comes to a finish. FRANCES has calmed down somewhat.)

NOA: Is it over?

FRANCES: *(Bravely.)* Yes. . . . All gone.

(She tries a reassuring smile, rallies even more as he returns the smile. He becomes little-boyish, impish, grinning.)

NOA: So, give me my pill. It's time.

(She reaches into her cloth bag and takes out a small pill bottle; she takes out a pill, offers it.)

NOA: I don't want it.

FRANCES: *(Playing along; it's an old game.)* You must. The doctor said.

NOA: 'A 'ole au makemake.[6]

FRANCES: The doctor insisted. Pono 'oe e inu![7] Every four hours.

---

[6]NOA: I don't want it.

[7]FRANCES: . . . You must take it. . . .

NOA: *(Hamming.)* Oh, all right! He mea pilikia ʻoe, e Palakika![8] *(He takes the pill.)* You know I can't swallow it dry like this . . .

(FRANCES reaches into the bag deeper, but stops as she sees CHARLES come in with a great wicker peacock chair which he sets down at the throne area. He comes to FRANCES on:)

FRANCES: Charles . . .
CHARLES: Yes, ma'am . . . ?
FRANCES: Could you bring some water, please? So my husband can take this pill?
CHARLES: Of course.

(He goes off. FRANCES'S hand, still in the bag, is now withdrawn. In it is a small bottle of whiskey. NOA gives her the pill, which she returns to its bottle; he uncaps the bottle, takes a big swallow. Then he continues to sip as they talk. The bottle is about a third full.)

NOA: That's better. Much better.
FRANCES: I'm glad.
NOA: You?

(He grins, offers her the bottle. She smiles and plays along, taking the bottle. A little dainty sip, coughs, returns the bottle.)

FRANCES: Much, much better.
NOA: I'm glad. *(He drinks.)* You seen the costumes they got back there?
FRANCES: Not yet.
NOA: The flowers are plastic. The *ʻilima* lei are yellow paper, and the capes and helmets.
FRANCES: Feathers are hard to get. There aren't many *mamo* or *oʻo* any more. . . .
NOA: How sad that sounds, just saying their names. *Oʻo, mamo, iʻiwi, oʻu* . . . a *mele kanikau* of birds' names. When I was a boy, there were thousands in the valleys.
FRANCES: *(Quietly.)* Noa, they started disappearing long before you were born.
NOA: I saw them, Frances, I saw them. . . .

---

[8]NOA: . . . What a bother you are, Palakika! . . .

FRANCES: *(Acquiescing gently.)* Yes, dear. Of course you did.

NOA: Thousands. Flying from tree to tree, everywhere—like green and yellow rain whipped by the wind . . . thrashed! . . . *(Softly.)* Crushed!

(The memory seems to have taken possession of him, and he stares straight ahead, lost in it. She is a little concerned.)

FRANCES: Noa . . . *(He is still "away." She touches his arm.)* Noa . . . Noa, dearest!

(He stirs back, looking down.)

NOA: *(Softly.)* And the killing wind is over, and the rain is over. But where did all those little lives go, Frances?

(He drinks. LYDIA enters at the back unnoticed. Seeing NOA drinking, she moves forward a bit and watches in angry silence.)

FRANCES: I guess to make feather capes and helmets for the *ali'i.*

NOA: *(More sadly than angrily.)* The damned—the goddamned *ali'i.* *(Sighs.)* I don't know. Maybe they're right. Maybe paper is better.

FRANCES: Anyway, under the right lights, they look real.

NOA: They crushed us, Palakiko. *(He looks at the bottle.)* It's almost empty.

FRANCES: *(Getting a wallet out of her bag.)* There's a liquor store down the road. I'll send Kamuela.

(She gets up to go, and for the first time they see LYDIA. NOA smiles, raises the bottle to her in a toast. He drinks, emptying the bottle. CHARLES comes in with a coffee cup of water.)

CHARLES: Sorry I couldn't find a glass, Mr. Napou.

LYDIA: *(To NOA.)* Don't you think you better hold off until after the rehearsal?

NOA: Can't.

LYDIA: We like to set a good example for our young people in the dance troupe. No drinking. Not even cigarettes. You notice anybody here even smokin' a cigarette?

NOA: It's medicine. Like haole drink because of snake bites. Hawaiians have to drink because of the *mo'o.* Lizards.

LYDIA: What's the lizards got to do with it?

NOA: Well, you see—there's lots of old Hawaiian *'aumakua* around. And sometimes they turn into a little *mo'o* and then the little *mo'o* gets very naughty. . . . And he comes and bites and drinks people's blood and souls. . . . So they own the people's *piko*—all their different kind *piko*. . . . You see, they want to live in your body. . . . (*Both his hands have cupped themselves over his crotch as he makes loud sucking noises. Then his right hand stretches out to* LYDIA.) And they do even worse things to women, especially *ali'i* women. Wiggle wiggle wiggle . . . (*His right index finger wriggles as he makes a single long sucking sound.*) They can suck your *ali'i* soul dry. *Ono!*

LYDIA: You're drunk.

NOA: Sure! Sure, that's the point! When the *mo'o* come—(*The finger wriggles.*)—wiggle wiggle wiggle, you think they suck my soul out? Never! They get only whiskey. And they get drunk. They pass out. . . . And my soul is safe. All my *piko*, safe . . . I'm still me. (*Suddenly he is very tired. He runs a hand across his eyes.*) Hurry up, Frances. The bottle is almost empty, and I think the *mo'o* are going to attack.

FRANCES: (*Genuinely worried.*) Yes.

(FRANCES *hurries off. The puzzled* CHARLES *brings the cup of water to him. Some of the cast are moving across the stage at the back from right to left.* CHARLES *offers the cup of water to* NOA, *who is again "lost."*)

CHARLES: (*Softly.*) Mr. Napo'o . . .

NOA: (*As if to himself.*) Na mo'o . . .

CHARLES: Your water.

(NOA *"realizes." He takes the cup of water.*)

NOA: Thank you. (*He raises the cup to* LYDIA.) May you always be safe from the *mo'o*.

(*He drinks the water.* CARL *is crossing at the back.*)

LYDIA: Carl, wait! I want to talk to you!

(CARL *moves to her, as she hurries to him.*)

NOA: And I want to talk to you, Carl. Come.

(CARL *leaves* LYDIA *and comes to* NOA, *who is pensively staring into his empty cup.* CARL *waits.* NOA *keeps staring into the cup.*)

CARL: Well—?

NOA: You know the old Hawaiian proverb?

CARL: Which proverb?

NOA: You drink too much water, bye'n'bye your pee gonna come rusty. . . . Very old authentic Hawaiian proverb.

(CARL *turns to go, is stopped by:*)

NOA: No, wait! *(Fishes in his pocket and brings out a folded piece of paper.)* That man who came to hire me yesterday . . . the lawyer. Tom . . .

CARL: Bruner.

NOA: Yes, he brought a script of your pageant. I read it. Something is missing. . . . When the royal court comes in and you're all in place—I wrote something for you to say.

CARL: *(Taking the offered paper and glancing at it.)* It's in Hawaiian.

NOA: You're a Hawaiian king, aren't you? A *mōʻī.*

CARL: Well—I'll try.

(LYDIA *gestures impatiently to* CARL, *who goes to her. They whisper, and they exit left.* CHARLES *reaches for* NOA's *empty cup;* NOA *seems to have slipped "off" again. He comes back at* CHARLES' *reach.*)

NOA: No, no. I'll keep it for awhile, thank you.

(NOA *studies* CHARLES' *face steadily. The direct scrutiny makes* CHARLES *uneasy.*)

NOA: *(As if to himself.)* Hapa.

CHARLES: *(Dutifully.)* Yes, sir.

NOA: Half-gone. Don't let them suck all your soul away. *(Pours a drink into the cup.)*

CHARLES: No, sir. . . . You want to start the run-through now? I think everybody is ready. . . .

NOA: *(A sigh.)* I can't wait.

CHARLES: Do you want the whole thing? I mean, there's great special effects and projections of rainbows and waterfalls and things like that.

NOA: *(Even more tired.)* It sounds beautiful.

CHARLES: Yes, sir, it is. Very beautiful.

NOA: *(Rising.)* No, thank you, Kale—we'll just have to get along with what we've got. That will be enough beauty for one afternoon.

(NOA is moving out front into the theater, leaving CHARLES alone on stage. He takes the cup and the bottle with him. His walk is a little unsteady.)

CHARLES: *(Calling off upstage.)* Bill—Bill—you guys! We're ready to start.

BILL: *(Off.)* Right!

(CHARLES crosses to downstage left, looks off.)

CHARLES: *(Yelling.)* Okay, Jimmy—ready on sound. We're going to start.

(The show lights are replacing the work lights. CHARLES takes a bench and places it in the court area at stage right. Across the back, three or four men in costume hurry from right to left. Then a great, splendiferous rainbow is projected against the cyclorama.)

CHARLES: *(Yelling.)* Bill . . . Bill. Not the rainbow. We don't want the special effects this time . . . Bill, can you hear me? I said, kill the rainbow!

(The rainbow is killed.)

CHARLES: *(Yelling.)* Okay! *(To front:)* You want the curtain, Mr. Naoupou?

NOA: *(From out front.)* No, thank you. Let's just pretend.

CHARLES: Yes, sir.

(The young man, FREDDIE, in a malo, *his T-shirt removed, moves into the background with a conch shell. He stands on the platform, silhouetted against the sky in the dim lighting. CHARLES addresses him as he moves to downstage left.)*

CHARLES: Okay, we're starting.

(FREDDIE strikes his pose.)

CHARLES: *(To offstage left.)* Places, people. . . . Ready, Jimmy?
JIMMY: *(Off.)* All set.
CHARLES: Okay. *(He picks up the bench, faces front.)* Curtain.

(He steps offstage with the bench. FREDDIE *raises the conch shell to his lips, blows three mournful notes. He moves off. Lights and romantic "Hawaiian" music. The pageant begins. The* ROYAL COURT *moves on. They move sedately to place themselves about the stage—the king and queen and court at the throne area, the attendants across the back. As they come:)*

VOICE: *(PA system.)* A-l-o-o-o-o-o-ha! Welcome to the golden shores of Paradise! . . . Welcome to the golden days of Hawai'i-nei when the *ali'i* reigned in their regal splendor over their loyal and carefree subjects. . . . Welcome to an Eden of perfumed flowers and dew-spangled days that reflect rainbows across azure skies. . . . Welcome to the land of true aloha, Hawai'i, the land of Love and Music and the Hula. . . .

(The HULA DANCERS *move on and down to left, where they arrange themselves prettily.)*

VOICE: The hula that captures the sway of the coconut palm, the falling of rain, the surge of the ocean, the sweep of the sky . . . the hula that captures Love, the heart and soul of Hawai'i-nei! . . . Welcome, travelers! Welcome, strangers—strangers no longer in the warm embrace of Hawai'i's a-l-o-o-o-o-ha!

(The music sweeps to a climax. The HULA DANCERS *rise—but* NOA *has come to the apron of the stage.)*

NOA: *(Loud.)* Hold it! . . . Stay seated please.

(The DANCERS *and the others begin to sit down.)*

NOA: No, no, just the dancers. The rest of you remain standing.

(The court remains standing, which obviously irks LYDIA. *The* DANCERS *sit.)*

NOA: This is where you read your speech, Carl. . . . Would you try it, please?

CARL: *(Taking out the speech.)* You want me to read it in Hawaiian?

NOA: Well, it isn't written in Japanese, is it?

CARL: No. E nā kānaka o ka 'āina . . .[9] *(He murders every word.)*

NOA: *(Correcting.)* E nā kānaka o ka 'āina . . .

CARL: E nā kānaka o ka 'āina . . .

NOA: *(Disconsolately.)* Try the next line, please.

CARL: *(It is worse than ever.)* Eia ka mo'olelo o Laupi'o lāua 'o Kea. He mau 'ōpio lāua.[10]

NOA: *(Correcting.)* Eia ka mo'olelo o Laupi'o . . .

CARL: Eia ka mo'olelo o Laupi'o . . .

NOA: Laupi'o—Laupi'o, not Laupio.

CARL: Look, Noa—if I understood what I was reading, maybe—

NOA: All right, all right. That first line: 'O kēia ka mo'olelo o Laupi'o lāua'o Kea a me ke ali'i 'ōpiopio 'o Kahililoa.[11] This is the story of Laupi'ohana Kea and—

(LYDIA, *out of patience, sits.*)

NOA: Please. You will sit when I tell you to sit. Not before.

LYDIA: I'm not going to stand up all the time that you're rehearsin' him with that stuff.

NOA: Stuff?

LYDIA: It's a big waste of time: nobody's going to understand it. Anyway, I'm tired.

CARL: *(Trying to calm things.)* Noa, why don't we rehearse it later, just the two of us. It's hard for me, you know, and there's no sense taking up those people's time.

NOA: *(Sighing.)* Okay . . . *(To the rest of the cast:)* his Hawaiian "stuff" makes our queen tired, so let's continue. Just read the last line of your speech, Carl, then all of you sit, and we'll go on with the hula dancers.

LYDIA: Good. *(Very deliberately, she stands up with a superior look in* NOA's *direction.)*

---

[9]CARL: . . . People of the land . . . *(He murders every word.)*
NOA: *(Correcting)* People—of—the—land . . .
CARL: People of the land . . .

[10]CARL: This is the story of Laupi'o Kea. They were young people—
NOA: *(Correcting.)* This is the story of Laupi'o . . .
CARL: This is the story of Laupi'o . . .

[11]NOA: . . . This is the story of Laupi'o and Kea and the young *ali'i*, Kahililoa . . .

CARL: He moʻolelo aloha—i hōʻole ʻia kēia.[12]

(The PAGEANT COURT *sits. Hawaiian music begins—a hula. The* HULA DANCERS *go into their first dance. They are slick, expert, commercial dancers who smile and smile and smile and smile and smile, catatonically. Partway through the dance, the needle gets stuck, and the phrase is repeated over and over—creating instant havoc among the* DANCERS. *They stop in consternation. Then the needle skips and slides gratingly across the record's surface.)*

JIMMY'S VOICE: *(Over the P.A. system.)* Shit!

(And silence. NOA *is slowly walking onto the stage, the coffee cup dangling from a finger of his left hand, the empty bottle in the other.)*

NOA: *(Calling offstage, controlled but inwardly fuming.)* Charles! Kale!

(Almost instantly, a very worried CHARLES *enters from downstage left.* NOA *is quite drunk.)*

CHARLES: Yes, Mr. Naupou.
NOA: Who is the genius in charge of the sound?
CHARLES: Jimmy.
NOA: May I see him please?
CHARLES: Yes, sir. *(Goes off left immediately.)*
CARL: Noa—so he forgot to turn the PA system off.

(He turns away, pacing, drawn into his angry self. The others are somewhat apprehensive. CHARLES *and* JIMMY *enter.* JIMMY *is a small, elderly Japanese-Hawaiian, cowed by everything and everyone.)*

CHARLES: This is Jimmy, Mr. Naupou.
NOA: *("Patiently.")* Kale, Kale, Kale. It is Napoʻo, not Naupou. Napoʻo—ana—a—ka—lā. The sinking of the sun. Sunset. It is a very beautiful name. Please say it right.
CHARLES: Yes, sir.
NOA: Say it after me . . . Napoʻo-ana-a-ka-lā.
CHARLES: Napoʻo-ana-a-ka-lā.

---

[12] CARL: It is a story of Love—denied.

NOA: *(Delighted.)* Wonderful! Perfect! *(To* CARL:*)* Take lessons from him! *(To* JIMMY, *pleasantly:)* So, this is Jimmy, the man who said that naughty word.

JIMMY: Look, the word jes' slip out. I didn' think about the PA system or nuthin'.

NOA: We know, we know.

JIMMY: I'm sorry.

NOA: But you mustn't be sorry. *(Holds out his hand.)* I want to congratulate you. You took the word right out of my mouth.

(JIMMY, *very perplexed, takes his hand.*)

NOA: You seem to be the only person here with any taste. So I thank you. *(At* JIMMY*'s even more perplexed look:)* No, I mean it, and I thank you. . . . That's all.

(JIMMY *goes off.* CHARLES *is about to follow him.*)

NOA: Charles, stay. *(A smile.)* We have work to do. *(To the* DANCERS:*)* Well, all right. Thank you very much. . . . Would you all please go to your dressing rooms or someplace until— well—until you hear when you are needed?

(The DANCERS, *whispering concernedly among themselves, go.)*

CHARLES: Don't you want to see the rest of the run-through, Mr. Nau—Napo'o?

LYDIA: We're wasting a lot of time.

(Generalized murmurs of agreement from the cast.)

NOA: *(To* CHARLES, *ignoring* LYDIA.*)* No, Charles. Enough is plenty. *(To the* COURT:*)* Would you be ready please for a rehearsal in—oh—half an hour?

(General murmurings of assent from the court.)

NOA: Very well. You're dismissed.

(NOA *drops the empty bottle in the trash box.* LYDIA *sweeps offstage right in imperious relief. The others leave too. Only* CARL *remains seated. As the others leave,* KAMUELA *comes in with* NOA*'s paper-bagged bottle.*

NOA *goes immediately to him, takes the bottle out of the bag. The stragglers among the cast see it all.*)

NOA: Just in time, Kamuela! Mahalo!
KAMUELA: Ua hōʻea mai nā mea aʻe, e ke kumu.[13]
NOA: *(Delighted.)* They've come? Maikaʻi. Ke launa nei ʻo Frances
    me lākou?[14]
KAMUELA: ʻAe.
NOA: Frances was worried they wouldn't come! Ke mākaukau
    lākou, e lawe mai lākou i loko.[15]
KAMUELA: ʻAe.

(*He goes.* NOA *comes back to* CHARLES *with his bottle and coffee cup.
From his throne,* CARL *watches* NOA *in deep concern.*)

NOA: Kale, my dear friend. I want you to do something for me—for
    all of us.
CHARLES: Yes, sir.

(NOA *sits, begins to open the bottle.*)

NOA: Go talk to the dancers, in their dressing rooms.
CHARLES: Yes, sir.
NOA: Thank them all very much for the *kōkua* they have given.
CHARLES: Yes, sir.
NOA: *(Pouring a cupful of whiskey.)* And tell them we don't need them
    anymore.
CHARLES: What?
NOA: *(Simply.)* Fire them.

(CARL *rises in concern as* CHARLES *looks to him, worried, for guidance.*
NOA *drinks, lost in thought.* CARL *moves to him.*)

CARL: You can't do that, Noa.
NOA: I'm not. Charles is. *(To* CHARLES *nicely:)* You can do it more
    gently than I can.

---

[13] KAMUELA: The others have come, *kumu.*

[14] NOA: . . . That's good. Is Frances meeting them?

[15] NOA: . . . Bring them in when they're ready.

CARL: Look, I know you agreed to do this pageant on one condition: that you can change anything you want. But there isn't time. We've only got a few days.

NOA: We'll be ready. We'll dance the story of Laupiʻo and Kea, a beautiful and sad story of two young lovers.

CARL: But how're you going to dance anything without dancers?

NOA: The young people of my *hālau* have arrived. Kamuela just said. They know the dances and the chants. . . . Your part—you, the queen, the court—all that will stay the same. (*To* CHARLES:) Please, tell the dancers.

(CHARLES *again looks at* CARL, *who sighs and nods assent.* CHARLES *goes offstage at right.* CARL *watches* NOA *drink.*)

CARL: Must you do that?

NOA: Does it bother you?

CARL: It bothers the others.

NOA: Lydia?

CARL: All of them. . . . Do you have to throw it in everybody's face?

NOA: *(Simply.)* I drink. I like to drink. I like to get drunk. So why hide it? I don't like lies, Carl.

CARL: But why must you do it here? You can get into bad trouble.

NOA: Why? Because I don't want to pretend that something rotten and cheap is good and beautiful! Because I don't want to pretend that these awful people really represent my people!

CARL: Even so, they are people. You offend them, they'll get back at you.

(NOA *is pouring another drink.*)

CARL: You can be fired, Noa.

NOA: You're the chairman. Would you fire me?

CARL: I'm only one vote. . . . Lydia has a lot of influence with the others on the board. She's an *aliʻi.*

(*A big Bronx cheer from* NOA.)

CARL: The others don't think like that. An *aliʻi* still means a lot to them.

NOA: You're an *aliʻi.*

CARL: They respect Lydia.

NOA: What? They don't respect you?

CARL: Noa, Lydia is a descendant of the Kamehameha line.

NOA: Just for that alone somebody ought to wring her neck. . . .

CARL: Look, if you feel this way, why did you take this job?

(NOA *only looks at him with a smile.*)

CARL: Are you trying to get back at me?

NOA: What for?

CARL: That night. Twenty something years ago. What I said.

NOA: You were very angry.

CARL: I had every right, I think.

NOA: Sure.

CARL: I fell in love. She wanted to come visit me. I send my good friend to bring her. And the two of them double-cross me.

NOA: They fell in love.

CARL: I'm not blaming you. Either of you. But if you had been me, wouldn't you have been angry?

NOA: That angry?

CARL: Yes.

NOA: Over a woman? No.

CARL: *(Hitting his stomach with a fist.)* For weeks—like, in here, something had turned to pus. I couldn't even puke it out. I just went on rotting. That's how much I loved her, Noa. And you stole her away from me.

NOA: That isn't what happened.

CARL: No?

NOA: No.

CARL: Then—what did?

NOA: She saw through you.

CARL: What does that mean?

NOA: You took advantage of a girl who hadn't ever even been kissed. Really kissed. By a man.

CARL: That's not the way I remember her kisses. Christ, she practically ate me alive.

NOA: That wasn't love. It was panic.

CARL: What!

NOA: Panic. That kind of girl always panics like that.

CARL: What kind of girl?

NOA: The kind of girl that calls it her pee-place. That's the kind of girl Frances used to be. Kisses—your hand on the right place—panic—and in goes the *mo‘o*.

CARL: Damn it, Noa, I loved her.

NOA: It isn't very hard to love a pee-place worth fifteen million dollars.

CARL: *(Not angry.)* I wasn't after her money.

NOA: Then—why did she leave you?

(There's a pause. CARL moves away, then turns back.)

CARL: She say that?

NOA: She didn't have to.

CARL: Did she?

NOA: *(A moment.)* No. I pieced it together. . . . Through all the years, asked myself: why? Of all people, why me? I'm not much; I know it. I never even finished elementary school. And Frances is an educated woman. I decided: she didn't run to me; she ran from you.

CARL: Pieced it all together.

NOA: Yes.

CARL: You don't really know.

NOA: No.

(Despite himself, CARL is getting angry. He calms down.)

CARL: Didn't you ever ask her?

NOA: I didn't have to. I had her.

CARL: *(Exhaling the residue of his anger.)* Well—it was so long ago. Why get sore?

NOA: I'm not sore.

CARL: Good. . . . Good. . . . I guess at the time I was pretty angry. But—time passes. You put things into their place. You go on. *(He pats NOA's shoulder.)* But if it helps—after so many years— believe me, I'm sorry. I'm sorry for everything I said that night. I'm sorry for everything I did afterwards.

NOA: It was for the best. If you hadn't fired me—if you hadn't gotten your friends to refuse me jobs, I would never have found myself.

CARL: Still, I am sorry.

NOA: Hilo i ka ua, kani lehua.

CARL: And what does that mean?

NOA: It means: The rains come pattering down, and the lehua blossoms fall. . . . Sorry doesn't stop the rain, and Sorry doesn't stop the lehua blossoms from falling. . . . Things just happen. We accept. *(He has poured another cupful. He takes a particularly long swallow.)*

CARL: I beg you again, Noa. Please don't make things worse.

NOA: Lydia can't hurt me, Carl. The lehua blossoms fall, with or without Lydia.

CARL: I'm not thinking only of Lydia.

NOA: Oh?

CARL: Noa, you're not well. . . . I can see it in your eyes.

NOA: See what?

CARL: Once in a while—they go blank; the life goes out of them.

NOA: *(A slight smile.)* A dead man.

CARL: *(Gesturing to the bottle.)* Keep that up, and you *will* be a dead man.

(NOA *finds this enormously funny. He laughs.* FRANCES *enters from the left.*)

FRANCES: E Noa, aia lākou maʻaneʻi.[16] The children!

NOA: I know. Kamuela told me.

FRANCES: He's bringing them in a minute.

(LYDIA, *followed by* CHARLES, *comes in from the right. She barely suppresses her rage.*)

LYDIA: Carl! I want you to call Keaka Ching right away!

(At the sight of her CARL *stiffens, waiting for the blow.)*

CARL: What is it, Lydia?

LYDIA: He fired our dancers. Charles said. Well, I told the dancers not to go. I told them to stay downstairs, in their dressing rooms, until we get this settled.

CARL: Well?

LYDIA: I want you to call Keaka and tell him you're firing him. . . . Then fire him! Right now.

CARL: I can't do that, Lydia.

LYDIA: Why not?

CARL: Because the board hired him. They're the only ones who can fire him.

LYDIA: Don't give me that! The board goes along with you. You and Keaka.

CARL: Lydia, I tell you, I can't.

---

[16] FRANCES: Noa, they're here! . . .

LYDIA: Why not? He comes here—in the first minute, he goes to the bathroom with a boy . . .

NOA: Two boys.

LYDIA: Look at him grin, look at him grinnin'. . . . They locked the door while they were inside.

FRANCES: Now, just a moment.

NOA: (*Sharply.*) Frances! Hiki iā ia ke ʻōlelo![17]

LYDIA: And right away he starts to drink. He used vulgar language in front of everybody. And he fires the dancers, like this was his pageant. He's filthy, and he's immoral, and he's a drunken man, and I will not allow him to—

FRANCES: (*Flaring.*) Shut up!

LYDIA: What?

FRANCES: I said, You shut up!

NOA: You must never yell at Hawaiian *aliʻi.*

FRANCES: (*Quivering but in control.*) I'm sorry for yelling, Hawaiian *aliʻi* lady. Akā, piʻi koʻu hūhū me ka maʻalahi. Ma mua, ʻo ʻoe ka mea ʻole loa. Ua lilo koʻu mau kūpuna iā ʻoe i ke aliʻi.[18]

LYDIA: Don't show off! Speak English!

FRANCES: All right. I'll speak English! What I said was: Once you were nothing. All of you. Until my people came. . . . We taught you how to read, we taught you how to live at a time when you would have been trampled under by other haole. We made you into buffoon images of English kings and queens. But the one thing we didn't have to teach you was arrogance. You needed no lessons in that! The Hawaiian *aliʻi!* And, my God, you can't even speak your own language!

LYDIA: Carl, shut this woman up!

FRANCES: (*Going right on.*) And here you are, locked in your make-believe world, this cheap—this pathetic—pageant. . . . I am real, my Noa is real, but who are you, you contemptible fake?

(*For the answer,* LYDIA *rushes at her, enraged.* CARL *steps in the way.*)

CARL: Lydia!

NOA: (*Crowing.*) Hu ke kani o ka ʻalala![19]

---

[17] NOA: Frances! Let her talk.

[18] FRANCES: . . . But it is easy for me to get angry. Once you were nothing. My ancestors made you *aliʻi.*

[19] NOA: My, how the crow squawks!

(He is on his feet shouting triumphantly. And from the left, KAMUELA *rushes in shouting with joy.)*

KAMUELA: E ke kumu, e ke kumu, e nānā aku 'oe, e nānā aku 'oe. Eia no lākou! Eia no lākou, e ke kumu.[20]

(And NOA'S DANCERS *sweep in, wildly exuberant, young Hawaiian boys and girls. They are dressed with almost total disregard for even the minimal conventions of dress. They bring bundles, drums, calabashes, bamboo sticks, half a forest of ferns, vines, maile, carrying them, wearing them, trailing them, waving them. And they all babble away in exuberant Hawaiian.* POKIPALA *moves away from the swirl and, with* KAMUELA, *watches.)*

NOA'S DANCERS: Aloha, e Noa . . . Aloha, e ke kumu . . . Pehea 'oe, e Noa? Hau'oli au . . . Hau'oli au e 'ike iā 'oe.[21]
NOA: *(With a whoop of joy; overlapping.)* Eia 'oukou! 'Ano 'ai kākou! 'Ano 'ai kākou! How come you're so late? No ke aha 'ano lohi 'oukou?

(The GIRLS *and* BOYS *cluster around* NOA *and* FRANCES — *in effect, sealing them off from the irate* LYDIA *whom* CARL *is still keeping from attack and talking to softly and intensely.)*

KALEO (BOY): E ke kumu, aia mākou i kekahi hale.[22]
NOA: A building!

KALEO: A ke'oke'o noho'i ia! 'O nā lumi apau, e ke kumu, ke'oke'o noho'i . . .

HI'IAKA: *(To* FRANCES.) Aloha aku 'o Makalena iā 'oe.
FRANCES: Akā, 'a'ole 'o ia e hele mai?
PI'ILANI: 'A'ole, e Frances. 'A'ole lākou i 'ae iā ia.

---

[20]KAMUELA: *Kumu, kumu,* look, look. . . . Here they are! Here they are, *kumu!*

[21]NOA'S DANCERS: Hello, Noa. . . . Hello, *kumu.* . . . How are you, Noa . . . E, Palakia, how nice . . . how nice to see you!
NOA: *(With a whoop of joy; overlapping.)* There you are! Welcome, welcome! [How come you're so late?] What kept you so long?

[22]KALEO (BOY): Oh, *kumu,* we were in a building.
NOA: [A building!]
KALEO: And it was white! All the rooms, *kumu,* all white . . .

HI'IAKA: *(To* FRANCES) Makalena sends her love.
FRANCES: But isn't she coming?
PI'ILANI: No, Frances. They wouldn't let her.

ANOTHER: A nui nā kukui, e ke kumu. Ma nā wahi a pau . . .

FRANCES: Who—who wouldn't let her come?

MALIA: The man in the white clothes, Frances. He kanaka haole. He was very nice.

(FRANCES *crosses to* NOA, *concerned.*)

FRANCES: Noa, Noa, did you hear? Makalena's not coming.

(*But* NOA *is too fondly intent on* KALEO, *his hands on the boy's cheeks.*)

MALIA: He wahi uʻi loa kēia, e Palakika![23]

(NOA *is tenderly kissing* KALEO.)

FRANCES: (*To* NOA.) Somebody's kept her back.
PIʻILANI: I kuʻu manaʻo, e hauʻoli ana kākou i ka hula ʻana maʻaneʻi.[24]

(FRANCES *turns to her as* NOA'S *kiss ends.*)

FRANCES: (*To* PIʻILANI.) Yes, we will be.
NOA: You've been eating sugarcane, Kaleo.
KALEO: Only a little, *kumu.*

(*In disgust,* LYDIA *sweeps out at right.* CARL *hurries after her.* NOA *moves to center stage.*)

ANOTHER: An' so many lights, *kumu.* . . . Every place . . .

FRANCES: [Who—who wouldn't let her come?]
MALIA: [The man in the white clothes, Frances.] A *haole* man. [He was very nice.]

[23] MALIA: What a beautiful place this is, Palakika!

[24] PIʻILANI: I think we will be happy dancing here, Palakika.

NOA: E nā keiki, nā keiki o kuʻu puʻuwai, pili kākou! Me kō kākou hula laʻa![25]

GIRLS: ʻAe, e Noa...pololei ʻoe....A e hula pono kākou maʻaneʻi.

NOA: (*To the* BOYS.) E oli! E oli pū kākou.

(*Some* BOYS *have gone over to make friends with the fascinated* CHARLES, *talking animatedly to him.*)

BOYS: ʻAe, e ke kumu, e oli kākou![26]

(NOA *forcefully begins the chant, joined immediately by* KAMUELA. *Then, at his signal, the other* BOYS *begin.* NOA *begins to dance, dances over to the* GIRLS. *Laughing, they join him in the dance. The* BOYS *who are with* CHARLES *begin to dance "at" him, taunting him good-naturedly to join them. It embarrasses* CHARLES.)

NOA: E hula, e hula! E hula kākou![27]

(*The hula continues joyfully.* GIRL 1 *is dancing with* NOA, *and her close-ness does something strange:* NOA *begins to dance erratically. Something is taking possession of him, something beyond his drunkenness. Scared a little, the* GIRL *backs away and turns to* FRANCES, *who, seeing, comes to* NOA. *The* OTHERS *are too caught up in their own dancing to notice.*)

FRANCES: Noa—Noa, enough. . . . Stop . . .

(*But* NOA'*s possessed dancing becomes more frantic. He is turning into a lizard.*)

FRANCES: Noa, Noa, dear, enough. . . . Enough! (*She reaches for his writhing arms.*)

---

[25]NOA: Oh, children, children of my heart, we are together again! With our sacred hula! [Note: The use of the heart as the center of emotions is believed to be a Western concept.]
GIRLS: Oh, yes, Noa. . . . You are right. . . . And we will dance beautifully here.
NOA: (*To the* BOYS.) Chant! Let us chant together!

[26]BOYS: Yes, *kumu*, let us chant!

[27]NOA: Dance, dance! Everybody dance!

NOA: Ka moʻo! E waiho wale i ka moʻo![28]
FRANCES: Lawa! Lawa!
NOA: E waiho wale iaʻu!
FRANCES: *(Frightened, near tears.)* You mustn't. You're not yourself. *(He slaps her hand away.)* Noa—please . . .

(She reaches for him. He grabs her arm, twists it behind her cruelly, spinning her around. She screams with pain. He shoves her away. She falls to the floor, stunned, weeping. CHARLES, *appalled, rushes to* NOA.*)*

CHARLES: Mr. Napoʻo!
NOA: *(frenzied)* E hopu iā ia![29]

*(*KAMUELA, POKIPALA, KALEO, *and others dash to intercept* CHARLES. *They grab him, pin him.* CHARLES *yells. The drumming and chanting have become wild, insane.)*

NOA: Hold him! E hoʻopaʻa iā ia no ka moʻo![30]

(The BOYS, *chanting wildly, have lifted* CHARLES *up so that he is in a prone position, despite his struggling.)*

NOA: Maikaʻi! E nānā i kona ʻoniʻoni ʻana! Makemake ʻo ia i ka hele ana ʻmai o ka moʻo![31]
FRANCES: *(Rushing to him.)* Noa, don't! Don't!

*(*NOA *is too far gone. He fights her off, but she keeps grabbing to pull him away.* CHARLES *keeps screaming. The* BOYS *themselves seem to have gone mad.)*

NOA: *(Screaming.)* E hoʻohuli iā ia, e hoʻohuli iā ia.[32]

---

[28]NOA: The *moʻo.* Leave the *moʻo* alone!
FRANCES: Enough! Enough!
NOA: Leave me alone!

[29]NOA: Grab him!

[30]NOA: . . . Hold him for the *moʻo!*

[31]Good! See how it wriggles! See how it wants the *moʻo* to come!

[32]NOA: Turn him around, turn him around!

(The BOYS *turn* CHARLES *around.* FRANCES *keeps trying to pull* NOA *away.)*

NOA: Kū a hele loa![33]

(And he shoves her away hard. The GIRLS *break her fall to the ground, cluster around her, jabbering in alarm. And then they are screaming, for* NOA *is upon* FRANCES *viciously, kicking her and kicking her and kicking her.)*

NOA: *(In a fury.)* E hoʻēʻē! E hoʻēʻē mai ka mana o ka moʻo.[34]

(He turns back to the BOYS *and* CHARLES. *Some* GIRLS *kneel down by the sobbing* FRANCES. *Others just run, crazily, hither and yon: little trapped animals in an invisible cage.* NOA *has moved close to* CHARLES. *They are partially masked by the* BOYS. *Whatever he does causes more intense screaming from* CHARLES. CARL *grabs* NOA. *The drumming stops.)*

CARL: Noa, Noa, for Christ's sake, Noa!
NOA: Carl . . . Carl . . . *(His pathetic dance continues, although it is dying down.)*
CARL: Get away!

(He shoves NOA *away.* NOA *sinks to his knees beside* FRANCES, *who is now kneeling, her hands to her face. The* GIRLS *have backed away.* CHARLES *breaks loose, rushes to attack* NOA.*)*

CHARLES: Damn you!
CARL: *(Intercepting and grabbing him.)* Hold it!
CHARLES: Let me at him.
CARL: Stop it, Charlie, stop it!

(He shoves CHARLES *away. The* MEN *grab him.* CHARLES *submits to tears of rage and humiliation.)*

CARL: Take him away.

---

[33] NOA: Get away!

[34] NOA: *(Stage direction.)* Stay away! Stay away from the power of the *moʻo!*

(*The* MEN *take* CHARLES *off.*)

MEN: (*Variously.*) Come on, Charlie. . . . Hey, man, come on. . . . Let's go. . . . Cool it . . .

(*They go off.* CARL *moves to* FRANCES.)

CARL: Frances . . . Frances . . .
FRANCES: Please go . . .
CARL: Are you all right?
FRANCES: Please go!

(CARL *shakes his head in sympathy and shock. The* BOYS *gently urge him off at stage right. They return during:*)

KAMUELA: *Kumu, kumu,* what is it?
POKIPALA: (*To* FRANCES.) Pehea ʻoe?[35]
FRANCES: (*Softly.*) Yes.
KAMUELA: You want us to call a doctor?
KALEO: Or maybe a kahuna?
FRANCES: No. He'll be all right, Kaleo.
KALEO: Ae.
FRANCES: Kamuela, take them. Then, when you are ready, come back. I want to rehearse Pokipala's hula.
KAMUELA: Ae . . . (*To the others:*) E hele mai me aʻu.[36]

(*They exit left. The rest of the troupe goes with them.* FRANCES *and* NOA *are alone. He finally sits up, his hands coming down from his face. He is drained; terribly, terribly drained.*)

FRANCES: It is over?
NOA: Yes. Over.
FRANCES: They kept Makalena back . . .
NOA: I heard. I guess the ʻaumakua don't want her. . . .
FRANCES: They don't seem to know yet. Any of them.
NOA: No. (*He runs his hand over his forehead, drunk, utterly spent.*)
FRANCES: I'll rehearse Pokipala and the others. You should rest.

---

[35]POKIPALA: Are you all right?

[36]KAMUELA: . . . Come with me.

NOA: No. I'll be all right. Pokipala doesn't dance with enough anger. He has to be shown how to be—*(He tries to rise, but he falters and sits quickly.)*—angry.... (FRANCES *reaches for him in quick concern.)* I am tired ...

FRANCES: One of the boys can help you to the dressing room downstairs....

NOA: No ... no, I can manage.... Just—weak—suddenly—so weak.... Who would have believed the *moʻo* still wanted to live so much.... But it's over.... It's really, really, over ...

FRANCES: *(Reaching to help him up.)* Come.... You must rest....

NOA: No.... You go on.... I'll just—rest—here.... Alone.... I want to be alone.... I have to be alone ...

FRANCES: All right ...

(She kisses him on the forehead, rises, and goes out at left. He remains very still, head bowed. Then, very softly, there is the sound of wind and rain. NOA *begins to chant; finally, the* AUTHOR *steps on, downstage right.)*

AUTHOR: (To audience.) Let me tell you about the day he died.

(The chant dies out. NOA *does not move.)*

AUTHOR: It was an afternoon. Villagers who lived near the foot-hills came to my mother, bringing word that Georgina's lover was dying. My father drove into the forest. He took me with him. When we found the tent, it had begun to rain—rain so thick it seemed to push the air away, leaving you stifled, obliter-ating Space, washing away Time.

(Sounds of wind and rain are out. And then we hear GEORGINA'S *wail.)*

AUTHOR: I seemed to sit at the very center of a formless Nowhere. And then I heard Georgina's voice rise out of that primal void in a wail ... *(The wail rises.)* ... and fade away, and rise again and again and again. Death had come into that hut.... I think I called out to her, "Georgina!" You know how children will do, out of quick pity, or fear maybe ... *(The wail begins to fade.)* ... but, of course, she couldn't have heard.... And so it went, all that lonely afternoon, that voice rising over the indifferent rain, crying out to a dead love, and dying back into the void. (Pause.) It is important that you know all this. *(He is about to go off but, remembering something, turns back.)* Oh—all that about Georgina keeping a diary and pressing flowers and playing Chopin and Mendelssohn and painting watercolors . . . Well, none of it is true. Georgina didn't do any of those things. I made those up for Frances. But she did go to Sydney once. I think that's where she met that merchant she walked out on to live in that forest with Noa. . . . *(He catches himself in the slip, shakes his head.)* Eech! I mean with that Samoan man. . . . Sometimes I get mixed up. I'm sorry.

(The lights fade quickly to black.)

ACT TWO

(About halfway through the intermission, KAMUELA, POKIPALA, *and* HIʻIAKA *come in from upstage left.* HIʻIAKA *sits nearby and watches* KAMUELA *instructing* POKIPALA *in the finer points of the hula. It is the love duet that* POKIPALA *and* HIʻIAKA *will dance later and so, from time to time,* KAMUELA *takes the girl's part as* HIʻIAKA *watches intently. They converse in inaudible whispers. Then, finally,* HIʻIAKA *replaces* KAMUELA. *She and* POKIPALA *dance,* KAMUELA *watching carefully. He seems satisfied with what is going on, turns, goes off at left.* POKIPALA *and* HIʻIAKA *continue practicing for the rest of the intermission. Toward the end of the intermission, the* AUTHOR *comes in with a bench that he sets in place. Then he goes to the throne area, gets the bench from there, brings it to the other, sets it. The two benches are set as they were at the start of Act One. The* AUTHOR *comes to the downstage end of the throne dais, sits there, and waits as the houselights fade slowly and* KAMUELA *returns with* PIʻILANI, MAILE, *and* KALEO. *They sit on the benches. The houselights are out, the Second Act begins.)*

AUTHOR: *(Matter-of-factly to the audience.)* The Second Act begins. *(He rises and moves downstage.)* In my grandfather's village, women kept the bones of their loved ones in the eaves of their huts, and on sunny mornings they would take their dead outside and rub them with coconut oil until they glistened in the sunlight. Often when I was a little boy, I would sit in the yard with a woman who cradled her child's skull against her bare breast and sang softly to it; he had been my playmate until one day he fell from a guava tree and gored himself on the broken end of a lower branch. I would sit with the woman and then, as the sunlight began to slant and wane, we would wrap my little friend in oil-soaked tapa cloth and take him back into the hut and hang him in a pandanus basket from the eaves. And I would whisper goodbye and go home, imagining him walking all the way by my side—or I would pause by a rotting coconut tree where lizards abounded and I would speak to the lizards as if I were speaking to my little friend. . . . You see, our dead—not just our dead on our small island but your dead here in Hawai'i and all the dead throughout all Polynesia—come to us in so many forms. In fact, in as many forms as there are living things. . . . And so we speak to them, with them . . .

The old men of my childhood spoke of our wandering ancestor, Tui Atua, who waited for girls on moonlight nights in the form of a handsome young man. He seduced them, and in the climax of their passion, the girls died. . . . But when Tui Atua met a handsome young man, Tui Atua became a beautiful girl who seduced the young man whose life streamed out of him in his final going. . . .

He/she is everywhere in the older Polynesian cultures. And even today some men contain him/her in them. They are our ancestors' familiars very often . . . men like Noa. . . . In them, we quicken into death; in them, we die into life. . . .

But they don't just come in the world of innocence or in the holocausts of the world of passion. . . . For many years now, I have known that they also come as words. And then, when the words cling to each other like lovers, they come as poems, as plays, and, when the heart is full, as song.

And so Georgina has come to me, over and over, since my childhood . . . and I have had to create, out of myself, a Noa, so that I might sing him/her into Frances.

It is the way of my dead.

Ladies and gentlemen, *Kanikau: A Pageant:* the Second Act.

(He steps off. POKIPALA *and* HI'IAKA *end their hula, come down to the benches, sit.)*

KALEO: Kamuela . . .
KAMUELA: *(Busy picking his toes.)* Mm?
KALEO: I feel funny.
KAMUELA: Why?
KALEO: We was all a little crazy . . . like the *kumu* . . .

*(*KAMUELA *looks at* KALEO, *then at the others.)*

OTHERS: *(Variously.)* Yeah, us, too, Kamuela. . . . It's a funny feeling . . .
KAMUELA: Don't think about it.

KALEO: But I'm scared, Kamuela. And the *kumu* is worse. And a little while ago, everything went away from me, like I fainted for a second . . . everything went away . . .

OTHERS: *(Variously.)* Us, too. . . . Yeah . . . I had the feeling, too, Kamuela . . .

(KAMUELA *rises, sits beside* KALEO, *whom he pulls close, comfortingly, arm around his shoulders.*)

KAMUELA: Listen, Kaleo—listen to me, all of you: we all got too excited. . . . Remember, sometimes when we're getting ready to dance, and we get too nervous and we breathe too much air too fast—and we get dizzy—even black out a little bit . . . well, it's like that. . . . Anyway, who has had anything to eat all day?

OTHERS: *(General murmurs of denial.)*

KAMUELA: You see. . . . Now, don't worry. After we rehearse here, we'll go find a nice place to eat. . . . (*To* KALEO:) Don't worry so much.

(KALEO *tries to smile.* KAMUELA *returns to his seat—and to picking his toes.*)

MALIA: Pokipala . . .

POKIPALA: Hm?

MALIA: I heard the *kumu* used to make love to himself—with a cucumber. Is that true?

POKIPALA: *(Indignantly.)* Naaaah! Ridiculous! *(Pause.)* Was one carrot.

MALIA: Oh. I heard was one cucumber.

POKIPALA: Crazy. Cannot with a cucumber.

MALIA: Can with a carrot?

HI'IAKA: Can. . . . Especially with the kine carrot got—you know—down the end is split—(*She makes a* **V** *with her downturned fingers.*)—like it got two legs. Can with a carrot like that. Cucumber is hard for hold. They never get those kine legs. . . . Need legs, you know.

KALEO: *(In quiet joy.)* I know.

PI'ILANI: For—give um.

KALEO: Yeah.

HI'IAKA: *(Together.)* Yeah.

KAMUELA: *(The quiet voice of authority.)* Was not a carrot. Carrot is haole. . . . Was a banana.

POKIPALA: Remember Aumea, the man was a dancer with the *kumu* a long time ago—used to come to visit?

GIRLS: Yeah.

POKIPALA: He told Kamuela an' me that, sometimes, in the old days, the *kumu* used to go out in the moonlight, naked, and then he would make a prayer to Laka—for Laka to come to him an' go inside his body... like a *mo'o*... an' then... (*Uncertainly to* KAMUELA:) ... banana?

KAMUELA: In the old, old days, instead of a man, our people offered a banana to the gods in the *heiau*. ... A banana is us ... all of us ... a banana is holy, sacred ... like you ... like all of you. ...

HI'IAKA: I thought Laka is a woman. A woman cannot—like that—like a man ...

KAMUELA: Laka was also a man. Man, woman, same thing, the *'aumakua* are like that. ... One minute man, one minute woman ...

POKIPALA: An' Aumea said, One time the *kumu* got *hāpai*.

GIRLS: Aue, no!

POKIPALA: He said.

PI'ILANI: Is that true, Kamuela ... ?

KAMUELA: I asked Frances one time if it was true. And she quick put her hand on my mouth, and she said: "Kamuela, you must never, never say this to the *kumu*. He must never know that you know. It is the most holy secret a man has got." Then she was quiet a long time, and then she said, "I had the baby."

MALIA: (*Awed.*) The *kumu* get *hāpai* and Frances had the baby?

KAMUELA: Yeah.

KALEO: Gee—hard, yeah?

PI'ILANI: What kine of baby?

KAMUELA: Boy.

HI'IAKA: Where's the baby now?

KAMUELA: *Make* ... Aumea said it was raining, real heavy rain, but you could hear Frances wail all afternoon, through the rain. ... Like she went *pupule*.

POKIPALA: Ssshh!

(*For* FRANCES *is coming on. There's still a strained quality about her.*)

FRANCES: Kamuela, everybody—are you all ready to begin?

DANCERS: 'Ae.

FRANCES: Well, get into your places.

(*The* DANCERS *move to place themselves.* FRANCES *turns to* POKI-PALA.)

FRANCES: Remember, you are an *ali'i.*
POKIPALA: 'Ae.
FRANCES: Your anger must show in your body.
POKIPALA: 'Ae.

(FRANCES *heads out front.*)

POKIPALA: (*To* KAMUELA *and* KALEO.) All right, come on, you guys.

(*Taking drums,* KAMUELA *and* KALEO *move to either side of him, close. He calls out front.*)

POKIPALA: Do I just start, Frances?
FRANCES: (*From front.*) No . . . Pi'ilani, you girls do the end of your dance. Before Pokipala's hula. Just the end.
PI'ILANI: Oh. Okay. . . . Come, Malia. . . . Hi'iaka, you goin' chant for us?
HI'IAKA: Sure.

(PI'ILANI *and* MALIA *move down more, conferring in whispers.*)

HI'IAKA: (*Out front.*) From any place?
FRANCES: (*From front.*) Just the last verse.
PI'ILANI: Okay. . . . (*To* HI'IAKA:) Okay.

(HI'IAKA *chants.* MALIA *and* PI'ILANI *dance—the closing part of a slow, sedate hula. The moment the dance is over, the drums explode in a frenzy;* POKIPALA *and the two drummers let out a scream of rage and pain, and they sweep downstage.* POKIPALA'S *hula is all* FRANCES *asked for: rage, physically expressed—angular, angry, stabbing. At the end,* POKIPALA *"collapses" spent.* FRANCES *comes back on stage.*)

FRANCES: Maika'i. . . . Ua maika'i kēlā.[1] But try to remember: Put all of your anger in your body, all of it. All the anger of an *ali'i* betrayed by two commoners . . .

---

[1] FRANCES: Good. . . . That was very good. . . .

POKIPALA: But he loved them also.

FRANCES: And it's over. *Pau.* When they fell in love and betrayed him, all the love goes out of the *ali'i*'s heart. You must remember that.

POKIPALA: 'Ae.

FRANCES: Kou ku'eku'e. E hula me kou ku'eku'e.[2] Don't keep them so close to your side. Stick them out more. *(She shows him.)* E like me kēia. . . . A laila, e ho'ā'o.

(POKIPALA *tries a few steps from his dance, with attention to his violent jabbing elbows. He stops.*)

POKIPALA: Poina au i ka manawa a pau.[3]

FRANCES: Well, don't forget.

PI'ILANI: It's hard to remember stuff in here, Frances. Hard to be serious.

FRANCES: Why?

PI'ILANI: Everything feels funny—an' fake—not like outside in the sunlight.

MALIA: Inā loa'a wale nā pua—nā pua 'i'o.[4]

PI'ILANI: Or even moonlight.

FRANCES: 'Ae, maopopo ia'u.[5] But there are no real flowers or moonlight in here. We simply have to imagine them both, like a dream. A laila, e komo i kō 'oukou lole hula. Noa will want to start very soon.

DANCERS: 'Ae.

(The DANCERS *go off at left—except for* KAMUELA. *He watches her sit in dejection, lost in concern. He comes back to her.*)

KAMUELA: Frances . . .

---

[2]FRANCES: Your elbows. Dance with your elbows. . . .[Don't keep them so close to your side. Stick them out more.] *(She shows him.)* Like this. . . . Now, try it.

[3]POKIPALA: I always forget.

[4]MALIA: If there were only some flowers—real flowers . . .

[5]FRANCES: Yes, I know. . . . [But there are no real flowers or moonlight in here. We simply have to imagine them both, like a dream.] All right, go get into your costumes. . . .

FRANCES: *(A little startled.)* What? . . . Oh, what is it, Kamuela?

KAMUELA: *(A little afraid to ask.)* Is something wrong?

FRANCES: Wrong? Why, what do you mean? Nothing's wrong, Kamuela.

KAMUELA: I mean—the *kumu*. His sickness.

FRANCES: It's not a sickness, Kamuela. . . . Noa is simply reaching out, calling to our gods to come into him out of the dark. And, from time to time, they hear him. They step out of the darkness, and he steps into the darkness, and they meet and are one, there at the edge, where the light and the darkness meet. He is bound by all of them and in that bond he is free. . . . I've told you all this before, all of you.

KAMUELA: Yes—but it's worse now. . . . Now—when he looks at me, at any of us—it's like he knows something—something terrible—and he doesn't want to tell us.

FRANCES: If the *kumu* has something—important—*(Despite herself, her voice catches.)*—to say, he will tell you—in his own good time. Now, do please go and get ready.

KAMUELA: Yes. *(He moves only a reluctant few steps away, turns back.)* What if—one time—he goes like that into the darkness and he can't come back, Frances? Sometimes I think that's beginning to happen—that he can't find his way back so easy any more. . . . *(She doesn't answer.)* What if, Frances?

FRANCES: *(Quietly.)* Then—then we'll just have to go to him, Kamuela . . . and go with him . . .

KAMUELA: . . . into the murmuring darkness?

FRANCES: If we love him.

KAMUELA: *(A moment; then:)* 'Ae. *(He moves away, and this time is stopped by:)*

FRANCES: Kamuela . . .

KAMUELA: 'Ae.

FRANCES: You said—murmuring darkness. . . . Why murmuring? *(He hangs his head.)* Come . . . come here . . .

(He moves to sit beside her. Very concerned, pity growing, she raises his face to hers, searching his eyes.)

FRANCES: You've heard them . . . the *'aumakua* . . . *(No answer.)* You know . . . *(She pulls him close, with great love; he clings to her.)* Oh, my precious! *(Pause.)* Your heart is fluttering like a little bird. . . . *(Pause.)* Don't be afraid . . .

KAMUELA: My heart breaks for them, Frances. . . .

FRANCES: Who?

KAMUELA: Kaleo and the others. . . . They are beginning to know
. . . they are so scared, Frances . . .

FRANCES: Take them to Noa. . . . He will know how to quiet
them. . . .

KAMUELA: 'Ae.

(She again lifts his face to hers.)

FRANCES: Say after me . . . I accept.

KAMUELA: *(Softly.)* I accept.

FRANCES: You are very dear to me . . .

KAMUELA: *(Softly.)* I love you.

FRANCES: And I love you, Kamuela.

(She kisses him tenderly. The kiss is over; she keeps regarding him gently.
CARL *comes in.)*

CARL: Fran— Oh, I'm sorry. Busy?

FRANCES: No.

CARL: Can we talk? It's important.

FRANCES: Yes. Of course.

(She nods to KAMUELA, *who rises and goes.* CARL *comes to her, sits. He
seems hesitant, not knowing how to begin.)*

FRANCES: What is it, Carl?

CARL: Are you all right? Charles told me Noa beat you. Kicked
you.

FRANCES: I'm all right.

CARL: Look, maybe it's none of my business—but—hell, it is my
business. Nobody's just going to stand back and watch a drunk
knock a woman around like that without—without making it his
business.

FRANCES: He didn't hurt me, Carl. He has never hurt me, and he
never will. Rest assured of that. . . . Is that what you wanted to
talk about?

(A pause.)

CARL: Lydia's on the phone, trying to locate various people on the
board, Keaka Ching and the others.

FRANCES: To fire Noa.

CARL: Yes. . . . Fran, I can head it off, but you've got to cooperate.

FRANCES: How?

CARL: You could both make it easier for me, if you'd apologize to Lydia. And to Charles.

FRANCES: How *is* Charles?

CARL: He's calmed down now. He's more embarrassed than anything else. . . . I think Lydia would take an apology in the right spirit. . . . It would have to be in front of everybody, of course.

FRANCES: The commoners groveling before the *ali'i.*

CARL: Fran, I've had a long talk with all of them. I've calmed them down for now. They've even agreed to go through with Noa's rehearsal.

FRANCES: On the condition that we apologize—in front of everybody.

CARL: You were both kind of out of line—you with Lydia, Noa with Charlie.

FRANCES: We don't grovel, Carl.

CARL: Look, I know how badly he needs this job. I know how badly strapped both of you are. . . .

FRANCES: You were the one who made the committee hire him. (*No answer.*) I thought as much. (*Still no answer.*) Why did you do it?

CARL: We needed someone.

FRANCES: There are a lot of other *kumu hula.* Tell me the truth, Carl . . . please.

(*A pause.*)

CARL: I saw you the other day. After so many long years. I guess I just started remembering.

FRANCES: Remembering what?

CARL: How we met. That party on your front lawn in Kaua'i—with all the dancing and the singing. . . . Our nights together. . . . All the nice memories started coming back.

FRANCES: Oh? . . . Where did you see me?

CARL: Downtown—waiting for a bus—

FRANCES: Why didn't you come over and speak to me?

CARL: Well, I was in my car. By the time I had parked and got to where you were, the bus had come—I could see you getting on. You left. But . . . well . . . I wanted to see you again . . . somehow . . .

FRANCES: The snows of yesteryear?

CARL: Maybe . . . *(A pause.)* You haven't been happy, Fran. It's written all over your face; it's in your voice. . . . You don't love him. You couldn't have.

FRANCES: *(Simply.)* I was in love with Noa once, when I left you for him. But I was young then, and I didn't know any better. Well, I learned. And we both left love behind, a long time ago.

CARL: Then, what keeps you tied to him—?

FRANCES: —to each other.

CARL: To a man who beats you. . . . It doesn't make sense.

FRANCES: I—agree with you. It doesn't.

CARL: Then—make sense. . . . Are you afraid that if you did try to make sense, you'd realize you made a terrible mistake?

FRANCES: In choosing Noa over you? Or in just doing what, God help me, I did.

CARL: Look—Fran—I did love you. I sincerely loved you. Believe me.

FRANCES: I believe you.

CARL: Then why?

FRANCES: Every time I have tried to put it into words, I've learned that the words were—just words. The life had been squeezed out of them, like pressed flowers.

CARL: Try anyway.

FRANCES: When I met Noa, it was as if, suddenly, I began to hear other voices.

CARL: What voices?

FRANCES: The voices of the dead. The dead we killed. And keep killing every day over and over. And I thought: when Carl and I have a baby, that baby will be destroyed, too. . . . The past cried Death, and the future promised only Death. . . . I heard those voices, Past and Future, in Noa, alive. . . . They lived in him; they spoke through him.

CARL: I don't understand. You keep talking in riddles, and I just simply don't understand.

FRANCES: I know that. . . . But then—you've never heard the voices. Words don't do any good.

CARL: You left me for a man who talks to the dead.

(NOA *enters at the back, his cup and bottle with him. Unnoticed, he stops and listens.*)

FRANCES: Not only to the dead. Noa talks to the night, as well. And to lizards. And to snails. To pieces of wood and *limu*, and to the empty nests of vanished birds. . . . He has talked to my tears and my excrement and he used to talk to the blood that monthly washed the promise of Life from my body. He talks beyond love and beyond hope. . . . He talks to the final sanctity of all things we see and hear and smell and taste and touch. . . . And he has placed me in the center of that sanctity, Carl. . . . And he is there, with me. Does that offend your good sense and your reason? Well . . . you have no idea how offensive Noa can be.

CARL: I'm getting a pretty good idea. And it's called insanity.

NOA: *(Moving down to them.)* Frances, my medicine is almost finished. *(He sets cup and bottle down on a bench, sits.)* Maybe if you go to that store now, you'll get back before we start rehearsal.

FRANCES: *(Rising.)* I don't have any more money.

NOA: Kamuela and the others probably have enough between them.

CARL: Goddamn it!

(Angrily he moves to them. Before either NOA or FRANCES realizes what is happening, he sweeps up the cup and bottle and moves to the trash box with them. He throws both in the box, turns to them, enraged.)

CARL: What's the matter with you people? It's like you don't want help. Somebody offers you aloha, and you just take it and smash it.

FRANCES: Maybe it's not help we want, Carl.

NOA: It's too late for that.

CARL: Then what is it, damn it? What is it you want?

NOA: *(Quietly.)* Frances, the children need your *kokua* with their costumes.

FRANCES: *(Softly.)* Yes. *(She starts off, is stopped by:)*

NOA: Frances. . . . They came to me. . . . We talked. . . . They know now. . . . They're afraid, a little . . . but they accept . . .

FRANCES: Thank you, Noa.

(She goes off left immediately. NOA looks steadily at CARL, who is a little challenged by it.)

CARL: You're—insane. Insane and drunk. A boor—that's what you are: a plain common honest-to-God boor!

NOA: *(Simply.)* If honest-to-God, that's fine. All gods like honesty of any kind. I know. I talk to them, too.

CARL: Christ, what conceit!

NOA: Why not? I've got a lot to be conceited about. . . . I'm a

Hawaiian. . . . But I guess you don't know what that means.

CARL: Listen, Noa, don't look down your nose at me. People like me—we're the real Hawaiians. We take the world as it is, we go out, we try. We don't sit around, whining and bellyaching about some great past we've lost. We work. We cope. The best way we can. In the real world. And we make it . . .

NOA: (*Always simply.*) You don't know what you've lost, Carl. And if you don't know that, you're not a Hawaiian.

(CARL *just stares at him. He shakes his head in a kind of wonder.*)

CARL: And you, of course—self-appointed kahuna to the dead— can do all this?

NOA: Of course. But only with your help.

CARL: (*Taunting.*) Oh? What do I do?

NOA: That pus inside—you puke it out.

CARL: A dead man can't puke.

NOA: Okay, I'll puke for you. But it'll hurt.

CARL: Well, then, if it's going to hurt, don't put yourself to any trouble, friend.

NOA: I didn't mean hurt *me*. I mean, it'll hurt you.

(*A pause. They face each other in silence,* NOA *smiling faintly.* CHARLES *comes in from the left.*)

CHARLES: Everybody's ready and waiting, Carl. Do you still want to start?

NOA: Want to start, Carl?

CARL: Do your damnedest, Noa.

NOA: Then, let's start Charles. Ask the court to come on stage, please.

(CHARLES *goes off right.* NOA *holds the look at* CARL, *smiles more broadly.*)

NOA: Won't you take your throne, Your Majesty?

(CARL *moves to his throne, sits.* NOA, *all brisk efficiency now, moves to the left.*)

NOA: *(Calling off.)* E Frances, e Kamuela, e Pokipala . . . e ʻoukou a pau. Mai. Pono no kākou e hoʻomaka.[6]

(He waits. From downstage right and upstage right, the COURT *and* ATTENDANTS *begin to straggle in. They remain at right, most of them in disgruntled silence, a few whispering. Meanwhile* FRANCES, KAMUELA, *and the others of* NOA's *troupe enter, more or less in a group. They are all in authentic ancient costume.* NOA *places some of them in position; he sends some other boys off.* LYDIA *and* CHARLES *move on from downstage right. She goes immediately to her throne, beside* CARL.*)*

LYDIA: *(To* CARL.*)* Are they going to apologize?
CARL: Don't worry. He'll apologize. Later. I promise you.

*(*NOA *finishes placing his people, and he turns to face the* COURT. *He is all affability.)*

NOA: Are we ready to begin, Kale?
CHARLES: *(Glumly.)* Yeah. Everybody's here.
NOA: Good—good. So, shall we start? . . . We're not going to go through your entrance again. . . . You enter, you are in place— and the *mōʻī* and the *aliʻi* sit. . . . Would you please get into your positions, after you enter?

(There is a rearrangement of places. CARL *and* LYDIA *remain seated.)*

NOA: Maikaʻi! Now, the *aliʻi* sit.

(The aliʻi *sit.)*

NOA: Then Carl—I'm sorry, *mōʻī*—you rise and read your speech in Hawaiian.

(With a sigh, CARL *starts to rise.)*

NOA: No, no, you don't have to do it now. . . . Later on. . . . So the speech is over, you sit. . . . And now come the commoners, begging the *aliʻi* to receive their poor offering . . .

---

[6]NOA: Frances—Kamuela—Pokipala . . . All of you. Come. We must begin.

(He *makes a quick signal. Drums. A chant. And from the left, prostrate, humbling themselves,* KAMUELA, POKIPALA, *and* KALEO *"drag" themselves toward* CARL *and* LYDIA.)

NOA: See how they come, Your Majesties! The common people—low, low as the dirt through which they drag themselves to lay their gift at your feet. *("Contemptuously," he shoves* KALEO *with his foot, indicating him.)* Here is Malalo, one of the *kauwā*, a nothing. . . . In your kindness, you let him live even though he has no land or house and must wander, homeless, from hovel to hovel, feeding on roots, less than a man, lower even than the pig you keep as a pet and suckle at your royal breast. . . . *(He shoves* POKIPALA *with his foot.)* And here is Aikelekele—a nothing who one day raised his eyes and dared to look into your eyes, forgetting his place. . . . Banished from his world, an outcast, living only at your whim, your aloha, an aloha he does not deserve. . . . *(He shoves* KAMUELA *with his foot.)* Finally, here is Kapihe, who cannot even die—a poor man, yearning for Death, knowing that for him Life ends not in Death, but in Nothingness. For only the *ali'i* have souls, and he—a poor commoner without a soul, a nothing—can only return to Nothing. . . . An outcast throughout Eternity. *(He waits.)* Well—?
LYDIA: Well, what?
NOA: Accept us. Here we are, your people, humble in the dirt before you, apologizing . . .
KAMUELA: Ke mihi nei . . .[7]
POKIPALA: Ke mihi nei . . .
NOA: . . . For living.
KALEO: Ke mihi nei mākou no ka ola 'ana.[8]
NOA: We come to you, apologizing for living, bringing you a gift from Laka—the story of the young lovers, Laupi'o and Kea and the young *ali'i* Kahililoa. . . . Accept it. *(He gestures to* LYDIA, *urging her to accept.)*
LYDIA: Well—so—I accept it.
NOA: Good! Wonderful! But—a little more—*ali'i*—in your voice. Remember, you are speaking to dirt—to filth. You are an *ali'i*.

---

[7]KAMUELA: Apologizing . . .
POKIPALA: Apologizing . . .

[8]KALEO: Apologizing for living.

LYDIA: I accept it!

NOA: (*Practically crows with delight.*) A laila, e hele aku, e ka mea 'ino, e ka lepo, e ke kūkae, e hele aku! E haʻalele i nā aliʻi![9]

(*He practically kicks the three "commoners" off the stage. Then* NOA *turns back to face* CARL *and* LYDIA.)

NOA: We bring you our poor gift of the hula, Your Majesties. The story of the young *aliʻi* Kahikiloa's love for the beautiful Kea. . . . You all know the story—of how love turned into jealousy and how jealousy turned into hatred, destroying all Life.

(*His arm sweeps down in a signal to the* MUSICIANS. *They begin drumming.*)

NOA: You remember the beginning: how Kahikiloa grew up on Oʻahu. In the valley of Kalihi. How he was favored with power and beauty, and how he spurned all women until finally, while visiting Kauaʻi, he came to Waimea, where the people were feasting and dancing and where he saw the beautiful young woman, Kea.

(*The villagers enter, dancing in stately fashion;* HIʻIAKA *is with them, dancing, the center of their aloha. And then* POKIPALA, *as Kahikiloa, joins the dance. As the dance goes on, he and* HIʻIAKA *come closer and closer.*)

NOA: Kahikiloa, the son of *aliʻi* . . . Kahikiloa, at whose shadow the commoners trembled . . . Kahikiloa, the brave—Kahikiloa, the beautiful—Kahikiloa, the loving . . .

(*He lets the dance end, and, as if in direct continuation,* POKIPALA *and* HIʻIAKA *are dancing a love duet.*)

NOA: And, dancing with the beautiful Kea, Kahikiloa was enflamed with passion, passion feeding passion, fire inflaming fire. (POKIPALA *and* HIʻIAKA *continue their love duet.*) And that night, he took her and, into the deepest valleys of her love, he poured out his fire. . . . And so, forest and fire consumed each other all night

---

[9]NOA: Now, go, filth, dirt, turd, go! Leave the *aliʻi!*

long, burning the skies of Waimea, blazing out moon and stars. . . . *(The dance is over.* POKIPALA *is gone.)* When morning came and Kahikiloa returned to Oʻahu, the fire within him still raged. . . . Nothing could still it. *(To* CARL:*)* You know the feeling, Your Majesty! You know the ache that rots and turns to pus here—*(He bangs both fists against his lower abdomen.)*—and you want to puke it out, but it just stays inside there, rotting.

(Uneasy, CARL *shifts his gaze from* NOA. *It falls—perhaps not by conscious design—on* FRANCES, *who, their eyes meeting, turns away.* CARL *looks down.)*

NOA: *(To* CARL.*)* You know—you know the story, of course. You all know the story. How he sent his friend, the commoner Laupiʻo, to fetch the beautiful Kea to him . . . Laupiʻo, the humble . . . Laupiʻo, the lowly. . . . And so, a canoe was brought . . .

(Male dancers in two lines of four move in from the left on either side of KAMUELA — *Laupiʻo in the canoe.)*

NOA: And Laupiʻo was taken in that canoe from Oʻahu to Kauaʻi and to Kea the beautiful.

*(*NOA *has moved to the side. He picks up a gourd and begins to chant. The "canoe" begins to move, with* KAMUELA *in the center.* KAMUELA *does not dance; the men do a "paddle hula." In a while, the musicians pick up the chant, and* NOA *is silent. Then the hula is over; the "canoe" has arrived.)*

NOA: And so they arrived at Waimea to be greeted with feasting and dancing.

(Again the villagers dance in, mingling with KAMUELA *and the paddlers.* NOA *has moved to* FRANCES' *side, stands there with her as the welcoming hula builds to its end.* KAMUELA *and* HIʻIAKA, *as Laupiʻo and Kea, are left alone, eyes downcast, standing very still.)*

NOA: And so they returned, Laupiʻo bringing the beautiful young Kea back to Oʻahu and to Kahikiloa.

(Slowly, side by side, KAMUELA *and* HIʻIAKA *begin to circle the stage, eyes always downcast. But as they move, their slow walk slowly begins to change—change more—and become, finally, a hula; they fall in love in dance.)*

NOA: And as they went—past cliffs, past valleys, across the channel waters, Love came to them—surprising them. . . . They arrived at Nanakuli on Oʻahu. . . . And they walked, dallied as they walked, across the island for Kalihi. And as they went, Love deepened, the Love that was to bind them forever. . . . The Love that was to destroy them . . .

*(*KAMUELA *and* HIʻIAKA *continue to dance. And then it is over. In the silence that follows,* NOA *moves slowly to face* CARL. *Then:)*

NOA: *(Quietly.)* Tell us the rest of the story, Carl.

*(*CARL *hesitates, uneasy in the attention that the rest of the* COURT *is now paying him. The hesitation grows, awkwardly.)*

NOA: *(Always quietly.)* It's your story, Carl. You taught me the story. Remember? . . . Tell us.

*(*CARL *stares at* NOA *in silence. He is angry, put upon—and silent.)*

JOSEPH: Oh, come on, Carl. If you know the story, tell it and let's get it over with.
KEOKI: Yeah, Carl, especially that part where the young *aliʻi* went to pour more hot lava into her valley!

(There's some laughter, cut short by:)

CLEMENT: Go on, Carl. Finish the story.
CARL: I don't know what he's talking about. It's his damned story.
NOA: You know, you know. What did Kahikiloa do when he found out about Laupiʻo and Kea?

*(*CARL *is about to explode; still, he fights it down.)*

ARTHUR: What're you getting sore about, man?
NOA: *(Intensely.)* Rage! The fire exploded into rage!

(The hula rehearsed earlier by POKIPALA *now bursts forth. It does not continue for very long before* CARL's *rage explodes. He is on his feet.)*

CARL: Stop it! . . . I said stop it!

*(*NOA's *signal stops the hula. The* DANCERS *all back away, but they do not exit.)*

CARL: *(To the* DANCERS.*)* Get out. . . . Get the hell out of here. *(The* DANCERS *do not budge.)* I said, get out! *(The* DANCERS *still don't make a move.)*
NOA: *(Softly.)* E lohe iā ia. E hele aku.[10]

*(*NOA's *troupe exits. A silence. The* COURT *is perplexed, even a little shocked, at* CARL's *excessive anger.* NOA *and* CARL *are "locked.")*

CARL: What the hell are you trying to do?
NOA: Why was he angry?
CARL: His girl had been stolen from him—by a friend he trusted.
NOA: *(Simply.)* No. You're telling it all wrong. Love stole both of them.
CARL: Okay, fine! If that's the story, fine! Let 'em go, good riddance. Why make such a big thing out of it? *(He starts to go off but is stopped by:)*
NOA: Because the young *ali'i* made a big thing out of it, Carl. . . . He wouldn't let them go. He went after them and after them and *after* them. . . . Do you remember the story now, Carl?
CARL: All right. Whatever it is, Noa, get it said. Get it all said!
NOA: It is quickly said, Carl.
CARL: Say it!
NOA: The young *ali'i* used his position to grind them into the earth. Finally, they went off into a valley—far from their people. They built their huts, planted their taro, tried to make a new life for themselves.
CARL: You go to hell. *(Once more he turns on his heel, and once more he is stopped.)*
NOA: There was a baby, Carl. A little boy!

*(*CARL *turns and faces* NOA, *who continues more evenly now.)*

---

[10]NOA: Obey him. Go.

NOA: The young *ali'i's*—from the night they first met on Kauai, the night of—panic.

(CARL's *consternation mounts. He looks at* FRANCES *in silent, shocked questioning. The* COURT *is whispering. From their concerned looks at* CARL, *it is obvious that they are beginning to catch on.*)

FRANCES: *(Quietly.)* It's true, Carl.

(*The silence is broken by* LYDIA *getting up. She is obviously concerned for* CARL, *is going to get him off the hook.*)

LYDIA: I think I would like some coffee—a little break.

(*The* COURT *breaks into murmurs of relieved agreement.*)

JOSEPH: *(Over the murmuring.)* Yeah, I think that's a great idea, Lydia. Little coffee break.
LYDIA: Come, Carl.

(*She takes* CARL's *arm. The others are about to follow. But no one moves more than three or four steps before they are stopped by:*)

NOA: He was a beautiful boy, Carl. And on his twenty-first birthday, he died. . . . He was murdered!

(*More concerned whispering from the* COURT. NOA *turns to one of the princesses.*)

NOA: You helped kill him, Lokalia.
LOKALIA: *(Moving forward, appalled.)* Me? What are you talking about?
CARL: What the hell is he talking about, Frances?
FRANCES: Lokalia, when you were teaching elementary school in Kane'ohe, do you remember a little boy who would never sit still in class?
LOKALIA: What's she talkin' about? Lotsa little kids don't sit still—
FRANCES: A little boy who wouldn't sit still because he was so excited by the joy and wonder of everything about him.
NOA: You killed him!
LOKALIA: You're crazy!
FRANCES: A little boy you hated—

NOA: —because he kept speaking Hawaiian in class.

LOKALIA: Look, I was supposed to make them all speak correct English.

FRANCES: Because you can't speak Hawaiian.

NOA: Is that why you hated him? Because a little boy made you feel guilty about being a Hawaiian?

LOKALIA: Look, I'm tellin' you, they're supposed to speak English. There was lotsa kids like that, didn' speak English so good.

NOA: There was lotsa kids like that! Then you admit it! Lots of kids —like Carl's son!

COURT: *(An ad libbed jumble of whisperings.)* Carl's son! . . . What's he talkin' about? . . . I thought this was just supposed to be a story! . . . I figured that's what he was holdin' back . . . the kid was Carl's son. . . . *(And so forth.)*

ARTHUR: *(Moving to challenge NOA.)* No fair! She said she didn't even know the kid. Why're you blaming her!

NOA: She didn't know any of the kids. That's the blame.

FRANCES: The not knowing, the not caring.

ARTHUR: Bull—!

NOA: You were guilty of it, too, the murder of Carl's son—by not knowing, by not caring.

ARTHUR: How the hell do I come into—?

NOA: Kamehameha School. The admission committee. You were on that committee.

ARTHUR: So?

NOA: The boy applied. His one dream was to attend that school—a school set up for his people. You turned him down.

ARTHUR: For Chrissake, not every Hawaiian kid gets into Kam School. So—he couldn't make it.

NOA: Because he didn't know haole history, because he couldn't write and read English well, because he didn't even know who was the President of the United States. . . . All he knew was *mele* and *oli* and chants about Kane and Laka and the stars Nana-mua and Nana-hope and Hoku-pa'a . . .

ARTHUR: A kid is supposed to know useful things—like math and history and geography and—

(Throughout the foregoing, CARL has been intent on NOA, his mind racing. Something has now snapped into place.)

CARL: Hold it, Arthur . . . I think I see what this guy's doing. *(He moves to face NOA.)* It's an old trick, Noa.

NOA: *(Softly.)* Very old.

CARL: Do you mind if I finish it?

NOA: *(The faintest of smiles.)* I was hoping you would. That was the deal: I puke, you suffer.

CARL: Childish tricks don't make me suffer.

NOA: Don't be too sure.

CARL: *(Smiles, assured.)* Okay—okay. . . . Lydia, would you go and call the museum, ask for Mabel Haleli'i?

LYDIA: I know Mabel.

CARL: In the museum library.

LYDIA: I know.

CARL: Ask her if there's such a Hawaiian legend as the one about the two young lovers named Laupi'o and Kea and a young *ali'i* named Kahikiloa.

LYDIA: Okay. *(She goes offstage right immediately.)*

CARL: *(To NOA.)* And so this boy was turned away from his people and his world.

NOA: Yes.

CARL: Clement . . .

(CLEMENT, *another prince in the* COURT, *moves to* CARL.)

CLEMENT: Yeah?

CARL: You were a councilman some years ago?

CLEMENT: Yeah?

CARL: And a Hawaiian boy came to you asking for help. Work. Nice boy. Beautiful. Talented.

CLEMENT: Jesus, Carl, hundreds of young guys used to come to me at that time.

CARL: Of course. That's the point! Like hundreds of kids who couldn't speak proper English came to Lokalia . . . and like hundreds of kids who weren't eligible applied to Kam School. . . . You turned some of them down.

CLEMENT: I helped some.

CARL: How?

CLEMENT: Well—there was always work for the City and County. I'd call somebody, pull a few strings, help out our people.

CARL: Garbage collecting.

CLEMENT: Yeah. Sometimes. Why not?

CARL: *(To NOA.)* Beautiful Hawaiians collecting garbage. How terrible!

NOA: *(Softly.)* Yes.

CARL: *(To the* COURT.*)* Don't you see what he is doing? . . . Joseph!

(JOSEPH *comes to him.*)

CARL: You work in a bank. Housing loans.
JOSEPH: Yes.
CARL: How many young Hawaiians come to you for a housing loan? Say, every month?
JOSEPH: Gee, not so many, maybe—but some, a few.
CARL: You may not know it, Joseph, but a young man came to you a few years ago, a young worker for the City and County. He wanted to buy a house. You turned him down.
JOSEPH: That happened often.
CARL: Of course it did. It could have been any young man. But Noa is trying to make this all apply to one particular young man: my supposed son. . . . Keoki!
KEOKI: Yeah?
CARL: You're in the cabinetmaking business.
KEOKI: Yeah.
CARL: Do you hire many Hawaiians?
KEOKI: Never. Not one.
CARL: Why not?
KEOKI: Well, because our people don't do cabinet work, that's why. Mostly, I hire Japs. Once in a while, a haole. But mostly Japs.
CARL: Keoki, my friend. Shame on you. You turned away my son. Poor kid—born a bastard, clobbered in school by incompetent teachers, denied higher education because he didn't really belong, refused land and a home in his own country, denied decent work so all he could do was collect the haole's garbage. . . . And it's all our fault. Right, Noa?
NOA: *(Quietly.)* That's right.
CARL: It all figures. *(To the* COURT:*)* Let me tell you something: When Tom Bruner went to offer Noa this job, Tom was really impressed by one thing: how interested Noa was in everybody in the cast. He kept asking Tom questions: who is this guy, what does he do, where does he work? *(To* NOA:*)* What did you do? Check us all out afterwards? *(No answer from* NOA.*)* Well, why don't you answer? That's it, isn't it? You checked us all out, then you made up this crazy story . . . *(To the cast:)* . . . to make you all seem guilty. *(To* NOA:*)* You know, you don't belong just in a booby hatch. You belong in jail.
NOA: *(Always quietly.)* You forgot one other person who denied him.

CARL: *(To the cast.)* Jesus Christ, I don't believe this nut. *(To* NOA:*)*
   And who's that?

NOA: You.

CARL: *(Almost laughs.)* I knew you would get around to that.

NOA: He finally came to you, too, Carl.

CARL: Of course he did.

NOA: Yes.

CARL: And, of course, I turned him down!

NOA: Yes.

CARL: How? How did all this happen?

NOA: You were getting a new show ready. For your tourists. You
   were looking for dancers. He came to dance for you.

CARL: He came and danced a beautiful old hula. Authentic. True.

NOA: Yes.

CARL: And I was auditioning for commercial dancers.

NOA: Yes.

CARL: I didn't hire him. He didn't fit in with the tinsel show-biz
   world of Waikiki. I hired trash and turned away gold.

NOA: Yes.

CARL: I rejected my people's heart and soul and rewarded a cheap
   parody of it.

NOA: Yes.

CARL: And a poor son is turned away by an unsuspecting father.
   What a heartbreaker! A real three-handkerchief heartbreaker!
   . . . Right, Frances?

FRANCES: He went away destroyed, Carl.

CARL: *(To her.)* You know as well as I do. There was no baby.

NOA: Then who was it Frances and I carried inside us, close to
   our hearts, and was born and grew up to be hurt by his own
   people?

CARL: Frances and you! Jesus! Jesus! *(He yells it, against his appalled
   rage.)* Nobody! Nobody was born! Nobody grew up! Nobody
   was hurt!

NOA: To you, a nobody. To us, everybody!

FRANCES: Our future. The future of our people.

CARL: Okay, then. Produce a birth certificate. Come to my office
   tomorrow with a birth certificate. Can you produce that?

FRANCES: There were only Noa and me in the hut. In our valley.
   No one else. . . . For me, the delivery was easy. For him, the
   labor was hard.

(Murmurs of consternation ripple through the cast.)

CARL: Let me get this right. He labored; you delivered.

FRANCES: Yes.

NOA: *(Together.)* Yes.

(CARL *looks at them an appalled moment and and then begins to laugh.*)

CARL: I can't believe it! I just can't believe it! *(A moment.)* And, of course, nobody ever saw this kid growing up. . . . Bring me one person who saw this kid growing up. Bring me one person who's ever seen him at all.

NOA: Lokalia . . . Arthur . . . Clement . . . Joseph . . . Keoki . . . you. . . . You all saw him.

CARL: We saw nobody.

NOA: *(Always quietly.)* Then who was it who went into the deepest part of the valley—

FRANCES: —after you had turned him away—

NOA: —and sharpened a short stake from a small branch of a koa tree—

FRANCES: —and, with that piece of wood, stabbed the hurt out of his broken heart?

NOA: Who was that, Carl?

CARL: *(Pointing at them, accusing, triumphant.)* You bring me a death certificate.

NOA: Who would have been interested in the death of a nobody?

FRANCES: Just another Hawaiian, Carl. Nobody really cared.

CARL: I thought so.

(LYDIA *comes back from stage right, smiling, self-satisfied.*)

LYDIA: Carl . . . Carl, I called the museum. *(All attention is focused on her.)* I talked to Mable.

CARL: And?

LYDIA: He made it all up. There's no legend like that.

(*Now the attention turns to* NOA. *In the accusing silence, they wait for his response.*)

NOA: *(Simply.)* It is the story of the lovers, Laupi'o and Kea . . .

(*From upstage right,* POKIPALA *and* HI'IAKA *appear. They are in white. Each wears a* kahoa.)

FRANCES: . . . and the wrath of the *ali'i*, Kahikiloa.

(Similarly dressed, KAMUELA *appears near the others.)*

NOA: It is a story about Love . . . Love despised, Love punished, Love neglected, Love forgotten . . .

(Similarly dressed, KALEO *and the other girls appear close by.)*

NOA: It is a story of how Laupi'o and Kea lived out their life of grief, and of how they finally died, heartbroken and forgotten . . .

(During the following, the rest of NOA*'s troupe appear near the others.)*

NOA: . . . and of how, even after death—
FRANCES: —even *in* Death—
NOA: —their spirits came in human form, and they went to the *ali'i* Kahikiloa, to remind him once again of the terrible need for that love.
FRANCES: And even in death, the *ali'i* denied them, and sent them away in anger.
NOA: It is a story of aloha—
FRANCES: —denied.
NOA: Of a child of Hawai'i—
FRANCES: —denied.
NOA: Of our life—
FRANCES: —denied.

(A silence. Then CARL *moves to them, everything about him deliberate. Feeling has gone, even anger. Only firm decisiveness is left.)*

CARL: You make me puke. . . . All right, just tell me one thing. Why? Why have you done all this? Just to get back at me? After all these years, to try to hurt me? And why now? *(There is no answer from* FRANCES *or* NOA.*)* What made you think you could get away with such an insane bunch of lies? *(No answer.)* I'm going to ask you again—just once more—why are you doing all this? *(No answer. To* NOA:*)* I stuck my neck out hiring you. I deserve an answer. *(No answer.)* Okay, that's it. You're fired. Right now. We don't need you any more.

(NOA *and* FRANCES *make no move to go. Nor does the troupe.*)

LYDIA: What's the matter with you? You're fired. We don't want you. Nobody wants you.

CARL: Good Christ, you've been told to go. Why the hell don't you go?

FRANCES: E hele mai, e kuʻu ipo. Pono kāua e haʻalele.[11]

NOA: ʻAe. *(To the troupe:)* We have done what we came to do. Let us go now.

(*As they go off left, the* AUTHOR *steps in upstage right. There is audible relief from the* COURT.)

COURT: *(Generalized babble.)* Well, I'm sure glad that's over. . . . What the hell was all that about? . . . Boy, that was weird. . . . Talk about *pupule.* . . . *(And so forth.)*

AUTHOR: They don't really go, you know. They never do.

CARL: *(Calling.)* Charlie! . . . Charles! *(He comes back to the cast. He is perhaps just a little too much "in charge.")*

AUTHOR: They linger in the mind.

CARL: Lydia, the dancers still downstairs?

LYDIA: Yeah. Sure. They're in that room—the greenroom—playing cards.

CARL: We've wasted a lot of time with these people.

LYDIA: Sure have.

AUTHOR: In the murmuring dark of our remembering, they hover—

(LYDIA *goes offstage as* CARL *turns to* CHARLES, *who enters.*)

CHARLES: Yes, Carl?

(CARL *moves to a bench, speaking to the cast over his shoulder.*)

CARL: Everybody take a break until we start. Half an hour.

AUTHOR: They wait for us to call . . .

(*The cast disperses stage right. On the bench,* CARL *takes out a checkbook.*)

---

[11]FRANCES: Come, dearest. We must go.

CARL: I just fired Noa, Charles. You're the boss now.
CHARLES: *(Gesturing to the left.)* I heard everything.
CARL: Got a pen?
CHARLES: Yeah.
AUTHOR: ... to reach out to them.

(CHARLES *hands a pen to* CARL, *who begins to make out a check.*)

CARL: Downstairs. Noa and Frances. They just went down.
CHARLES: Yeah. I saw them go down the steps.

(CARL *looks over his shoulder to where the cast was. Everyone is gone. He returns to making out the check.*)

CARL: They'll be with their dancers in their dressing room. . . .
   Give this to that boy. Kamuela.
AUTHOR: ... in pity... in love ...

(CARL *finishes writing the check, tears it off. He offers the check to* CHARLES.)

CARL: It's for all of them. I'm sure Kamuela will make Noa take it . . .
CHARLES: The bastard doesn't deserve any kindness from you, Carl.
CARL: Noa's a sick man, Charles. A sick and dying man. I don't excuse what he did—but—Christ, did you see, there at the end? He was talking to thin air, like there were other people there . . . sick. . . . Explains a lot.

(*The* AUTHOR *moves to downstage right.* CARL *shakes off his troubled thoughts, hands the check to* CHARLES *again.*)

CARL: Take it to Kamuela.
CHARLES: *(Reluctantly.)* Well . . . okay. *(He takes the check.)*
CARL: And don't forget. We begin again. In half an hour.
CHARLES: Sure.

(CHARLES *goes off at upstage left.* CARL *sits for a few moments, then, quite depressed, he rises. The* AUTHOR *watches him go to the right, pause for a moment as he regards the* mōʻī's *throne, then continue dejectedly off at upstage right. The* AUTHOR *turns to address the audience. The lights fade, leaving him in the spots.*)

AUTHOR: The morning after he died, the men of our village buried Georgina's lover there in the foothills. By noon, it was all over. Even the rain. My mother sent some women from our house to help Georgina move. She was to come and stay with us; she had nowhere to go now. The women didn't want to go into the forest. They were scared. They were afraid they would see him there. You see, our people believe that the dead never go immediately into the darkness. They return to their loved ones one more time, for one last lingering look, before they go. . . . And they never go far. . . . They are as near as the heart's calling. But my mother insisted, and the frightened women went and when they got to that tent in the foothills, they found no Georgina. . . . They searched, they called. To no avail. The women knew then: he had come for her. He had taken her. . . . They left that sad and frightening place. . . . The next day, some men, searching farther into the forest, found her. She was on the ground, leaning back against an ohi'a tree; a knife was beside her. . . . She had broken off one end of a branch, sharpened it with the knife, and— *(His control falters; he has to stop.)* Well, I think you know what happened. . . . *(A moment.)* But it wasn't until later that day that they found the most heartbreaking thing of all. . . . It was towards evening; they had laid Georgina to rest beside Noa, there in the forest. And when the men went back to the tent, inside, in one corner, hanging, was a calabash. . . . In it they found a bottle—a bottle of coconut oil, scented with sandalwood, and some—some wads of tapa soaked with the oil, and—and the anointed bones of a small child—a little girl, a little boy. I don't know. . . . *(A moment.)* A few nights later, I heard Georgina's cry of loss again. It woke me, and I sat up in the darkness of my room, listening to the darkness whispering around me, like echoes of her cry. Then I became that little boy: Years later, remembering her, thinking of her loss that was now mine, as well, trying to put the murmuring of her voice into words, asking over and over, "What was it? What flew away, out of our lives?" I could think only of . . . *(The spots begin to fade slowly.)* o'o . . . mamo . . . i'iwi . . . o'u. . . . A *mele kanikau* of birds' names. . . . Where did all those little lives go? Where, Georgina?

(The stage is dark.)

ACT THREE

(The AUTHOR *walks on and addresses the audience.)*

AUTHOR: And so I reach out to them, the way I did that afternoon in the foothills when she cried out her terrible loss over the crushing rain and I, alone in the car, called out, "Georgina!"— you know, the way children will out of quick pity, or fear maybe . . . reaching out for the other. . . . That is what a play is, I think, all a poem is: a reaching out for the other, an act of faith, an act of love . . . and I know now: Poets do not search for final meanings; we act; we celebrate. Poets aren't philosophers; philosophers are. Poets can only, when they reach out beyond words, touch what is real, what is near, and they are touched by that nearness. . . . They celebrate the ordinary: the flash of a bird's wing in the morning sun; the salty taste of love; the small death in the forgetting of a name; a dear voice that will never, never come again. . . . Poets remember, they always speak of what is gone, and they celebrate in spite of the hurt of that loss. They know about parting. . . .

*(*CARL *walks on and sits on the bench at downstage left.)*

AUTHOR: And so we begin our goodbyes by insisting that bliss lies about us, in the ordinary and the mundane, now . . .

*(*KEAKA CHING *enters from the left—a big, affable, Chinese-Hawaiian businessman.)*

AUTHOR: . . . in the world of hard fact, your world, mine, and of Mr. Keaka Ching, vice-president of the Jubilee Festival Committee . . . summoned by Lydia . . .

(He steps off. CARL *rises, shakes hands.)*

KEAKA: Hello, Carl.

CARL: Hi . . .

KEAKA: What's going on around here? My secretary got a hold of me down at the Outrigger. Something about Lydia.

CARL: It's all right, Keaka. It's all been taken care of.

KEAKA: What's the matter? Lydia pulling her Lili'uokalani act again?

CARL: No, it's not Lydia this time.

KEAKA: (Amused.) It's not Lydia? What's happening? The world coming to an end?

CARL: No. It's Noa. . . . He and Lydia just didn't hit it off.

KEAKA: Who?

CARL: Noa Napo'o. The *kumu hula*. . . . Despite you guys, I went ahead and hired him.

KEAKA: He was here?

CARL: Yes. This afternoon. With his—uh—wife and hula troupe.

KEAKA: What time this afternoon?

CARL: Oh, hour and a half ago. Maybe two.

KEAKA: You're kidding me. You're putting me on. (*Affable, confused, he scratches his head.*)

CARL: What do you mean?

(CHARLES *comes in, check in hand.*)

CHARLES: Carl—there's nobody downstairs. Anywhere.

CARL: Have you looked in their dressing room?

CHARLES: I looked everywhere.

KEAKA: For who?

CARL: Noa and his troupe.

CHARLES: Carl—something weird's happened to their dressing room. It's as cold as an icebox. . . . Clammy.

CARL: Well, turn the air conditioner off.

CHARLES: It *is* off . . . I turned it off this morning. . . . And the room looks like nobody's been in it for months. Nothing's been touched; nothing's been moved.

(*As if materializing out of nowhere,* NOA *appears from behind a pillar in the background. He is in the costume of a* kumu hula *of long, long ago. He stands very still, his head bowed.*)

CARL: What are you talking about?

CHARLES: Carl . . . this morning I mopped that floor. It was a mess. And I took a rag and wiped the dust off the mirrors and the dressing tables, everything. . . . The dust is back now, on every-thing, like I never cleaned anything. It's like nobody was ever in that dressing room today.

KEAKA: Nobody was. . . . At least, not Napo'o and his group.

CARL: What do you mean?

KEAKA: I mean . . . Noa Napo'o is dead, Carl.

CARL: What?

(FRANCES *materializes from behind another pillar. Like* NOA, *she stands very still, head bowed.*)

KEAKA: He, a haole woman, and his hula troupe. . . . The brakes went out on their truck—on a dirt road in the hills—North Shore someplace. . . . They went off the cliff—a two, three hun-dred foot drop.

CHARLES: When?

KEAKA: Late this morning.

CHARLES: Jesus!

CARL: I don't believe you.

KEAKA: It's been on the radio for the last two hours.

CARL: They were here, I tell you. (*He rushes to the trash box upstage left, urgently rummages through it.*)

KEAKA: What are you doing?

CARL: An empty whiskey bottle—a cup. . . . He was drinking. (*He keeps searching, his urgency mounting into frustration.*)

CHARLES: They were here. We all saw them.

(CARL *overturns the trash box. Wads of paper, paper cups, empty soft-drink cans, a newspaper, and so forth—but no cup, no whiskey bottle.* CARL *just stares down at the mess.*)

CARL: But I threw them in here myself.

KEAKA: (*The faintest of smiles.*) I'm not doubting you.

CARL: Then—what was it? What's been going on? That was Noa—that was Frances I saw . . . (*Points to* CHARLES.) . . . that he saw . . . everybody saw.

KEAKA: (*The smiles turning into a chuckle.*) Maybe it's some trick, eh, Carl? People pretending to be Noa and his troupe?

CARL: I know them. It was Noa. It was Fran.

KEAKA: (*The chuckling grows.*) Of course you do. . . . Do Lydia and the others know them?

CARL: Not until today.

(KEAKA's *growing amusement is now quite open. There is no hint of censure; he is genuinely amused.*)

KEAKA: I've got to hand it to you. You sure got some imagination.

CARL: I didn't imagine anything.

KEAKA: *(Laughing.)* Boy, you are convincing. You're really convincing! You, too, Charlie. But this doesn't come out of my publicity budget, you know. Not a crazy trick like this . . .

CARL: Publicity!

KEAKA: *(Amused always.)* It was your bright idea. You foot the bill!

(CHARLES *looks at the check in his hands.*)

CARL: My God, you think I set it all up—a publicity stunt!

KEAKA: Noa Napo'o, a haole woman, and a dance troupe were killed in an accident on their way here. . . . And their ghosts appear to their people, at the rehearsals for the famous Jubilee Festival Pageant, for one last farewell and—to what? I know. To bless our pageant.

(*He laughs. During the following,* NOA's *troupe materializes from behind pillars in the background, all in their old costumes. They, too, remain very still, heads bowed.*)

KEAKA: I buy the whole thing! But then I'm Hawaiian, and we're supposed to believe in Madame Pele and dead warriors marching to the sea and a *kahu* being called in to exorcise the spirits of the Hawaiian dead who jinx the stadium at Halawa. Stuff like that. I buy it all. . . . And the newspapers have a field day. The tourists eat it up. . . . What do the young people call 'em now? Auras? . . . The only thing is, Carl, the only question is: will Lydia and the others buy it?

(CARL *has sat down and is lost in his own troubled thoughts.*)

KEAKA: *(To* CHARLES.) Where *is* Lydia?

CHARLES: In her dressing room. Downstairs.

KEAKA: I suppose I should let her know I'm here. *(To* CARL:) Want me to tell her about the accident? They're all going to find out soon enough, anyway.

CARL: *(Softly.)* Do what you want, Keaka.

KEAKA: Okay. *(To* CHARLES:) Want to show me?

CHARLES: Sure. (*He moves to* CARL, *hands him the check.*) Here's your check, Carl.

(CARL *takes the check.* CHARLES *leads* KEAKA *off at right.* CARL *slowly tears up the check, then crumples the two halves.*)

KAMUELA: *Kumu* . . .
NOA: Yes, my son.
KAMUELA: I remember now.
POKIPALA: And I, *kumu*, I remember.
OTHERS: We remember . . .
KAMUELA: . . . the falling . . .
POKIPALA: . . . the steep falling into the murmuring dark.
FRANCES: Are you afraid?
KAMUELA: Only of the murmuring.
HIʻIAKA: Why do they murmur, *kumu?*
PIʻILANI: Who—?
OTHERS: Who murmurs in the murmuring dark?
NOA: Those are the dead who have gone on before us.
POKIPALA: What are they saying?
NOA: That they grieve for the living . . . and it is their grief that frightens you.
FRANCES: And there is no rest from that grief.
NOA: Ever.
KAMUELA: Why are we still here?
POKIPALA: Why can't we go?
FRANCES: We are not free to go yet, dear.
NOA: He keeps us here.
OTHERS: Why?
NOA: He remembers.

(CARL *stirs, stares straight ahead, deeply moved.*)

CARL: (*Remembering.*) The story of Laupiʻo and Kea—and of how their spirits went, even in Death, in human form to the *aliʻi*, Kahikiloa, to remind him once again of—Love. (*He bows his head.*)
FRANCES: Look, Noa, he is weeping.
HIʻIAKA: Is it for us he weeps, *kumu?*
NOA: He weeps for himself, Hiʻiaka.
CARL: (*Straight ahead.*) And even in Death, Kahikiloa denied them and sent them away from their land and from their people. . . . Aue! (*He covers his face.*)

KAMUELA: *Kumu*—I can feel it: his weeping.
POKIPALA: And I, *kumu*. He weeps in me . . .
OTHERS: In us.
FRANCES: Only be patient.
HIʻIAKA: How it hurts, Frances. . . . What a terrible hurt he suffers.
FRANCES: Be patient, dear.
KAMUELA: Will it end, *kumu,* when we go beyond the murmuring dark?
NOA: No, my dear. . . . That is our fate—to grieve their grief, without rest.
KAMUELA: I thought it would be different. An end of suffering and pain.
HIʻIAKA: But it hurts so much, *kumu*. Is it really forever?
NOA: Yes, my darling. For as long as there is life.
KAMUELA: *Kumu*—I think I am beginning to understand now.
NOA: Are you still afraid?
KAMUELA: No. I don't think so. Only—
NOA: Only?
KAMUELA: My heart is breaking, *kumu*.
NOA: Yes. Now you understand, my darling.
FRANCES: And so, receive. Accept. Grieve for the living—accept.
NOA: There is no other rest.
TROUPE: ʻAe.
FRANCES: There is no other Death.
TROUPE: ʻAe.

(CARL*'s hands come down from his face. He is a profoundly altered man.* LYDIA *comes in from the right with* CLEMENT, JOSEPH, KEOKI. *All have changed back into their royal costumes for the pageant. They are all grim, angry.*)

LYDIA: Carl! We want to talk to you.
CARL: *(Very softly.)* Yes.

(*They position themselves around* CARL, *who remains seated.*)

POKIPALA: Will they learn, *kumu?*
NOA: Learn what, beloved?
POKIPALA: That it is our hearts that break—for them?
KAMUELA: Don't they have pity?
TROUPE: For us?
NOA: They won't learn that until they learn pity for each other.

LYDIA: Carl, Keaka just came downstairs.

CARL: I know.

CLEMENT: He told us. About Noa. It's a pretty cheap trick you pulled.

KEOKI: Look, we do things like this pageant for the dignity of our people.

CLEMENT: We don't like these cheap Waikiki publicity stunts. It's—it's—

KEOKI: —undignified.

CLEMENT: Yeah. Undignified.

CARL: *(Quietly.)* Did Keaka tell you that? That it was all a publicity stunt?

JOSEPH: He didn't have to.

KEOKI: What else could it be?

CARL: *(Always quietly.)* It could have been our people—come back from Death—to speak to us—to tell us something.

CLEMENT: Bull! You expect us to swallow that?

KEOKI: Come off it, man.

JOSEPH: Cheap shot, Carl! Cheap shot!

LYDIA: You wrote the script for that man who was supposed to be Noa Napoʻo. You planned the whole thing. You attacked me, Joseph, Clement, Keoki, the others. You said dirty things against your own people.

KEOKI: What were you trying to prove?

CLEMENT: What made you think you could get away with it, anyway?

CARL: I don't know.

LYDIA: Well, I know. Everything that awful man said was you. You speaking. Your ideas. What you think about us. How you feel about your own people . . . including the vulgar stuff. You thought it all up. You made him say it.

JOSEPH: We're disappointed in you, Carl.

CLEMENT: Really disappointed.

LYDIA: We're disgusted with you.

KEOKI: You're one bad Hawaiian, Carl.

LYDIA: Look at me. I said, Look at me! (CARL *does.*) You don't belong to us. Do your hear me, Carl?

CARL: *(Softly.)* I hear you very well.

LYDIA: So we kick you out! (CARL *looks away.*) Don't look away. Look at me! (CARL *does.*) Your people kick you out, Carl. You are not a Hawaiian. I'm going to see to it that every decent Hawaiian is going to know about you—and avoid you. . . . And

you're fired from this pageant, Carl. You are a disgrace to
our *ali'i*.

CARL: Noa and Frances were right. You are arrogant. And ignorant. And you won't allow anything to shake you out of that
ignorance.

(LYDIA *glares at him, makes an ugly derisive, spitting sound, and turns
on her heel, going.*)

CARL: Sure! Walk away from it. Live in your make-believe world of
ali'i and crowns and thrones. Turn your backs on the awesome
truth about ourselves that has happened, here, right here, before
our eyes, this afternoon. . . . Well, I don't turn my back any
more, Lydia. My dead are all around me now. There is no hiding
from them. I know my loss now. Do you hear that? All of you!
Our dead are around us, reaching for us, speaking to us—and I,
for one, am going to listen. From now on, I'm going to listen
every moment of every day of my life.

(*There is a pause.* LYDIA *looks at him evenly. She moves to him, faces
him squarely. And spits in his face. She sweeps off in regal pride, followed
by* CLEMENT, JOSEPH, *and* KEOKI. CARL *sits in resigned sorrow.*)

KAMUELA: Does he really hear us now, *kumu?*
NOA: He hears.
FRANCES: He pities.
HI'IAKA: The hurt is getting worse, Frances. I want to go now, into
the darkness . . .
POKIPALA: Take us away, *kumu.*
NOA: Speak to him first, children. Comfort him.
KAMUELA: Carl . . .
HI'IAKA: Friend . . .
POKIPALA: Brother . . .
ALL: Beloved . . .
KAMUELA: We love you.

(*The lights are going down.* CARL *remains seated, staring straight ahead.*)

HI'IAKA: Aloha . . .

(NOA, FRANCES, *and their troupe begin to move away, going back into
the darkness.*)

FRANCES: We leave you with our aloha.

POKIPALA: Our aloha which is in the blessed earth of Hawai'i.

TROUPE: And in all that is of the earth.

KAMUELA: And in the air and the sky of Hawai'i.

TROUPE: And in all that is of air and sky.

POKIPALA: And the seas of Hawai'i . . .

TROUPE: And in all that is of the sea.

HI'IAKA: Aloha . . .

FRANCES: Ha'ina 'ia mai ana ka puana.[1]

TROUPE: Ha'ina.

NOA: Ha'ina 'ia mai ana ka puana.

TROUPE: Ha'ina.

(They are gone into darkness. CARL rises slowly, dejectedly. He moves to the spot where NOA had been standing. He touches the pillar. CHARLES comes in from the left.)

CHARLES: Carl—they want to start. *(He gestures off left.)*

CARL: I'm not part of the pageant any more, Charlie.

CHARLES: I know. Lydia told me. . . . She's talked Keaka into being the king.

CARL: Yeah. . . . Well, put on a good show, Charles. *(He starts for the right.)*

CHARLES: Carl . . .

(CARL stops, looks back. Until now we have not noticed something CHARLES has in his hand. He moves forward and puts it on the bench. It is the coffee cup.)

CARL: *(Resigned.)* Where was it?

CHARLES: In the tool cabinet, backstage, where I always keep it. . . . *(A pause.)* I know what I know, Carl. Nobody can take that away from me any more. . . . Jesus, for the first time in my life, I feel like— *(His voice catches.)* —I feel like a Hawaiian, Carl.

(A STAGEHAND comes in from the left to clean up the trash box mess.)

---

[1]FRANCES: The summary refrain is being told.

TROUPE: Being told.

NOA: The summary refrain is being told.

TROUPE: Being told.

CARL: Well—give them all my aloha, Charles.
CHARLES: *(Quietly, evenly.)* Fuck 'em.

(CARL goes off at stage right. CHARLES watches the STAGEHAND sweep up. Then he looks off.)

CHARLES: *(Calling up.)* Billy . . . Billy, you ready up there? *(The bounce and eagerness have gone out of him.)*
BILL: *(Off.)* Oh . . . okay.

(A moment, and the cyclorama lights come up.)

CHARLES: A little more. *(The lights come up a little more.)* That's it!

(The STAGEHAND finishes. He goes off taking the trash box with him.)

CHARLES: Oh—and Bill . . .
BILL: *(Off.)* Yeah?
CHARLES: Lydia wants us to do the whole thing, okay? The flowers and stuff. Everything. Even the goddamn rainbow.
BILL: *(Off.)* Right on!

(CHARLES moves to the left, picking up the cup. He calls off.)

CHARLES: *(Calling.)* Okay, Freddie. Places.

(The young man, FREDDIE, comes on with his conch shell. He takes his place as before on the back platform. CHARLES waits until he is positioned. Then:)

CHARLES: Curtain.

(CHARLES steps off. FREDDIE raises the conch shell to his lips, blows three times. He moves off. The lights come up. Music as before. The COURT, with KEAKA as the mōʻī, moves on. The pageant begins. This time, however, projections against the sky counterpoint the narration: rainbows, huge lurid flowers, waterfalls, sweeping beaches, and so forth.)

VOICE: *(PA system.)* A-l-o-o-o-o-ha! Welcome to the golden shores of Paradise! . . . Welcome to the golden days of Hawaiʻi-nei when the *aliʻi* reigned in their regal splendor over their loyal and carefree subjects. . . . Welcome to an Eden of perfumed flowers and dew-spangled days that reflect rainbows across azure skies. Welcome to the land of true aloha, Hawai'i, the land of Love and Music and the Hula.

(The pageant DANCERS *move on and down to the left, where they arrange themselves prettily.)*

VOICE: The hula that captures the sway of the coconut palm, the falling of rain, the surge of the ocean, the sweep of the azure sky . . . the hula that captures Love, the heart-and-soul of Hawai'i-nei. . . . Welcome, travelers! Welcome, strangers— strangers no longer in the warm embrace of Hawai'i's a-l-o-o-o-o-ha!

(The music sweeps to a climax. The court *sits. The* DANCERS *rise. Hawaiian music begins and the* DANCERS *go into their first hula. All smiles, they dance—and dance—and dance. The lights and music begin to fade slowly, as the* DANCERS *keep dancing more upstage. Their "going" is, to the perceptive eye, a duplication, more or less, of* NOA *and his troupe's "going." . . . And, as they dance, the music and lights fading always, the* COURT *begins to "disappear" one by one. When the stage is dim and close to dark, the music all but a whisper, the* DANCERS *virtually spectral dancers, the* AUTHOR *steps on at downstage left into a spot. There is silence. Then, far away, a chant begins.)*

AUTHOR: So it is over. . . . But listen . . . always listen. . . . And remember. For it is only in our remembering that we can make our *mele*, like houses of words into which our dead can move and live again and speak to us. . . . Oh, remember! *(A moment.)* Goodbye, then, my precious Georgina. . . . I have made this *mele kanikau*, a tattered tent against the indifferent rain, so that Love might once again cry out its loss through me. . . . *(To the audience:)* O listen to their voices! If you would only listen to them. . . . It is in you they grieve; it is through you they speak. . . . *(He extends his hands, cupped, as if at the end of a hula.)* HA'INA 'IA MAI ANA KA PUANA.[2] *(Eyes lowered, he pulls his hands back, folded, as if in prayer, softly:)* Rest, then, Georgina, rest.

(The lights fade out. When they come up again, the stage is empty.)

---

[2] AUTHOR: . . . The summary refrain is being told.

A Play

A PLAY

CAST

JAMES ACTOR/ JAMES ALAMA

THE HARD HAWAIIAN MAN ACTOR/ THE HARD
HAWAIIAN MAN

JULIA ACTRESS/ JULIA BRANDT

AH KIU/ AH KIU ACTOR

PELE ACTOR/ OLD WOMAN

SEVERINO/ SEVERINO ACTOR

SOFT HAWAIIAN MAN

YOUNG HAWAIIAN GIRL ACTRESS/ YOUNG HAWAIIAN GIRL

MĀHŪ

Place: A stage in Hawai'i

ACT ONE

(The play is set in the living room of the old Alama house, high above the slopes of Volcano, Hawai'i. It is a spacious old room, with old koa and wicker furniture, a large pūne'e *at right center stage backed by a table of matching length. The room suggests a private museum, for Hawaiian artifacts of rare value are everywhere tastefully displayed. There is a staircase at upstage left and a fireplace at the right. In the back wall is the front doorway; beyond it the spacious veranda. [Visitors enter from upstage left.] To the left of the front door, a large picture window through which vegetation is seen. At upstage right, an arched entrance to the off-stage dining room. At downstage left, another arched entrance, this one to a hallway. There are closets: one by the fireplace, one by the front door, and one at the left. Fine old kerosene and oil lamps used to provide light at night; they are now electrified.*

At curtain rise: the set is far from finished, although the basic furniture is in place. Most of the back wall, all of the staircase corner and stairs, some of the left wall, and almost none of the right wall are finished. The fireplace stands alone where the right wall should be. The old-fashioned telephone on an end table at left center stage has no cord whatsoever, not even for the earpiece. Backstage, a clutter of flats, ladders, potted plants, and the like. Off the set, at upstage right by a dim work light, there's an improvised dressing table with a crate for a seat, a makeup kit, PELE*'s wig and costume. The flat immediately to the right of the front door closet isn't in place, and we see that the right wall of the closet itself is practical: that is, it swings open, to right, so that one can enter or exit the closet behind the set.*

A few minutes before the play starts, JAMES ACTOR *is seen entering the closet from the right, visible through the gap made by the out-of-place flat. He opens the closet door and steps out from the closet, examines a hinge, steps back into the closet, moves out of it at the right of it, and is revealed in the gap. Another actor, the* HARD HAWAIIAN MAN ACTOR, *moves in from right center off and goes to the out-of-place flat. He and* JAMES ACTOR *move it into place,* JAMES ACTOR *remaining behind the set. Just before the flat is in place, we see* JAMES ACTOR *step into the closet and pull the closet right-hand wall into place. He reaches out for the closet door, shuts himself in the closet.*

The HARD HAWAIIAN MAN ACTOR *finishes with the flat; it is in place. He exits at right, goes out of sight.*

The closet door opens. JAMES ACTOR *has disappeared, and, in his place,* JULIA ACTRESS *steps out. She closes the closet door, comes down to an end table by the* pūneʻe, *takes a playscript from the table, and exits with it downstage left.*

Moments pass. Then the general stage lighting dims to suggest dusk. The lanterns and lamps come on.

A handsome, cultured Hawaiian man enters from behind the stairs and takes his place at the table that backs the pūneʻe: *immaculately groomed; casually—but obviously expensively—dressed. He pours sherry from a cut glass decanter into two glasses. His speech is slightly affected, "actorish," but there is something engagingly warm about him. His name is* JAMES ALAMA. *In a moment,* JULIA BRANDT *enters from the left. She obviously worships him. She comes in holding the play manuscript against her breast. She is obviously awed.)*

JAMES: Well—? How do you like my new play?

JULIA: It's—incredible!

JAMES: Yes, of course, but did you like it?

JULIA: It's a masterpiece.

JAMES: I didn't ask what it is, Julia. I asked if you liked it.

JULIA: Liked it! James, I can't find the words to tell you what a remarkable play you've written!

JAMES: Here. I find sherry wonderfully conducive of vocabulary, however redundant. *(He offers a glass of sherry.)*

JULIA: Thank you. *(She puts the manuscript down, is about to sip—but stops.)* No. A toast first. *(She raises her glass. He takes his.)* To my beloved James Alama, who, with his latest play, has become not only an artist and more than a genius—and so, the voice and soul of the Hawaiian people.

JAMES: Well, your aim is a bit shaky on syntax, my dear, but unerring in sentiment.

(They sip. She takes up the manuscript again, sits on the couch.)

JULIA: There is so much in it, James. Do you know what I like best? More than the skill?

JAMES: More than the skill?

JULIA: Yes.

JAMES: Good heavens! I yearn to know!

JULIA: The audacity of it! Who else would dare to write a play about our beloved Queen Liliʻuokalani—I mean, for once without sentimentality or condescension—and bring it off so triumphantly?

JAMES: Oh, who, indeed?

JULIA: That first entrance of hers—so regal, so dignified, yet so womanly. However did you do it?

JAMES: Oh, I just sat here, evening after evening, about this time, staring at the door, and I tried to imagine what it would look like if she actually walked in, out of the dusk—like a goddess of old . . . *(Indicates the main door to the porch.)* A goddess, yes . . . but a woman, as well, of infinite grace, infinite poise, moving majestically into this room from the garden outside.

JULIA: And with all that—she's so—so sexual, James! Imagine! A sexy Liliʻuokalani! But you've managed it so sweetly, so tactfully, with all of your usual good taste.

JAMES: In these pornographic times, one needs the reticence . . .

JULIA: Those lovely Hawaiian metaphors that suggest so much!

JAMES: *(Delighted.)* You noticed, you naughty girl!

JULIA: And the way the metaphors sing themselves into poetry so often!

JAMES: "Sing themselves into poetry!" How beautifully you put it, Julia!

JULIA: It's a line in the play. But it's true!

JAMES: Oh, I'm not refuting your point. It's very well taken.

JULIA: Thanks to your play, part of that great woman is given to me, as a part of myself. . . . And when the play is done, audiences — our people—will say: There it is. Our imperishable majesty. Returned to us at last. *(She kisses him lightly.)* Be proud of yourself, James. You deserve it. You mustn't be so endearingly modest.

JAMES: Oh—I feel more relief than pride, Julia. It is as if, with this one play, I've discharged all my debts. My debts to this house where I was born and raised. My debts to my father and mother, God keep them always, and to my ancestors. My debts to my people. All over and done with. All paid.

JULIA: And beautifully paid, James. In full.

JAMES: So! . . . Do you know what I'd like to do next?

JULIA: Marry me, of course. You promised.

JAMES: I mean—after that.

JULIA: No, dear—what would we like to do next?

JAMES: Go back to my beloved Italy. We would like to wash away all memory of past bondage in the clear blue waters of the Adriatic. Then, travel; blessed travel. We would like to rinse our eyes and ears clean with quiet contemplation of the cathedral of Chartres. We would like to walk over fields in the Cotswolds, under an exaltation of singing larks. We, in brief, are just going to wander, freely, throughout the civilized world. And then—guess what?

JULIA: What, my darling?

JAMES: And then, I shall write a book, a hymn of joy, called "A Song for Julia." It will be a thousand pages long, and it will be one sentence: I love you. Over and over and over, on every page . . . I love you, I love you, I love—

JULIA: Oh, James!

(And they kiss. AH KIU, a very old and wizened Chinese servant, comes in carrying wood for the fireplace. JAMES and JULIA rise from the pune‘e. AH KIU pays no attention to them, places the wood by the fireplace, begins to lay logs for a fire.)

JULIA: What are you going to do with all this after you sell the house? *(She means the Hawaiian artifacts.)*

JAMES: Oh, I don't know. Give it all to the Bishop Museum, I suppose. Although what they'd want with termite-ridden idols and moth-eaten *kāhili* is beyond me.

JULIA: Oh, dear—!

JAMES: What?

JULIA: I forgot. I've something to confess.

JAMES: Oh?

JULIA: Well, in the study, while I was reading the play—

JAMES: Yes?

JULIA: That calabash by the sofa . . . I knocked it to the floor, accidentally.

JAMES: The great big one, on the end table?

JULIA: Yes. It broke—dozens of little pieces. . . . I hope it wasn't particularly valuable.

JAMES: It's from the third Kamehameha's time. A little before, as a matter of fact. It's terribly old.

JULIA: That old?

JAMES: Yes. Dried out. Brittle.

JULIA: No wonder it broke so easily.

JAMES: Yes. Care for more sherry?

JULIA: No. As a matter of fact, I'd better be going.

JAMES: Must you?

JULIA: It's getting dark.

JAMES: Can't you stay the weekend?

JULIA: James, I've already been here for days. I've got other things to do.

JAMES: With the play finished, I have nothing to do.

JULIA: You've earned a rest. From me, too. *(She puts her arms around him.)*

JAMES: I wish you would stay.

JULIA: Can't. *(She pecks a kiss.)* I'll get my things.

JAMES: Want me to come upstairs, too?

JULIA: Ab-so-lute-ly no.

(Another peck, and she goes to the stairs and up. JAMES watches her go, then he pours himself another sherry. He sips, watching AH KIU light the fire.)

JAMES: Do you need some help, old friend?

(AH KIU's face—a mask of disgust and betrayed hurt—tightens; he over-concentrates on his work.)

JAMES: I asked you a question, Ah Kiu. *(AH KIU's mask goes tighter, the work becomes more stubborn.)* Oh, well, if you're going to pull your pigheaded act. *(He sits, sips his wine, stealing an occasional glance at the old man.)* I finished the play. . . . At three o'clock this afternoon. . . . Julia thinks it's wonderful. *(AH KIU goes on working.)* It's about Queen Lili'uokalani. How she comes back to life today, and enters the lives of ordinary Hawaiians, reviving them spiritually by reminding them of their past greatness. . . . Julia insists it's a masterpiece. *(No response.)* She has wonderful critical judgment! *(Nothing.)* All right, is it because I'm selling the house? *(Nothing.)* Look, every beam and post and board is hollow, like paper! One of these days it's going to come crashing down around your pointy *Pākē* ears. . . . *(Nothing.)* Well, it isn't as if you're not going to have a place to stay. Julia insists that you come and stay with us—in Honolulu. . . . We'll travel a lot. . . . You're getting too old to live alone. . . . *(Mumbling.)* Too old and too pigheaded, if you ask me.

(Still no response. AH KIU lights the fire. Sighing, JAMES gets up, sets his glass aside, moves to the old man, by the fireplace.)

JAMES: You don't really like her, do you? You're jealous of her. . . . You still think of me as the little boy you took care of all through the years . . . here, in the same house you came to when you were a boy . . . and you're jealous because she's taking me away! Is that it? *(No response. JAMES picks up a piece of wood.)* Here, let me help you. . . . That's it, though, isn't it? . . . Well, she really wants you to come and stay with us. And it was entirely her idea. Really. *(No response. The fire has caught well.)* I had thought—during the past few days, you would get to be friends, and you would see how kind she— *(Something about the piece of wood in his hands makes him stop.)* Good heavens, Ah Kiu: Look! *(He offers the piece of wood. AH KIU doesn't look.)* It's a face. A woman's face. See?

(Not looking, AH KIU takes the piece of wood.)

AH KIU: Bullshit! *(He puts the wood in the fire.)*
JAMES: Okay. Be stubborn! *(He goes back for his wineglass, moves to the decanter.)* But when you're in Honolulu and you get to know Julia better— *(He is pouring another glass of wine.)* —you'll wonder why you spent all these years cooped up in this—

(He stops, for a very strange thing is happening: the soft sound of a woman sobbing in heartbreak is heard. It seems, for a few moments, to come from the fireplace. Then, spreading, from upstairs.)

JAMES: What the hell?

(JAMES moves toward the stairs, looking upstairs, around, in rising consternation. For now the sobbing has grown in volume and seems to be coming from everywhere. Meanwhile: from behind the flats, backstage, the PELE ACTOR moves slowly out to sit at the dressing table upstage right. He begins to put on his makeup as PELE. During the ensuing minutes, he will transform himself into a shriveled old crone, dressed in a raggedy, patched mu'umu'u, shawl, old army boots, and old leaf hat.
The sound of sobbing has become quite loud. JAMES is about to dash up the stairs, even as AH KIU reaches into the fire and snatches out the piece of wood he has just put in. Instantly the sobbing ceases, stopping JAMES on the lowest steps. AH KIU moves to the table with the piece of wood.)

AH KIU: *(Babbling.)* 'O kēia ka mea— kēia lā'au—ua 'ike au iāia ua 'ike au i kō ka lā'au uē 'ana—ua 'ike au i kō ka maka uē 'ana![1]

JAMES: *(Hurrying to him.)* What are you babbling about?

AH KIU: *(Putting the piece of wood down on the table.)* Me see! . . . Ua uē ka maka. Ua uē ka lā'au. He mea weliweli ia![2]

JAMES: Speak English!

AH KIU: Me see! *(He points to the piece of wood.)* Lady cry! Wahine face she go . . . *(He imitates the sobbing.)*

JAMES: That's ridiculous. *(He reaches for the piece of wood to examine it. It burns his hand.)* Ouch! *(He shakes his hand in pain.)* Damn thing's like a hot griddle.

AH KIU: Mai ho'opa iāia! He lapu kēia! He 'uhane kēia![3]

JAMES: How come your hands didn't burn when you picked it up? *(AH KIU only shakes his head, mystified, scared.)* Put your hand on it.

AH KIU: No.

JAMES: I said, put your hand on it.

AH KIU: He 'elemakule au. 'A'ole au hō'eha i kekahi kanaka i ko'u wā e ola ana. No ke aha kou hō'eha ia'u?[4]

JAMES: Do as I say.

(He grabs AH KIU*'s hand, slams it down on the piece of wood.* AH KIU*, anticipating the heat, screeches. But* JAMES *keeps his hand on the piece of wood, and a look of surprise and relief spreads over* AH KIU*'s face as he realizes he isn't burnt.)*

AH KIU: No burn! No fire!

JAMES: All right.

Kneubuhl's original typescript included the stage direction "(in Hawaiian)" with the English lines. The Hawaiian has been added for this publication.

[1]AH KIU: It was this—this piece of wood—I saw it—I saw it crying—I saw the face crying.

[2]AH KIU: . . . The face was crying. The piece of wood was crying. It's terrible!

[3]AH KIU: Don't touch it! It's a ghost! It's a spirit!

[4]AH KIU: I'm an old man. I never hurt anybody in my life. Why are you trying to hurt me?

(AH KIU *withdraws his hand.* JAMES *screws up his courage, then very gingerly touches the piece of wood. Instantly he withdraws his hand in pain. For a moment they look at each other mystified. Finally:*)

JAMES: Put it back in the fire. (AH KIU hesitates.) Go on, go on— put it back in the fire. (AH KIU *takes the piece of wood to the fire. Again he hesitates.*) Put it in!

(AH KIU *sets the piece of wood in the fire. He steps back beside* JAMES. *Then, softly, the sobbing is heard again. It grows louder rapidly.* JAMES *kneels down to watch the wood closely. He gets up, more stunned than ever. He gestures to the fire.*)

JAMES: Take it out!

(AH KIU *quickly does. The sobbing stops. He sets the piece of wood on the mantle.* JAMES *sits, his senses defeated.*)

JAMES: Where did you get that piece of wood, Ah Kiu? *(No answer.)* The wood—you find what place? Where?
AH KIU: Me no fine. Severino, he fine wood.
JAMES: Go get him, bring him here. Hurry! Wikiwiki! Chop chop!

(AH KIU *starts to go, but stops as* JULIA *comes down the stairs with her bag. He stares at her briefly.* JULIA *notices his intensity, which puzzles her a bit.* AH KIU *goes out.* JAMES *goes to* JULIA, *who puts her bag down and moves to him.*)

JULIA: What's wrong with Ah Kiu? He gave me such a funny look. . . . Is something the matter?
JAMES: Matter? No—no, should anything be the matter?
JULIA: No. *(She slips into his arms, close.)* I wish I didn't have to go. *(But concerned, she steps back, touching his arms and chest.)* James, you're shaking like a leaf! What is it?
JAMES: Just—oh—you know . . .
JULIA: *(Smiling, moving closer, wrapping her arms around his neck.)* Why, you darling insatiable monkey, you . . . *(She pecks a kiss.)*
JAMES: Mind?
JULIA: I like it. I like it very much.

(*She kisses him hard and long. In his dressing area, the* PELE ACTOR *turns the light off. He can be seen going straight back where he is lost among the flats, shrubbery, and so forth.* AH KIU *and* SEVERINO, *a young Filipino, come in from the porch.*)

JULIA: Promise you'll never be satiable.

(She kisses him hard and long again. AH KIU *and* SEVERINO *stop at the sight of the kiss.* SEVERINO, *instantly overwhelmed by embarrassment, crosses himself quickly, covers his groin with his plantation hat, and starts to go out. But* AH KIU *catches his arm, swings him around back into the room, as the kiss ends.*)

JULIA: *(Studying* JAMES *and puzzled.)* Something is wrong. You look funny.
JAMES: Just—sad to see you go.
JULIA: Pet! *(She pecks another kiss, then reaches for her bag. He reaches too.)* No, no, I can manage. *(She sees* SEVERINO *and* AH KIU.) Besides, I think you're needed.

(JAMES *turns and sees* SEVERINO *and* AH KIU.)

JAMES: Come in, Severino. *(He gestures to an area by the fireplace.)* There. I'll only take a moment. *(He turns, takes* JULIA*'s bag from her, takes her arm. As they go to the door:)*
JULIA: Goodbye, Ah Kiu. (AH KIU *only scowls at her.)* Keep smiling.

(She and JAMES *go out onto the porch. Then we see them through the large window. They stop and kiss, and* SEVERINO *moves closer to watch.)*

SEVERINO: *(In his own Filipino language.)* Do they always do that without shame?
AH KIU: *(In his Chinese.)* Idiot! You know I can't understand your silly language.

(Outside, JULIA *and* JAMES *break.* JULIA *takes her bag and goes.* SEVERINO *hurries back to the fireplace area, and* JAMES *comes in.)*

JAMES: All right, Severino. There is something I want to know.
SEVERINO: Yes, sir.
JAMES: You gathered the firewood this afternoon. *(He points to the wood.)* That.
SEVERINO: Yes, sir.
JAMES: Where did you get it?

SEVERINO: *(Very heavy Filipino accent.)* I collected the wood from the porest.

JAMES: What part of the forest?

SEVERINO: Where the figs are.

JAMES: Figs? What figs?

SEVERINO: Pigs? No sir, not pigs. I know there are no pig trees in this vicinity. . . . Figs. You know, the pore-pooted animal: oink - oink - oink!

JAMES: I see.

SEVERINO: Tha-tha-tha-that's all, pokes. Forky Fig.

JAMES: Yes, yes, I understand. *(He moves closer to the fireplace.)* While you were chopping the wood, handling it, touching it, did you notice anything unusual?

SEVERINO: Oh, yes, sir.

JAMES: What?

SEVERINO: *(Shy.)* Oh, sir—

JAMES: What?

SEVERINO: One of the figs—a very big fig—was— *(He giggles, covers his mouth, turns away in embarrassment.)*

JAMES: What?

SEVERINO: —was trying to have the lob-appair with— *(He is too embarrassed to go on.)*

JAMES: With—?

SEVERINO: —a fiece of wood.

JAMES: *(Pointing to the piece of wood on the mantle.)* This piece of wood? Take a careful look. Don't touch it.

(SEVERINO *moves to the piece of wood, looks.*)

JAMES: You'll notice—the grain suggests a woman's face.

SEVERINO: I know.

JAMES: Then you've seen it before. You collected it.

SEVERINO: Yes, sir. The fig was very prustrated.

JAMES: When you touched it, was it hot?

SEVERINO: Oh, yes, sir, the fig was extremely h—

JAMES: I didn't mean the pig—

SEVERINO: I would like to remind you, sir, there are no pig trees there.

JAMES: All right, fig! I didn't mean pig! *(He collects himself.)* Was the fiece of wood hot?

SEVERINO: *(Scratching his head, looking at* JAMES *puzzled.)* Sir—?

JAMES: *(Sighing.)* Oh, Lord! Look, Severino, I want you to do something. . . . I want you to pick that piece of wood up.

(SEVERINO *looks at the piece of wood, looks back at* JAMES, *in growing bewilderment.*)

JAMES: Go ahead. Do as I say.

(Quite perplexed by the request, SEVERINO *moves to obey. His hand goes slowly to the piece of wood. But just before the hand touches it there is a piercing, terrified call from outside—*JULIA'*s voice.)*

JULIA: *(Offstage.)* James! James!

(She appears at the porch window, dashing for the front door. JAMES, AH KIU, SEVERINO *all rush to the door.* JULIA *runs in, terrified and shaken.* JAMES *grabs her.)*

JAMES: Julia! What is it?
JULIA: *(Near tears.)* An old woman. I hit her.
JAMES: Where?
JULIA: Right in the '*ōkole!*
JAMES: Damn it, Julia, where?
JULIA: Down by the gate. She was walking along the side of the road.
JAMES: Is she hurt?
JULIA: I don't know. She's just lying there in the gutter! Ass over teakettle!
JAMES: Christ! Severino, Ah Kiu!

(AH KIU *and* SEVERINO *dash out, then* JULIA *hurries after them.* JAMES *goes to the door and watches them go. Then he notices that slowly, very slowly, the lanterns are beginning to dim. He moves quickly to the nearest one. But then, suddenly, the fire in the fireplace flares up, dies down, flares up higher, dies down to normal again.*

Meanwhile: offstage at right, a big SOFT HAWAIIAN MAN *enters into the spill and stops some distance from the set itself, near the* PELE ACTOR'*s dressing table. He wears only a* malo, *but he is wreathed and wrapped in vine and fern: a crown, wristlets, anklets; long trailing strands from his neck, upper arms. He preens, minces, as the slow rise and fall of the fire intensifies.)*

SOFT MAN: *(Imitating the ring of the telephone.)* Bring-bring! Bring-bring-brrringgg! *(Ad lib.)*

(JAMES goes to the phone and picks it up.)

JAMES: *(Into the phone.)* Hello. . . . Yes, this is—
SOFT MAN: Bring bring bringgg! Bringgg brrringgg—!
JAMES ACTOR: *(To him impatiently.)* All right, all right! I've picked it up!

(The SOFT HAWAIIAN MAN disappears at right.)

JAMES: *(Into the phone.)* Yes, this is James Alama. . . . Oh, hello, Mrs. Brandt . . . Julia just left. I mean, she's having a little trouble with her car. . . . No, nothing serious. . . . We'll have it all fixed and see she gets home safe and sound . . .

(Simultaneously, JULIA ACTRESS and the actors' general lighting come in, she from the porch.)

JULIA ACTRESS: Hey. . . . Can we take a break here?
JAMES ACTOR: *(To himself.)* Christ, not again!
JULIA ACTRESS: Well, I'm not alone in this, you know. The others have got their gripes too . . .

(JAMES ACTOR moves to the pūne'e, taking the phone receiver with him. He idly twirls it up, catches it over and over.)

JAMES ACTOR: Okay, okay, but why pick on me? I didn't write this damned play.
JULIA ACTRESS: Look—we're all in this together.

(From all around, the cast—except for the PELE ACTOR and the SOFT HAWAIIAN MAN—appear: AH KIU, SEVERINO, the HARD HAWAIIAN MAN, and the YOUNG HAWAIIAN GIRL.)

JULIA ACTRESS: And we're going to have to do something about it. Including you.
JAMES ACTOR: Great! So what're we going to do, including me?
JULIA ACTRESS: Walk out in protest. We've all talked it over. We've all agreed.

(General agreement from the others.)

JAMES ACTOR: But what about—? *(He gestures to the* PELE ACTOR*'s dressing area.)*

HARD MAN: Madam Queen? Who cares what he thinks?

AH KIU ACTOR: She.

YOUNG GIRL ACTRESS: It.

JAMES ACTOR: *(To* JULIA ACTRESS.) I thought you said we were all in the same boat.

JULIA ACTRESS: Okay, he wants to stick it out.

AH KIU ACTOR: Damn fool likes the play.

YOUNG GIRL ACTRESS: Why not? How often does a *māhū* female impersonator get to play a big fat part like this?

JULIA ACTRESS: But that's it! That's the thing: Why did they cast a female impersonator? Why not an old Hawaiian woman?

AH KIU ACTOR: Yeah. Shit, with some sense of dignity.

JAMES ACTOR: But funny.

YOUNG GIRL ACTRESS: Screw "funny"! Pele is sacred to us. . . . She's not supposed to be a clown—

JULIA ACTRESS: We're being made to look ridiculous by some racist, pretentious son of a— *(As if the question had never occurred to her before:)* Who wrote this goddamn play, anyway?

(She looks at everyone, searching, challenging. And an odd thing happens: everyone looks down, avoids her looks, as if, in not knowing the answer to the question, they shared some common guilt or shame. She holds her look at JAMES.)*

JAMES ACTOR: So—why pick on me?

JULIA ACTRESS: 'Cause I think you know something—something you're keeping to yourself.

JAMES ACTOR: Like?

JULIA ACTRESS: I don't know. But you're not leveling with us. I've felt it all along. . . . There's something about this play you know and you're keeping it from us . . .

JAMES ACTOR: Look: is it the play, the casting, what?

JULIA ACTRESS: Both!

(Ad libbed agreement from the others, except for SEVERINO ACTOR, *who has become very withdrawn.)*

JULIA ACTRESS: We want a rewrite and a Hawaiian woman to play Madam Pele, or we quit, walk out.

HARD ACTOR: We're fed up.

JULIA ACTRESS: Tell your friend the playwright. A new Pele by tomorrow, rewrites by tomorrow night, or *pau*.

JAMES ACTOR: *(Almost yelling.)* Damn it, I don't know the playwright, I don't even know who he is. And I had nothing to do with the casting.

AH KIU ACTOR: Bull! . . . You tell him: no more cheap shots at us Hawaiians! *(To the others, quickly:)* And no cracks from anyone, okay? I was born right here in Hawai'i, like all of you: and I'm just as Hawaiian as any of you . . . *(To SEVERINO ACTOR:)* Right?

SEVERINO ACTOR: *(Softly.)* I guess.

HARD ACTOR: Hey, calm down, man, take it easy.

JULIA ACTRESS: *(Together.)* Of course you are, of course!

YOUNG GIRL ACTRESS: Right on, brother! All right!

(A pause.)

AH KIU ACTOR: *(Nailing it down.)* Okay!

JULIA ACTRESS: All right. Come on. *(She goes to the front door. Although the door itself has not been installed, she grabs the nonexistent knob, turns back to JAMES ACTOR.)* Tell him! *(To AH KIU ACTOR:)* Come!

(She goes out. The HARD HAWAIIAN MAN ACTOR goes downstage right to the closet there, steps inside, closes the door after himself. The YOUNG HAWAIIAN GIRL ACTRESS goes up the stairs and off. AH KIU ACTOR goes to the front door, is stopped by:)

SEVERINO ACTOR: Just a minute! *(AH KIU ACTOR turns at the door.)* You said you were born where?

AH KIU ACTOR: Right here in Hawai'i-nei.

SEVERINO ACTOR: I know. But where?

(Puzzled, AH KIU ACTOR scratches his head as he tries to remember.)

AH KIU ACTOR: *(Gives up; emphatically.)* What's it to you? Right here in Hawai'i! *(Pronouncing it with a "W.")* *(He is about to go, turns back, correcting himself.)* Havai'i. *(He goes out, closing the door after himself. He moves along the porch to the left and off.)*

(The lights are going down to where they were before the ACTORS' *interruption. The fireplace begins to glow hot and hotter.* SEVERINO ACTOR *sits very still.* JAMES ACTOR *has been watching him intently.)*

JAMES ACTOR: *(Gently.)* What are you thinking?

*(*SEVERINO ACTOR *looks at him in troubled questioning. He avoids* JAMES ACTOR*'s look.)*

SEVERINO ACTOR: He didn't know where he was born.

JAMES ACTOR: That happens, especially with old people. They forget.

SEVERINO ACTOR: He isn't old. That part he plays is old. Ah Kiu is old. But not him. *(He is pointing to where the* AH KIU ACTOR *sat.)* He didn't forget. He doesn't know.

JAMES ACTOR: So he was born in some valley, some old plantation village. His birth was never registered. He doesn't know.

SEVERINO ACTOR: His folks woulda told him—even when he was a small kid . . . folks like to know where they were born, where they came from . . .

JAMES ACTOR: *(Giving up, lamely.)* So maybe he was an orphan.

*(*SEVERINO ACTOR *is now looking intently at* JAMES ACTOR, *who doesn't quite meet the look.)*

SEVERINO ACTOR: *(More perplexed than accusing.)* You're making excuses for him. . . . Why?

*(*JAMES ACTOR *now returns the look directly, but he doesn't answer.)*

SEVERINO ACTOR: You do know something. She's right: you're hiding something from us.

(The look continues. JULIA ACTRESS *has come onto the porch from upstage left.)*

JULIA ACTRESS: *(Impatiently.)* Are we going on, or do you want us to call the whole thing off right now?

JAMES ACTOR: *(Still intent on* SEVERINO ACTOR.) Yeah. . . . We're starting. Right now.

JULIA ACTRESS: About time.

(She moves back off at upstage left. JAMES ACTOR *moves closer to* SEVERINO ACTOR.)

JAMES ACTOR: Look. Would you mind? *(He turns, looks upstage right, downstage right, as if searching for someone. He gestures right as he speaks to* SEVERINO ACTOR.) That other guy, the chubby one with the maile and ferns all over him—he seems to have disappeared.... I'm supposed to be talking to Mrs. Brandt, Julia's mother, and as long as the phone hasn't been rigged to ring yet, well, Chubby was helping out—you know—making like a phone.... Would you mind?

SEVERINO ACTOR: *(Sighing.)* No—of course not.... *(He rises.)* Right now?

JAMES ACTOR: They're waiting.

SEVERINO ACTOR: Yeah.... Well.... *(Imitates ringing phone.)* Bring ... bring ... bring ... bring ... Bring-a-ring-a-ring ... Bring bringgg ... *(And so on.)*

(He backs off behind the staircase, and JAMES *picks up the phone. The fire's pulsating rise and fall is at its peak.)*

JAMES: *(Into phone.)* Hello.... Yes, this is James Alama.... Oh, hello, Mrs. Brandt.... Julia just left. I mean, she's having a little trouble with her car.... No no no, nothing serious.... We'll have it all fixed and see she gets home safe and soond.

("Soond?" Well, he's rattled by the sight of AH KIU *and* SEVERINO *bringing the* OLD WOMAN *between them: a crone. The mu'umu'u she wears can be seen now to be incredibly tattered and patched; her long white hair is in leaf-and-twig disarray. She moans. She lifts her army-booted feet six or so inches off the ground as she walks.* JULIA *follows.)*

JAMES: Here! Here! Bring her here!

(They ease the OLD WOMAN *down onto the* pune'e. JULIA *is already headed for the liquor.)*

JAMES: Should we call a doctor?

JULIA: I don't think she's really hurt. Just badly shaken up. A little brandy should help.

(The OLD WOMAN, *frail and weak, watches* JULIA. JAMES *moves close to her.)*

JAMES: Are you all right?

(*The* OLD WOMAN *sinks back weakly, moaning.*)

JAMES: Hurry with that brandy, Julia.
JULIA: Yes, coming . . . (*She hurries back with the brandy and snifter, pouring even as she comes. She fills the glass almost to overflowing, hands it to* JAMES.) Here.

(JAMES *offers the snifter to the* OLD WOMAN, *holding it in both hands for her.*)

JAMES: Now, sip a little of this. It'll do you good.

(*He places the snifter against her lips, tilts it gently so that she may sip. The* OLD WOMAN *does, but then her hand comes to the base of the snifter and tilts it up more. She gulps.*)

JAMES: Hey! Easy!

(*The hand tilts the snifter up even more. She drains it.* JAMES *hands the snifter to* SEVERINO, *who returns it.*)

JULIA: Is she going to be all right?
JAMES: When that brandy takes hold, she's going to be more than all right. (*To the* OLD WOMAN:) What's your name?
OLD WOMAN: Ka'ula o ke'ahi.
JAMES: Well, we're feeling better, aren't we?
OLD WOMAN: 'Ae.
JAMES: My name is James Alama. James Dixon-Wentworth Alama . . . and this is my fiancée, Julia Brandt.
JULIA: How do you do?
JAMES: And Julia and I are dreadfully sorry about what happened.
JULIA: I just didn't see you. You were there so suddenly! A little wisp of fog, and, like out of nowhere, there you were.
OLD WOMAN: 'Ae.
JULIA: It was too late for brakes.
OLD WOMAN: 'Ae.
JAMES: But what are you doing so far up the mountain? There isn't another house for miles. And it's almost dark.
JULIA: She's lost, she saw the house lights, she headed this way off the road, and—

(The OLD WOMAN, *with a groan, sags back into the chair.)*

JULIA: James!
JAMES: *(To the* OLD WOMAN.) What is it? Do you feel in pain?
OLD WOMAN: *(Faintly.)* Inu . . . Inu . . .
JAMES: What?
OLD WOMAN: Inu.
JAMES: *(To* JULIA.) What does that mean?
JULIA: How should I know?

(Moments before, AH KIU *has started to pour brandy into the snifter.)*

AH KIU: Drink. Inu. *(He moves to the* OLD WOMAN *with the drink. To the* OLD WOMAN:) Eia kekahi mea inu nāu.[5]
OLD WOMAN: *(Brightening immediately.)* 'Aue! 'Ōlelo Hawai'i 'oe!
AH KIU: 'Ōlelo Hawai'i au ma ko'u wā li'ili'i a hiki i kēia manawa.

(He offers the drink. She takes it, drinks in long gulps. Meanwhile:)

JULIA: I didn't know Ah Kiu spoke Hawaiian.
JAMES: Ah Kiu came here over sixty years ago, as a boy. Lots of Hawaiians worked for us then. My grandfather taught him. *(To the* OLD WOMAN:) Slower, slower! *(But the* OLD WOMAN *goes right on drinking.)*
AH KIU: She goin' be okay, Kimo, okay. You no worry.
SEVERINO: She's going to be flastered.

(The OLD WOMAN *has finished the drink. She hands the glass back.* AH KIU *takes it. There is an almost beatific grin on her face.)*

OLD WOMAN: Maha— *(She suppresses a hiccup.)* —lo! *(Then, sing-song:)* Mahaaaaaaaaalo![6] *(And she leans back and grins especially for* AH KIU:) 'Olu'olu nō 'oe.
AH KIU: 'A 'ole pilikia.

---

[5]AH KIU: . . . Here's another drink for you.
OLD WOMAN: You speak Hawaiian!
AH KIU: I have spoken Hawaiian since I was a boy. . . .

[6]OLD WOMAN: . . . Thank you. . . . *(And she leans back and grins especially for* AH KIU:) You are very kind.
AH KIU: You're welcome.

OLD WOMAN: (*To* JAMES.) I have so much aloha for you, my dear!

JAMES: Thank God! I was beginning to think you didn't speak English. . . . Look, you must tell us. What are you doing this far up here?

OLD WOMAN: (*To* JULIA.) An' you too, my dear! I have so much aloha for you, too. . . . Such nice smile . . .

JAMES: Yes, but would you please tell why it is you're—

OLD WOMAN: (*To* JULIA.) . . . But no enough nā ū! (*To* AH KIU:) 'Alu'alu loa! Hiki i kekahi kanaka ke pahemo no ka mea, 'a'ohe ka mea no ka ho'opa'a 'ana.[7]

AH KIU: (*Laughs.*) Hiki iā ia ke kā'ili me kona mau niho!

(*She goes off into gales of laughter to* JAMES' *and* JULIA'*s increasing perplexity.* AH KIU *is howling, too, so that he doesn't even know* SEVERINO *has taken the snifter from him.* SEVERINO *drinks.*)

JULIA: James, she's drunk!

JAMES: You don't say!

JULIA: She mustn't!

JAMES: Tell her!

(*He moves away in exasperation. Meanwhile,* AH KIU *has noticed that* SEVERINO *has his glass. So what! Still chuckling, he drinks from the bottle.*)

JULIA: (*To the* OLD WOMAN.) Don't you think you'd better lie down? You've been hit by a Volkswagen!

OLD WOMAN: (*Delighted.*) In the '*ōkole. (Confidentially.*) Tha's awright, my dear, 'cos you know why? My '*ōkole* hard, tha's why. Jes' like lava rock.

(*She,* AH KIU, *and* SEVERINO *find this very funny. As they laugh, the* OLD WOMAN *takes the glass from* SEVERINO, *drinks.* SEVERINO *takes the bottle from* AH KIU, *drinks, gives it back.* AH KIU *drinks, pours for the* OLD WOMAN, *who has emptied her glass. Meanwhile,* JULIA *has gone to* JAMES.)

---

[7]OLD WOMAN: . . . breasts. (*To* AH KIU:) So flat! A man could slide off with nothing to hold onto!

AH KIU: (*Laughs.*) He could hang on with his teeth!

JULIA: James, you must do something. She's getting out of hand.

JAMES: Give me the keys to the car.

JULIA: What're you going to do?

JAMES: Drive her down to Hilo.

JULIA: The keys are in the car.

JAMES: Okay. (*He marches back, resolutely, to the* OLD WOMAN.) Now, look, I want you to listen to me. (*But she is flirting with* SEVERINO.)

OLD WOMAN: (*To* SEVERINO.) You nice!

JAMES: I said, listen to me.

OLD WOMAN: (*To* SEVERINO.) I got so much aloha for you, my dear.

JAMES: (*Exploding.*) Listen to me!

(*It is the first time anyone here has heard* JAMES *so aggressive, so loud. Instant, awed silence.*)

JULIA: (*Awed.*) James!

JAMES: (*Taken aback by his own violence, but going on.*) Yes, well. . . . Now, I—I want you to—consider—something. You've been in an accident. You've been hurt. Now I think we should get you to a doctor. Down in Hilo. Just to be sure. So I suggest to you—that you—I—drive down the hill—and then—

(*The* OLD WOMAN *is still looking at him with the same "awe" brought on by his shouting. She is quite lost.*)

OLD WOMAN: (*Frail again.*) An' den—?

JAMES: Why . . . then, I'll take you home, if the doctor says it's all right.

OLD WOMAN: Home—?

JAMES: Yes . . . I imagine your—husband?—children?—are worried about where you are. It's getting dark. . . . Your little grandchildren, hmm?

OLD WOMAN: 'Ae. An' great-gran'chirren . . .

JAMES: (*Supportively.*) Well, now, you don't say! So we'll get you back safely to them and show them that great-grandmama is all safe and sound—

JULIA: —and swacked!

JAMES: (*Going right on.*) —won't we? So what do you say we get up and get going?

OLD WOMAN: (*Very subdued.*) An' great-great-gran'chirren . . .

JAMES: *(Surprised.)* Yes! . . . Well, even so . . .

OLD WOMAN: *(Softly, wistfully.)* An' great-great-great-gran'-chirren . . .

JAMES: *(!)*

JULIA: Now, really.

(And suddenly the OLD WOMAN is weeping into her hands.)

OLD WOMAN: Ua hāʻule lākou. . . . Kaʻu mau moʻopuna a me nā moʻopuna a kaʻu mau moʻopuna a me kā lākou mau moʻopuna. . . . ʻAʻohe home . . .[8] An' my great-great-great-great-great-gran'chirren too. . . . Ua hāʻule ka poʻe a pau.

JULIA: *(Touched by the weeping.)* James, the poor dear!

JAMES: *(Trying to comfort.)* Now, now, now, now, now. You mustn't upset yourself so. Everything will be all right!

OLD WOMAN: Ua hoʻopio ʻia nā ahi.[9] Ua hala nā loina kahiko . . . ʻAuana wale i kēia manawa . . . ʻImi i ka home . . . A mālama ʻole ka poʻe a pau i kēia manawa. . . . *(She goes on weeping.)*

JAMES: *(Lost.)* Ah Kiu?

AH KIU: *(Already on the verge of tears.)* Lady say, all her chirren an' gran'chirren and great-gran'chirren and great-great-gran'chirren all dead . . .

JULIA: Oh, no!

AH KIU: Yes, an' her great-great-great-gran'chirren all dead too. An' she got no more home. . . . An' she walk walk walk every place, lookin' for a home. . . . An' nobody care . . .

JULIA: James, I think I'm going to cry, too.

AH KIU: An' her great-great-great-great-gran'chirren all dead too! *(And he bursts into tears.)*

JULIA: Oh! *(And she is crying.)*

JAMES: Jesus.

(JULIA, all compassion, sits beside the OLD WOMAN, puts an arm around her.)

---

[8] OLD WOMAN: All dead. . . . All my *moʻopuna* and the *moʻopuna* of my *moʻopuna* and their *moʻopuna*. No home. [An' my great-great-great-great-great-gran' chirren too. . . .] All dead, everybody . . .

[9] OLD WOMAN: All the fires dead now, all the old ways gone. . . . Wandering now . . . Only wandering . . . Looking for a home . . . And nobody cares any more. . . .

JULIA: There, there. . . . You mustn't, you simply mustn't . . . *(And bawls all the harder.)*

OLD WOMAN: Oh, my dear, I got so much aloha for you.

JULIA: And I have so much aloha for you, too, my dear! *(They are in each other's arms.)*

AH KIU: *(Overwhelmed.)* Severino!

(SEVERINO enfolds the weeping AH KIU in his arms. And he has developed a bad case of the sniffles.)

JULIA: Oh, James! It's so pitiful!

JAMES: She's drunk!

JULIA: She's lost and lonely and hurt—

JAMES: —and loaded! Swacked, you said.

JULIA: I've never seen you like this. You're being spiteful and mean!

JAMES: Look at her!

JULIA: *(Flaring in her own way.)* I am looking at her. And what I see is a poor old woman scared out of her wits.

JAMES: *(Loud, angry.)* Nonsense!

JULIA *(Shouting.)* Please don't shout at me!

(The OLD WOMAN weeps more, perhaps upset by the quarrel. AH KIU and SEVERINO are now all wide-eyed attention.)

JAMES: *(Shouting.)* I am not shouting!

JULIA: I've never seen you like this!

JAMES: It is impossible for anybody to have great-great-great-great-grand—

JULIA: *(Shouting.)* You're mean, James, mean and cruel to this poor old Hawaiian woman. . . . *(Another outburst from the OLD WOMAN; JULIA pulls her close.)* There . . . there . . . don't worry. You'll be all right. Nobody's going to drive you down the mountain to Hilo and just leave you there with no place to go. . . . We'll just go on upstairs and put you in a nice bedroom of your own, all warm and comfy. . . . And then, in the morning, we'll see what—

JAMES: For God's sake, Julia!

JULIA: *(Flaring.)* I thought you wanted me to stay the night.

JAMES: Oh!

JULIA: *(To the OLD WOMAN.)* Come . . . James is just being awful.

OLD WOMAN: Oh no! Oh no! *(She is quite "up." She moves to JAMES.)* I got so much aloha for you! *(She touches his cheek with either hand, turns back to* SEVERINO, *touching his face.)* An' I got so much aloha for you, my dear. . . . *(Then she moves to* AH KIU, *her fingers touching his mouth.)* 'Oko'a ke aloha o nā mea 'ē.[10]

(She turns back to JULIA, *who holds out her hand for her. The* OLD WOMAN *reaches for it—and misses it by a mile, stumbling a little.* JULIA *catches her.)*

JULIA: *(A nervous laugh.)* Careful!
JAMES: *(Clenched teeth.)* Julia, I absolutely forbid this!
OLD WOMAN: Auē! You folks so nice!
JULIA: *(Resolutely.)* Come! *(She leads the* OLD WOMAN *to the stairs and up.)*
JAMES: Julia, come back down here. . . . You don't just turn the house over to any old— *(Beside himself.)* What's come over you? Julia! *(But* JULIA *and the* OLD WOMAN *have gone out of sight at the top turn of the stairs.)* Oh, damn!

(He stomps back to SEVERINO *and* AH KIU, *who has a drink poured and ready for him.* JAMES *takes the offered drink on his angry way to the couch where he sits. He drinks.)*

JAMES: Who is that silly old crone, anyway?
AH KIU: Pele.
JAMES: *(Ranting on.)* What right has she got to barge into other people's homes and—what did you say?
AH KIU: Pele.

*(*JAMES *makes a spitting sound of disdain; turns away; drinks.)*

SEVERINO: *(To* AH KIU.*)* Are you referring to Madame Pele, the goddess op the bolcano? The sister op Hi'iaka, goddess op the hula?
AH KIU: *(To* JAMES.*)* Pele . . .
SEVERINO: *(To* AH KIU.*)* . . . who pucked with the fig?
JAMES: *(To* AH KIU.*)* Do you think I'm going to sit here and swallow—*(To* SEVERINO:*)* What pig?
SEVERINO: Fig.
JAMES: Fig.

---

[10]OLD WOMAN: . . . The love of the different is different.

SEVERINO: The fig god, Kamafua'a.

JAMES: Where did you hear that?

SEVERINO: In the tales of Hawai'i. . . . Everybody knows that. Kamafua'a and Pele make lob up the mountain, down the mountain, make the valleys and the deep ravines—

JAMES: The what?

SEVERINO: Ravines. In their ecstasy.

JAMES: You're drunk. Both of you.

AH KIU: *(Picking up the manuscript of* JAMES' *play.)* Ha ha ha! You suppose to know so much about Hawai'i. You suppose to write a play. *(Imitates* JULIA, *holding the play to his chest as she did earlier:)* Oh, James, it's soooo beautiful. You write a wonderful play, James. *(As himself:)* You write stink! Don't even know one thing about Pele.

JAMES: I don't let silly heathen facts hamper the flight of my creative imagination. That play is about the glory of Lili'uokalani and not about some silly Stone Age savages' belief in a—

AH KIU: Big words. Big words! Ever since you was one small boy, you always use big words when you don't know you ass from you 'ōkole . . .

JAMES: Enough! I have heard enough! I'm not going to stand here and listen to another— *(He is moving to the stairs, and is stopped there by:)*

AH KIU: The piece of wood cry! You hear. All the house cry!

JAMES: It was the wind.

AH KIU: No wind. Pele.

JAMES: *(Coming back, fuming.)* Wind! *(Mumbling.)* House crying, figs pucking fieces of wood, goddesses getting knocked ass over teakettle into gutters by a Volkswagen. . . . It's ridiculous!

(And a strange, eerily sad moan rises out of nowhere and fills the room. It is mournful, but no human voice ever so mourned.)

JAMES: What's that?

(They all listen. It comes again.)

JAMES: Jesus!

SEVERINO: Joseph!

(The moan comes again and keeps repeating during the following. On the stairs, the YOUNG HAWAIIAN GIRL appears, her hair down past her shoulders. She is dressed in shorts, tight T-shirt; she is physically luscious.)

JAMES ACTOR: All right all right all right. . . . Look, before we continue: when are you going to come down those steps naked . . . bare-ass naked . . . like the script says?

YOUNG GIRL ACTRESS: This is only a rehearsal. You just got a dirty mind, wanna see me naked all the time . . .

JAMES ACTOR: The longer you put it off, the harder— *(He stops instantly.* AH KIU ACTOR *grins at him in naughty glee.)*

AH KIU ACTOR: *(Singsong teasing.)* Go on, go on. . . . Finish the sentence like a big boy.

(The YOUNG GIRL ACTRESS *takes a pillow from the* hiki'e *and hurls it at* AH KIU ACTOR. *He dodges it, leaving the stairs open, and the* YOUNG GIRL ACTRESS *goes stomping up the stairs.)*

JAMES ACTOR: *(Yelling after her.)* The—the—more difficult—it will get later when you have to do it before an audience.

(He picks up the pillow and brings it back to the hiki'ee *as* AH KIU ACTOR *applauds.* SEVERINO ACTOR *watches shyly.)*

AH KIU ACTOR: Very good. "More difficult" is very good.

JAMES ACTOR: And you're no help. You know how shy she is. *(Yells up the stairs:)* Now, we'll take it over again. I'm sorry I interrupted the scene. *(To* AH KIU ACTOR:) And you cooperate, okay?

AH KIU ACTOR: That girl is going to get me into terrible trouble one of these days. Old dog, new tricks. *(They are taking their places. In* JAMES ACTOR's *direction:)* Da's why "more difficult," you know.

JAMES ACTOR: Okay, okay. Cut it out!

(They are in place, JAMES *crossing from the stairs.)*

JAMES: House crying, figs pucking fieces of wood, goddesses getting knocked ass over teakettle into gutters by a Volkswagen. . . . It's ridiculous!

(And a strange, eerily sad moan rises out of nowhere and fills the room. No human voice ever so moaned.)

JAMES: What's that?

(They all listen; it comes again.)

JAMES: Jesus!
SEVERINO: Joseph!

(The moan comes again and keeps repeating during the following. On the stairs, the YOUNG HAWAIIAN GIRL *appears, her hair down past her shoulders. The three men play as if she were, indeed, naked: open-mouthed, bug-eyed astonishment. She moves down the stairs.)*

SEVERINO: And Maria!

(The YOUNG HAWAIIAN GIRL *moves down and crosses to a chair. She sits facing the men.)*

YOUNG GIRL: Aloha!

(The stunned men cannot answer. SEVERINO *covers his crotch with his hat. The moaning has stopped. Finally:)*

JAMES: *(Aspirately.)* Who—are—you?
JULIA: *(Calling from upstairs off.)* James!
JAMES: Oh, God! She can't see you naked like this. I mean—it's not done!
JULIA: *(Offstage, calling.)* James!
JAMES: It's not decent. Please! You must go. Get dressed. At once. Outside. Oh, Lord! *(Points to the upstage closet.)* Ah Kiu, the closet! Open it! *(To* YOUNG HAWAIIAN GIRL:*)* Please, get up! Oh, please! *(She remains seated, cheesecaking a bit, naughtily exuberant.)* Very well. . . . Excuse me.

(He picks her up bodily. She likes it, snuggles, an arm going around his neck. AH KIU *has the closet door open.* JAMES *carries her, but halfway to the closet her lips find his—and stick! Now, as he shoves her into the closet, the last thing to get unstuck is her mouth.* JAMES *closes the door quickly. And* JULIA *comes hurrying down the stairs worried. The men move away from the closet.)*

JULIA: James! The old woman! She's gone!
THE THREE MEN: Gone!?
JULIA: Yes. I was in the upstairs hall, getting a quilt for her bed. I went into her room, and she's gone.
JAMES: Well, she didn't come down here. *(To* SEVERINO:*)* Did she?
SEVERINO: Oh, heavens to Betsy, no!

AH KIU: Never. She never come. Never.

JAMES: We were here all the time, weren't we?

AH KIU: Yes, sir!

SEVERINO: *(Together.)* Yes, sir!

JULIA: Then she must've gone down the back stairs.

(She hurries out at left. The moment she is gone, JAMES hurries to the closet.)

JAMES: We've got to get her out of here!

(He opens the closet door; the closet is empty. The three men exchange mystified looks; then they react as if something has happened at the closet downstage right. Actually, the door is supposed to have opened—but it hasn't.)

AH KIU ACTOR: *(Loud.)* Okay, open the door and come out, Knucklehead! We're waiting!

(The closet door remains closed. SEVERINO ACTOR moves to the closet, opens the door; the closet is empty.)

AH KIU ACTOR: Where the hell is he!

JAMES ACTOR: *(Disgusted.)* Probably wrapping some more vines and ferns around his pecker. You two guys continue. I'll go see. *(Goes off at downstage right.)*

SEVERINO ACTOR: Just the lines. Okay?

AH KIU ACTOR: Okay, okay, I'm one big fat lovable *māhū*. *(Steps into the closet, closing the door after himself.)*

SEVERINO ACTOR: *(Loud.)* Okay. He opens the door. *(Indicates the closet upstage right.)* The closet is empty. As the three men exchange mystified looks, the door to the closet by the fireplace opens. *(The door opens. Out steps the AH KIU ACTOR.)* Out steps the plump, soft, delightfully effeminate Hawaiian Man, still bedecked in his vines, ferns, and flowers, and little else.

AH KIU ACTOR: Aloha!

SEVERINO ACTOR: *(Amazed, moving closer.)* The *māhū* waves a long-stemmed flower before Severino's nose.

AH KIU ACTOR: *(Pantomiming it.)* You—nice!

SEVERINO: *(In his Filipino accent.)* Oh, now I have seen everything. I have seen a *māhū* with my own eyes.

SEVERINO ACTOR: The *māhū* flicks the flower across Severino's face coquettishly.

AH KIU ACTOR: Oh. *(He flicks the flower across* SEVERINO's *face coquettishly.)* I got so much aloha for you, my dear!

SEVERINO ACTOR: He bats his eyes at Severino, then throws the flower to Severino's feet.

*(*AH KIU ACTOR *doesn't bat his eyes, but he pantomimes throwing the flower.)*

AH KIU ACTOR: You naughty.

SEVERINO ACTOR: He turns and goes back into the closet, closing the door after himself.

(Which AH KIU ACTOR *does.* JAMES ACTOR *comes back from the right, worried.)*

JAMES ACTOR: Can't find him anywhere. He was here: I saw him. Earlier. Where's Ah Kiu?

*(*SEVERINO ACTOR *indicates closet.)*

SEVERINO ACTOR: We just ran through the lines.

JAMES ACTOR: *(Still looking off right, puzzled.)* What happened to that guy?

SEVERINO ACTOR: Maybe he quit. He's been saying he was going to. Like the others.

JAMES ACTOR: Fat chance! The only way you can get rid of that ham is to write him out of the play. . . . Well, when we get to his other scenes, just go through them as if he was here. Okay?

SEVERINO ACTOR: Okay.

JAMES ACTOR: *(With no conviction.)* He may show up.

SEVERINO ACTOR: *(He won't.)* Yeah.

(And JULIA *comes back in from the left, more worried now.)*

JULIA: James, it's getting too dark outside. *(She crosses right.)* I'll need a flashlight.

JAMES: The flashlight! It's upstairs, Julia!

JULIA: Nonsense, dear! I put it in this closet this afternoon.

(She has reached the closet downstage right. She opens the door, steps back with a little cry of surprise. The HARD HAWAIIAN MAN, *now in a business suit, steps out. He has the stub of a cigar in his mouth. In his hand is*

a flashlight. He closes the door after himself, gives the flashlight to the astonished JULIA, *and goes out at left. During this:)*

HARD MAN: He makana no ka wahine. . . .[11] 'Ano wīwī akā hiki ke ho'omomona iā ia. . . . Kekahi aloha.

(And he is off. They all stare after him in wonderment, especially JULIA. AH KIU *enters the set from the darkness at the right.)*

JULIA: Who was that?

JAMES: It's him. . . . Somebody . . .

SEVERINO: Lookin' por the old woman.

JAMES: Yes, it's somebody looking for the old woman.

JULIA: In a closet?

JAMES: You know how she is. Drunk. You never know where she'll be hiding . . .

JULIA: *(Going to the upstage closet.)* But who is he? When did he get here?

JAMES: He just popped in. Out of nowhere.

JULIA: Well, he's certainly very handsome.

JAMES: Yes, dear.

JULIA: Is that old raincoat of yours still in here? It's starting to drizzle a little outside.

JAMES: Yes, dear.

(She opens the closet. Standing in it is the OLD WOMAN. *The brandy has taken maximum effect.)*

OLD WOMAN: Howzit!

JULIA: There you are! *(She brings the* OLD WOMAN *out.)* James, I thought you said she didn't come in here.

JAMES: We didn't see her. Did we, Ah Kiu?

AH KIU: No. Ah Kiu no see.

JULIA: How could you have missed her, if you were here all the time, as you said?

JAMES: She must've—*(He gives up with a sigh.)*

OLD WOMAN: *(To* JULIA.*)* You so sweet, my dear.

---

[11]HARD MAN: . . . A present for the woman. . . . A little skinny, but we can fatten her up. . . . Don't worry, woman. . . . A little aloha for the stomach and the stomach gets fat . . . fat . . . fat fat fat fat fat . . .

JULIA: Yes, well, sweet or not, I'm quite quite cross with you. You worried me, terribly, dashing off like that. . . . Ah Kiu, please help me get her back upstairs.

(AH KIU *comes over;* JULIA *turns back to the* OLD WOMAN.)

JULIA: You've been very very naughty.

(AH KIU *takes the* OLD WOMAN*'s arm.*)

OLD WOMAN: (*To* AH KIU.) I like you. . . . You naughty?
JULIA: Bring her along, Ah Kiu.

(AH KIU *leads the* OLD WOMAN *as they go,* JULIA *following. Partway up the stairs,* JULIA *lets them go on ahead and out of sight. She looks back to* JAMES.)

JULIA: James, I think there is something wrong with that old woman.
JAMES: What do you mean?
JULIA: She has a funny smell . . . a very odd smell . . . about her.
JAMES: Like?
JULIA: I don't know . . . an acrid sort of smell . . . like burnt-out matches. . . . Well, she probably just needs a good bath. . . . Oh, and James—!
JAMES: Yes?
JULIA: I'll ask Ah Kiu to bring dinner up on a tray. Is that all right?
JAMES: Of course.
JULIA: I don't want to leave her alone tonight. Not for a moment. She might get hurt wandering around—fall down the stairs, something. . . . There is some more brandy in the upstairs parlor, isn't there?
JAMES: Yes, dear.
JULIA: That'll put her out. . . . See you later.
JAMES: You bet.

(*She smacks a "kiss" to him; he answers. She goes up the stairs and out.* JAMES *moves to the couch, sits.* SEVERINO *comes and sits beside him.*)

SEVERINO: Mr. James . . .
JAMES: (*In deep, troubled thought.*) Mmm?
SEVERINO: I'm scared.

JAMES: Of—?

SEVERINO: I'm apraid of the *māhū*.

JAMES: Don't be.

SEVERINO: I am innocent, I am not naughty . . .

JAMES: He can't get you to do anything you don't want to do, Severino. Relax.

SEVERINO: I cannot relax. *(Pats his heart to calm it down.)* I am having the falfitations ob the heart.

JAMES: Damn it, Severino, that's your trouble. Anybody says any-thing to you, you jump. Like you're afraid of your own shadow.

SEVERINO: I know. I know.

JAMES: Well, stop it. Just stop it. Build up your ego. There's no trick to it. Just tell yourself you're not going to be so scared of things, and that's half the battle won.

SEVERINO: What do I tell to myself?

(JAMES looks at him, shakes his head, sighs.)

JAMES: Well. . . . Okay. Repeat after me . . .

SEVERINO: Yes, sir!

JAMES: I am Severino.

SEVERINO: I am Severino.

JAMES: I am important in this world . . .

SEVERINO: I am important in this world . . .

JAMES: God made me in his image. . . . I am in God . . .

SEVERINO: God made me in his image. . . . I am in God . . .

JAMES: And God is in me.

SEVERINO: And God is in me.

JAMES: So I will stand unafraid . . .

SEVERINO: So I will stand unapraid . . .

JAMES: I will fear no evil . . .

SEVERINO: I will peer no evil . . .

JAMES: No one can put ideas I don't want in my head . . .

SEVERINO: No one can foot ideas I don't want inside my head . . .

JAMES: No one can put words in my mouth . . .

SEVERINO: No one can foot words in my mouth . . .

JAMES: Or make me do what I don't want . . .

SEVERINO: Or make me do what I . . .

(They stop, for there comes the sound of a hula gourd, as if a dance were about to begin. Then another gourd. And more. JAMES ACTOR enters at the top of the stairs.)

SEVERINO: Oh, fleece! *(Terrified.)* No more! No more!

JAMES ACTOR: *(Sore.)* What the hell is the matter with that girl! *(Calls.)* Hey! Hey! Where are you?

(And the YOUNG HAWAIIAN GIRL *appears at the lanai window from the left. She is struggling to get into a flesh-colored body stocking; a kimono covers her nakedness.)*

YOUNG GIRL ACTRESS: I'm sorry. . . . I'll be with you in a minute. . . . How do they expect people to get into these damn things?

JAMES ACTOR: You're supposed to be naked. Really naked!

YOUNG GIRL ACTRESS: *(Shrieking back.)* It'll look naked, *lemu!* *(Mumbling in frustration and rage, she half-hops, half-stumbles, off-stage at left.)*

JAMES ACTOR: *(To himself.)* Damn her.

(The actors' lighting, which started fading in from the start of the inter-ruption, is now at full. JAMES ACTOR *has moved over to the* pūne'e *and plunked himself down in a sulk.* SEVERINO ACTOR *waits a while, but he too is very upset.)*

SEVERINO ACTOR: Can I ask you something?

JAMES ACTOR: *(On the verge of being fed up.)* Okay, shoot. What?

SEVERINO ACTOR: You won't get angry?

JAMES ACTOR: *(Angry.)* Why the hell should I get angry? *(He sinks back on the* pūne'e, *his forearm going over his eyes.)* Jesus! . . . Okay, what's your question?

SEVERINO ACTOR: *(Carefully.)* Where were you born?

*(*JAMES ACTOR *sits up a little too fast, as if caught with some secret. He looks steadily at* SEVERINO ACTOR *perhaps a little afraid himself.)*

SEVERINO ACTOR: You don't know either, do you?

JAMES ACTOR: *(With slow, firm emphasis.)* I was born in—in— Lahaina, Maui. *(A little too much emphasis.)* April 7th, 19 . . . *(A little confused, he lashes back defensively.)* Who cares, anyway?

SEVERINO ACTOR: Because when you asked that guy who plays Ah Kiu and he didn't know, I asked myself when I was born, and I didn't know. . . . It was like I never asked that question of myself before. Like it was a brand new idea I never thought of before. . . .

(JAMES ACTOR *can't answer* SEVERINO ACTOR'*s hurt, scared look; he looks down, tense.*)

SEVERINO ACTOR: *(Softly.)* You were lying, weren't you? . . . You made that date up, just then, like somebody just put those words in your mouth for the first time . . . just then.

(JAMES ACTOR *doesn't respond, seems utterly withdrawn.* SEVERINO ACTOR *comes slowly to him, stops by the end table on which lies* JAMES' *manuscript.*)

SEVERINO ACTOR: What's your name? (JAMES ACTOR *just looks at him.*) The others—I don't know their names either. They don't know. *(A moment.)* Why didn't I think of that before? Why is it only now, right now, like wondering when I was born—you—that Ah Kiu guy . . . *(A moment.)* What's going on? *(A moment.)* I'm scared. Like the others. . . . They don't really want to quit, they don't really care about all that Hawaiian stuff. . . . That's just an excuse to hide the fact they want to run away from something that's making them scared but they don't know what. . . .

(JAMES ACTOR *gets up, moves away. Idly he picks up the "magical" piece of wood.*)

SEVERINO ACTOR: People keep talking about dead Hawaiians . . . in a dead culture . . . the living dead . . . *(A moment.)* Is that it?

(JAMES ACTOR *returns the piece of wood to the mantel, faces* SEVERINO ACTOR.)

SEVERINO ACTOR: Are we dead? . . . And we're beginning to forget who we were?
JAMES ACTOR: No.
SEVERINO ACTOR: I read someplace, it happens like that. We wait until, little by little, everything that was life is only a whisper—a murmur—and then, if we're lucky, even the murmuring disappears, and there's peace and rest at last. . . . And we sleep like undreaming children waiting for that beautiful morning when our Father wakes us gently to his Love. . . . That's it, isn't it?
JAMES ACTOR: *(Gently.)* No.
SEVERINO ACTOR: Then what is it?

(His hand has gone, absently, onto the manuscript. Idly he makes as if to move it. JAMES ACTOR *is instantly to him.)*

JAMES ACTOR: *(Loud, urgent.)* Don't touch that!

SEVERINO ACTOR: *(Recoiling, surprised, a little hurt.)* I was only—

JAMES ACTOR: Just—don't touch that . . .

SEVERINO ACTOR: Is it so terrible?

JAMES ACTOR: I don't know. . . . Not for sure. Not yet . . . *(He sits, shaking his head, a deeply troubled man.)*

SEVERINO ACTOR: *(A statement, not a question.)* You're scared out of your mind.

JAMES ACTOR: When I first suspected, I was scared. Like I've never been frightened in my whole life. But as I started to get a little more sure I was right, and I thought about it more, it started to get, well, kinda funny; a little.) *(A mirthless attempt at a laugh.)* I have this idea that the surer I get, the funnier it gets. . . . That it'll end up in howling laughter . . . *(A pause.)* No . . . I'm not scared any more, but I really don't know how I feel . . . how to feel. . . . But when I do know, I'll tell you what I know—or think I know . . .

SEVERINO ACTOR: *(After a pause.)* Just one thing, if you are sure of the answer . . .

JAMES ACTOR: Okay.

SEVERINO ACTOR: We are not dead.

JAMES ACTOR: No, we're not.

SEVERINO ACTOR: Then, we are alive . . . ? You're sure? (JAMES ACTOR *obviously is at a loss*.) Are we?

JAMES ACTOR: *(Quietly.)* We're as alive as we'll ever be.

*(*SEVERINO ACTOR *goes to the front door. His perplexity weighs as heavily as ever.)*

SEVERINO ACTOR: From the top again?

JAMES ACTOR: Might as well.

SEVERINO ACTOR: Yeah . . . *(He is about to "open" the door to go out on the porch, but is stopped by:)*

JAMES ACTOR: There's something else. . . . Don't tell the others any of this. . . . I don't want them bugging me before I'm ready to tell. . . . It would only scare them more maybe. . . .

SEVERINO ACTOR: *(Sighing.)* Okay . . .

(The YOUNG HAWAIIAN GIRL *appears on the porch as* SEVERINO *steps out onto it. Her preparations are over; she is in body stocking and kimono.)*

YOUNG GIRL ACTRESS: Okay. I'm ready.
JAMES ACTOR: *(Mumbling.)* It's about time.

(The YOUNG HAWAIIAN GIRL ACTRESS *goes off at left.* SEVERINO ACTOR *is already back in the living room, close to* JAMES ACTOR, *quite agitated.)*

SEVERINO ACTOR: *(Whispering.)* She heard!
JAMES ACTOR: *(Normal voice.)* No, she didn't.
SEVERINO ACTOR: *(Whispering.)* She did, she did. She was right behind that flat, she's there now.
JAMES ACTOR: She's supposed to make her entrance from up there . . .

(He points up to the entrance at the top of the stairs, and the YOUNG HAWAIIAN GIRL ACTRESS *steps out into view at the top of the stairs.)*

YOUNG GIRL ACTRESS: Ready.
JAMES ACTOR: *(To her.)* Okay. We'll go on. We'll take it from the sound cue.

(The GIRL *steps off.)*

JAMES ACTOR: *(To* SEVERINO ACTOR.*)* See . . .
SEVERINO ACTOR: But I saw her— *(Gestures vaguely to the porch.)* How could she get up there so fast?
JAMES ACTOR: Goddamn it! I told you I didn't want anybody buggin' me until I was ready to explain. . . .
SEVERINO ACTOR: *(A moment.)* Sorry . . .

(He goes and takes his place, just before the YOUNG HAWAIIAN GIRL'S *entrance.* JAMES ACTOR *takes his. The lights change back to the "scene setting." Now there comes the sound of a hula gourd, as if a dance were about to begin. Then another gourd joins in, then more gourds. And more.)*

SEVERINO: Oh, fleece! *(Terrified.)* No more! No more!

(The sound keeps building, as does SEVERINO*'s terror. And the* YOUNG HAWAIIAN GIRL *appears at the top of the stairs. She comes down the stairs, approaches* JAMES*, who falls to his knees in awe, as does* SEVERINO*. It is obvious that beneath her simple kimono, the* GIRL *is naked. Meanwhile:)*

SEVERINO: I am Severino. I am important in this world. God made me in his image. I am in God. And God is in me. So I will stand unapraid. I will peer no evil.

(The lights are fading as the GIRL *stands before* JAMES*. She opens her kimono, revealing herself to him.* SEVERINO*'s panic jumps up a few more notches.)*

SEVERINO: No one can foot ideas inside my head. . . . No one can foot ideas inside my head. . . .

(She enfolds JAMES *in her kimono.)*

SEVERINO: Oh, heavens to Betsy!

(The lights go to black. There is a full-throated cry of ancient triumph from a chorus of men—Mua. Mua! It is repeated, again and again. And then there is silence. House lights reveal an empty living room.)

ACT TWO

(The lights come up to full morning light. On the pūneʻe, JAMES *is fast asleep. The* pūneʻe *is a mess. He reaches over and amorously pulls a pillow closer, hugging it. A moment. Then* SEVERINO *is seen through the large porch window. He moves cautiously, peering into the living room first before he heads for the front door. He enters the living room. He looks around, particularly at the stairs. He is scared and exhausted. There is a slow moan of contented delight from* JAMES, *calling* SEVERINO'S *attention to the* puneʻe. SEVERINO *comes closer.)*

SEVERINO: *(Softly.)* Sir . . . sir . . .

(That sound of deep satisfaction from the sleeping JAMES *comes again.* SEVERINO *scratches the sole of* JAMES' *foot.)*

SEVERINO: Sir. . . . Is she gone?
JAMES: *(Asleep.)* Again.
SEVERINO: *(Immediately dutiful.)* Oh—yes, sir . . .

(He sits, back to JAMES, *on the edge of the* pūneʻe, *turns to* JAMES' *feet, tickles one. Delighted,* JAMES *reaches up behind him, pulls him down.)*

SEVERINO: Oh, sir!

(Struggling and flailing! As JAMES *is now also tickling him—and* SEVERINO *is very ticklish—his protests are interrupted by wild giggles.)*

SEVERINO: Stop! . . . Please! . . . You have made a terrible mistake! . . . No . . . don't do that! . . . Help!

(And JAMES *is awake, freeing* SEVERINO, *who backs away. It takes a moment for* JAMES *to wake fully.)*

JAMES: Oh, God! *(Then he remembers.)* Oh, God!! *(He beams, shakes his head in delighted wonder. Then he starts to laugh in delight, running his hand over his face. He turns suddenly and makes a loud animal snarl.)* Aaaaargh! *(He buries his face in a pillow, bites it, all fangs!)*

SEVERINO: I could hear all the lib-long night! Boom boom boom! *(Only a moan of deep delight from JAMES.)* I may conclude, therepore, sir, that the lady was satispactory . . . ?

JAMES: *(Coming up for air.)* Satisfactory—satisfactory—sa-tis-fac-to-reeee! *(He really sees SEVERINO for the first time. His face falls.)*

JAMES: You look awful!

SEVERINO: Yes, sir. Por me, the evening was not very satispactory.

JAMES: What happened?

SEVERINO: That *māhū* . . . I ran por my life.

JAMES: *(Chuckling.)* Did he catch you?

SEVERINO: Not yet. I hide in the fig-sty. And he came close in the dark. Jesus, Joseph, and Maria, I said, what am I going to do? And he came closer. And I go, Oink! Oink! Oink!

JAMES: You do that very well.

SEVERINO: The *māhū* think so too, because he went away.

JAMES: Well, that was good.

SEVERINO: *(In despair.)* No, sir, that was not good.

JAMES: No?

SEVERINO: No, sir. . . . The fig began to make lob to me. I ran por my life.

JAMES: I wouldn't go hiding in the sties again, if I were you. You might get hurt. A couple of those boars are pretty wild.

SEVERINO: Not as wild as the *māhū*, sir.

JAMES: *(Together.)* . . . as the *māhū*. . . . Yes, I know. Still, don't do it again.

SEVERINO: Yes, sir.

JAMES: Where's Julia?

SEVERINO: She went to Hilo, early this morning. Shop.

JAMES: *(Worried.)* She didn't take the old woman with her, did she?

SEVERINO: No, sir. The old lady is upstairs asleep. (JAMES sinks back with a relieved smile.) I wish Miss Julia to take her. Quick!

JAMES: Now now now, Severino. She is very old, very frail. We can't just throw an old person like that out into the street, now can we?

(AH KIU comes in from outside with a basket.)

JAMES: Ah, good morning, Ah Kiu!

AH KIU: Good morning. *(Sets the basket on the table.)*

JAMES: What've you got there?

AH KIU: Me go get ʻōhelo . . .

JAMES: Really—?

AH KIU: Yes.

JAMES: Let me try one. *(Reaches over, takes a berry, bites it.)* Good lord! It's rather like cranberries . . .

(He stops—for at the top of the stairs, the OLD WOMAN *has appeared.* JAMES *rises respectfully. The* OLD WOMAN *comes down the stairs.)*

JAMES: Ah, good morning!

(The OLD WOMAN *smiles at him, and, passing* SEVERINO, *pinches his fanny.)*

OLD WOMAN: Oink! *(She continues for* JAMES.)

JAMES: Did you sleep well?

(The OLD WOMAN *breaks into laughter, sitting in a chair.)*

OLD WOMAN: *(To* AH KIU.) ʻO wai i hiamoe?[1]

AH KIU: *(Laughing.)* Pōloli ʻoe, ʻea? *(He brings the basket of* ʻohelo *berries to her.)*

OLD WOMAN: Mahalo iā ʻoe!

(She sets the basket on her lap and begins to eat the berries—leaves, stems, and all. JAMES *and* SEVERINO *watch wide-eyed.)*

JAMES: Well, Severino—why don't you start cleaning up the bedrooms upstairs . . .

*(*SEVERINO *darts a worried look up the stairs.)*

JAMES: Go along. . . . Madam Pele will be down here with me all the time. We've got a lot to talk about.

---

[1] OLD WOMAN: Who slept?

AH KIU: *(Laughing.)* You must be hungry. *(He brings the basket of* ʻōhelo *berries to her.)*

OLD WOMAN: Oh, thank you!

SEVERINO: Yes, sir . . . *(Goes up the stairs warily.)*

JAMES: Ah Kiu, is there some coffee? *(He thumbs a secret "Get out!")*

AH KIU: Oh, yes. . . . Oh, yes. . . . Ah Kiu go make.

(He goes off at left. Alone with the OLD WOMAN, JAMES *is suddenly a little nervous.)*

JAMES: Well . . . *(He sits. She goes right on with her breakfast.)* I—uh—I . . . It isn't often that I have had the great pleasure—honor—to . . . uh . . . *(Clears his throat.)* I mean—a goddess—I've never —*(A delicate choice.)* —welcomed—a goddess in my house before . . .

OLD WOMAN: Was a nice welcome?

JAMES: It was— *(Pulls himself in check.)* —a privilege.

OLD WOMAN: Was nice. *(She resumes eating.)*

JAMES: I had no idea—I mean, I had heard about you before, of course—I mean, who hasn't?—but I had no idea that—that you would be real and—you'd show up here. . . . *(She is too busy munching.)* Fancy being hit like that by a Bug. . . . *(She stops, looks at him.)* I mean, a Volkswagen. . . . *(She is still puzzled.)* Volkswagen . . . Julia's little car. It's called a Bug. Affectionately.

OLD WOMAN: Right in my poor ol' 'ōkole. *(She sets the basket aside, rising.)*

JAMES: We're terribly sorry.

OLD WOMAN: All black an' blue. You like see? *(She is about to flip up the back of her skirt to show.)*

JAMES: Oh no no . . . ! I take your word for it.

OLD WOMAN: Was sore, you know.

JAMES: Yes. *(She sits.)* Julia says she didn't see you. . . . You were suddenly there.

OLD WOMAN: I never see that folks' wagon, tha's why. . . . My eyes, you know. . . . They weak now.

JAMES: And it's understandable that Julia wasn't on the lookout for you . . . for anyone really. . . . No one ever walks this far up . . .

OLD WOMAN: I walk e'rry place now. . . . Walk . . . walk . . . walk.

JAMES: All alone?

OLD WOMAN: One time, I get one small 'īlio. . . . One little dog. White. But—auē!

JAMES: What happened to it?

OLD WOMAN: Awful! . . . Terrible! . . . Stink!

JAMES: What?

OLD WOMAN: One day . . . you know, over in O'ahu . . . close Le'ahi place, okay?

JAMES: Okay.

OLD WOMAN: Okay. . . . I goin' walkin' along, mindin' my own business. . . . Nice day, you know. . . . Plenty Hawaiian birds singin', sun shinin', . . . so nice. . . . My little 'ilio beside, go— *(Her hands become four legs pattering along.)* pitpitpitpitpitpit . . . *(The hand-dog's hind leg—fifth finger?—lifts:)* Psssst! *(The hand-dog continues on its pattering way.)* Pitpitpit pitpitpit. *(Lifts.)* Pssst! Then suddenly, yeh? Was one wagon. . . . Some other folks' wagon. . . . An' one man get one net an' he come get my little 'ilio in the net an' put him in those folks' wagon. . . . I run, I say, "Hey, stop! . . . What you doin'?" An' he say, "No get license . . . no get license!" And prrrrrrrr, he go away with my little 'ilio and I never see him again. . . .

JAMES: But that's awful. . . . Didn't you go to the pound and pay the—well, whatever you had to pay—and get your little dog back?

OLD WOMAN: *(After a pause.)* What's that, one license?

JAMES: It's like—well—you have to pay a kind of tax—to get a permit—to own a dog. . . . It's the law.

OLD WOMAN: Was one real skinny guy, you know. . . . You know what?

JAMES: What?

OLD WOMAN: I think that skinny guy went eat 'um. . . . *(Sighs.)* So, now, jes' walk . . . walk e'rry place . . . noplace . . . jes' me alone . . . jes walk . . .

JAMES: *(Quite touched.)* And you came here.

OLD WOMAN: *(Softly.)* 'Ae . . .

JAMES: But—why? . . . Why, from all the houses in Hawai'i, did you pick this one?

OLD WOMAN: I like for see my friends again. . . . I walkin' along, out there, an' I think about Kamapua'a. . . . An' then, I know Kamapua'a is here . . . I can smell him.

JAMES: My God, the pig sty!

OLD WOMAN: An' so I was comin' . . . smellin', smellin' . . . an'— aaaaaaagh!—right in the 'okole!

(JULIA comes in from the porch, all chipper, with a shopping bag. JAMES sees her.)

JAMES: Speaking of the devil.

(JAMES *rises as* JULIA *enters the living room.*)

JULIA: *(Brightly.)* Good morning, good morning. . . . (*To the* OLD WOMAN:) See you're up! Did you sleep well?

OLD WOMAN: Lilybit.

JULIA: You didn't make a sound. Why, it was almost as if you weren't there, all night.

JAMES: Severino said you drove down early . . .

JULIA: I don't know what you expected to live on over the weekend. Anyway, I had to see my mother. She was terribly worried.

JAMES: Did you—you know—say anything?

JULIA: Of course not. I told her you were sick and—and the phone wasn't working. . . . I think she knew right off that I was lying. She probably checked the phone company the moment I left. . . .

JAMES: Mothers are like that. Clairvoyant. . . . Besides, she called last night—just when the accident happened—I told her your car wouldn't start. . . .

JULIA: You could've told me.

JAMES: Things started getting pretty wild. I just forgot . . .

JULIA: Thanks. . . . So, I met Ray Tanaka at the supermarket.

JAMES: Oh?

JULIA: I asked him and his wife—I always forget her name—

JAMES: Fumiko . . .

JULIA: . . . Fumiko up for tea this afternoon.

JAMES: Oh, Lord! Did you have to?

JULIA: They were driving up this afternoon anyway with the papers about the house. . . . Ray's people have all signed. So, I thought: a pleasant tea, you sign, we'll celebrate, and—(*She gestures to the* OLD WOMAN.)—they can save me another trip down.

JAMES: What do you mean?

JULIA: They'll take the old lady down, when they go. . . . I've decided to stay the weekend.

(AH KIU *comes in with coffee, which he sets on the table.* JULIA *doesn't see the disappointment and dismay on* JAMES' *face.*)

JULIA: Oh, coffee! *(She helps clear the table.)*

OLD WOMAN: Who's that Tanaka?

JAMES: He's—helping with some papers. . . . Business.

(The OLD WOMAN *looks at* JULIA, *who is busy with the coffee. The look is cold, hostile.)*

JULIA: Thank you, Ah Kiu. That'll be all . . .

*(*AH KIU *looks at her, cold, hostile; turns and exits left.)*

JULIA: It's nothing to worry about, dear. It's just business. Real estate. . . . Would you care for some coffee? . . . Good heavens, I still don't know your name!

*(*JULIA *is offering her a cup of coffee. But the* OLD WOMAN *only looks at her, then rises, and without a word goes to the stairs, goes up, and off.* JULIA *is, naturally, both surprised and concerned.)*

JULIA: What—? . . . Did I say something wrong?

JAMES: I suppose.

JULIA: But what's wrong with asking if she wanted a cup of coffee?

JAMES: I think it's about the Tanakas.

JULIA: What's so terrible about the Tanakas?

JAMES: You said they'd take her down to Hilo. I think it's that.

JULIA: I'm sure it's no imposition. Ray and his wife are very sweet—

JAMES: I don't think she wants to go at all.

JULIA: It can't be helped. She surely doesn't—

JAMES: It isn't as if she had a place to go. As you said last night, she really is kind of pathetic. . . .

JULIA: Last night was last night. She looks perfectly all right now.

JAMES: It's—upsetting—just tossing her out like that.

JULIA: *(Looking at him a puzzled moment.)* Are you thinking of letting her stay on here?

JAMES: *(Too quickly.)* No! . . . No, of course not.

JULIA: You sound like it.

JAMES: Well, now that you suggest it . . .

JULIA: I—suggest—it?

JAMES: I mean—there's more than enough room. . . . You know, when I was a kid, we once slept thirty-six people here for a birthday party that—

JULIA: James, the movers are coming day after tomorrow. . . . Except for the two bedrooms upstairs, on this side—all the other rooms are empty. . . . Even the bunkhouse outside—everything: all crated up, except for Ah Kiu's and Severino's rooms. . . .

JAMES: Well—there's this *pūne'e.*

JULIA: James . . . James! What's come over you? Why this sudden concern over an old woman—a total stranger?

(A moment. He pats the pūne'e, *by his side.)*

JAMES: Julia. . . . Come and sit down. . . . There's something I've got to tell you. About that old woman. Something rather incredible, I'm afraid.

JULIA: *(Concerned.)* What is it?

JAMES: Please sit down.

(She sits near him, quite worried.)

JULIA: You don't look well, James.

JAMES: I want to tell you who that old woman really is. . . . Now, I don't know what you think of the supernatural, what other people call superstitions . . . but, believe me, Julia, there's an awful lot that science and so-called common sense can't explain. . . .

JULIA: So?

JAMES: Well, who is Man to say that his existence is the only kind of existence there is . . . ?

JULIA: Who, indeed?

JAMES: I mean, after all, perfectly intelligent people believe in the immortality of the soul. People believe in the devil and angels and—things like that. . . . So isn't it logical that those different kinds of beings live in worlds—existences—that are different from ours?

JULIA: *(Completely at sea.)* Very logical, dear.

JAMES: *(Moving closer to her, pressing it all home.)* Well, isn't it just as logical, then, to assume—isn't it inevitably true—that, from time to time, a being from one of those other existences could—does —cross over into ours?

JULIA: Are you all right, James?

JAMES: Of course I am. . . . And I suppose if one of them should cross over, she'd have to assume the physical characteristics of our world . . . appearances, speech—even—say—pidgin English . . .

JULIA: She?

JAMES: Yes.

JULIA: *(Catching on.)* All right, James: who is she?

JAMES: That—old—woman—is— *(He shakes his head, can't do it.)*

JULIA: *(Quite bored now.)* Oh, for God's sake, James, spare me this excruciating suspense. . . .

JAMES: Julia, that old woman is—well—is Pele. *(She only stares at him.)* The Hawaiian goddess of the volcano.

(JULIA keeps looking at him, then suddenly breaks into laughter.)

JAMES: Don't do that! *(But she goes on laughing, in real merriment.)* I said don't do that! *(She goes on laughing.)* Stop it, Julia!

JULIA: *(Through her laughter.)* You can't be serious!

JAMES: *(Furious.)* Damn! *(Angrily he rises, moves away, to pour himself another drink.)*

JULIA: *(Worried.)* You are serious. *(She goes to him, reaches for his arm.)* Oh, James, I am sorry. It's so unlike you to believe such nonsense, and naturally I—Now I have gotten you angry. *(She moves to his chair, sits on the arm.)* I don't want you to be angry. Not after last night. *(She begins to fuss with his hair.)*

JAMES: What about last night?

JULIA: *(Fussing, nuzzling.)* It was so—so daring of you—to come to me like that, in the dark, knowing that old woman was in the very next bed! You were so—sure—like never before. So strong. So—in command!

JAMES: I—what?

JULIA: Were magnificent!

JAMES: You're making it up! *(He gets up, getting angry again.)* I was down here. On that *pūneʻe.* All night!

JULIA: That's ridiculous. . . . You came upstairs. To me.

JAMES: That's ridiculous. *(He points to the* puneʻe.*)* I was there. All the time. . . . Alone!

JULIA: James, it's mean to tease me like this.

JAMES: I'm not teasing. I tell you, I was there.

JULIA: Just because I laughed at that nonsense about Madam Pele doesn't give you the right to—

JAMES: *(Exploding.)* It is not nonsense!

JULIA: Nonsense! Nonsense!

(There's a shriek of terror from offstage at the top of the stairs. Then, down the staircase, comes SEVERINO *in terror.)*

SEVERINO: Help! . . . Oh, sir! Oh, Miss Julia! Save me!

JULIA: Severino! What is it?

SEVERINO: *(Darting behind her and* JAMES.*)* The *māhū!* Look! *(There is, of course, no one on the stairs.)*

JULIA ACTRESS: Well, where is he?

JAMES ACTOR: Gone.

JULIA ACTRESS: Gone?

SEVERINO ACTOR: We think he quit.

JULIA ACTRESS: (*To* JAMES ACTOR.) I'm not surprised. The way the play made fun of *māhū*. Good for him. . . . So—what do we do?

JAMES ACTOR: Pretend he's here.

JULIA ACTRESS: That's ridiculous. Look, what's the point in going on? If the whole thing is falling apart like this, what's the use?

JAMES ACTOR: Those rewrites you wanted: maybe he's being written out of the play.

JULIA ACTRESS: Well, that's a good idea. Finally! That's not all that needs to be changed, but it's a beginning. . . . (*To* SEVERINO ACTOR, *pointing to stairs:*) Okay. Cue.

(SEVERINO ACTOR *goes halfway up the stairs, waits until* JAMES ACTOR *and* JULIA ACTRESS *are back in their places, then he comes down as before:*)

SEVERINO: Help! . . . Oh, sir! Oh, Miss Julia! Save me!

JULIA: Severino! What is it?

SEVERINO: (*Darting behind her and* JAMES.) The *māhū*! Look! (*He points to the empty stairs.*)

JULIA: (*Scared.*) James! James, who is that man? Why has he got all those ferns wrapped around himself?

JAMES: Pele!

JULIA: Will you stop this ridiculous game, or whatever it is you're playing!

JAMES: (*Angry.*) Nobody's playing games!

SEVERINO: Oh, flease, flease! He is comin' down!

JULIA: (*Striding angrily to the foot of the stairs.*) You get out of this house! (*A moment, then more forcefully.*) I said get out of here! . . . I don't care what you are or who you are! (*She grabs a* kāhili *from beside the steps.*) You aren't wanted here, you aren't welcome here! (*She bangs the "*māhū*" on the head with the* kāhili.) Get out!

(*The "*māhū*" flees up the stairs,* JULIA *pursuing and banging him on the head.*)

JULIA: Get out! Get out! Get out and stay out!

(The "māhū" is gone, routed. JULIA *comes down the stairs, angrily jamming the* kāhili *back into its stand.)*

JULIA: James, go upstairs at once. Send that man and that old woman away.
JAMES: I've been trying to tell you—
JULIA: Right now!
JAMES: —they're the same person.
JULIA: What?
JAMES: They're the same person.
SEVERINO: And another man and a girl with *susu* out to here!
JULIA: What are you talking about?
JAMES: It's Madam Pele. She can turn herself into three other people.
JULIA: *(On the verge of angry tears.)* James, once and for all, I beg you, stop this stupid joke!
SEVERINO: Oh, it is not a joke, Miss Julia! It is Madam Fele!
JULIA: *(Almost hysterical.)* Both of you! Stop it! Stop it at once!
SEVERINO: There! Look!

(For the YOUNG HAWAIIAN GIRL *has appeared at the top of the stairs. Again the gourds. She moves down only a step or two.* JAMES *is immediately entranced,* SEVERINO *is concerned, and* JULIA, *seeing, goes deeper into anger and confusion.)*

SEVERINO: It is Madam Fele!
JULIA: *(Weeping.)* I don't care who they are! Get rid of them! James, send them away! Go upstairs and send them away!

(The YOUNG HAWAIIAN GIRL *raises her hand for* JAMES.)

SEVERINO: Oh, no! Miss Julia, you must not!
JULIA: Why mustn't I? *(To* JAMES:*)* Get these awful people out of here! At once! *(But she is speaking to* JAMES' *back, for he is already moving to the stairs.)*
SEVERINO: *(To* JULIA.*)* Please! Tell him to stay! He must not go upstairs.

(Halfway up the stairs, JAMES *reaches for the* YOUNG HAWAIIAN GIRL'*s hand.)*

SEVERINO: Oh, Mr. James, come back! Come back!

(But hand-in-hand, JAMES *and the* YOUNG HAWAIIAN GIRL *go off at the top of the stairs.)*

JULIA: *(Practically screeching.)* Severino, what is all this? It's cruel to play such horrid tricks on me!

SEVERINO: It is not a trick, Miss Julia. That is really Madam Fele.

JULIA: *(Screaming, stomping.)* Stop it! Stop it! Stop it!

*(*AH KIU *enters for the coffee things.)*

JULIA: Ah Kiu! Who are these people! That old woman, that girl . . .

SEVERINO: —and the *māhū* . . .

JULIA: —and the *māhū* . . .

SEVERINO: And the man.

JULIA: What man?

SEVERINO: That man who make lob to you las' night.

JULIA: *(A gasp.)* Who?

SEVERINO: You saw him. *(He indicates the closet downstage right.)* In the pether cape. He came from there an' gave you the plash-light.

JULIA: *(Really frightened now.)* What are you talking about?

SEVERINO: He came upstairs to you. Las' night.

JULIA: It was James!

SEVERINO: The man. You said he was magnificent.

*(*JULIA *sinks into a chair, stunned, looking imploringly at* AH KIU*.)*

JULIA: Ah Kiu?

AH KIU: Everybody was all Pele.

(He is about to take up the coffee tray when the OLD WOMAN *appears at the top of the stairs.)*

OLD WOMAN: Eh, Ah Kiu! Wait! Wait!

*(*AH KIU *puts down the tray. The* OLD WOMAN *comes down.)*

OLD WOMAN: E lawe mai i ka ʻōmole iaʻu. Ke ʻike nei ʻoe, ʻo ka ʻōmole pōkole me ke ahi ma loko.[2]

---

[2]OLD WOMAN: Bring the bottle to me. You know, the short one with the fire inside.

(She comes to the foot of the stairs. AH KIU *takes the bottle of brandy to her.)*

AH KIU: 'O ke ahi no ke akua wahine o ke ahi. A ke mamake nei au i nā ho'okupu mai ke kai mai a mai nā kuahiwi mai.[3]

JULIA: *(Dashing to them in a rage.)* Oh, no, you don't! Give me that! *(She grabs the* OLD WOMAN*'s wrist with one hand, the bottle with the other.)* You give me that bottle, and you get out of here! I don't care who you are, you get—

(And she stops in surprise. She stares at the OLD WOMAN. *The bottle is still in the* OLD WOMAN*'s hand. For a moment, the two women just look at each other,* JULIA *in shocked disbelief, the* OLD WOMAN *with a slightly mocking smile. Then, very deliberately, the* OLD WOMAN *offers her arm, almost daring, to* JULIA. *Then, with something like awe,* JULIA *reaches once more for the* OLD WOMAN*'s wrist. She feels it. The* OLD WOMAN*'s smile never alters.* JULIA*'s awe deepens. She releases the wrist, and she remains stockstill as the* OLD WOMAN *turns and goes up the stairs with the bottle.* AH KIU *picks up the tray and heads for the dining room.)*

AH KIU: *(Mumbling.)* 'O Pele nā mea a pau. Hele mai nā mea a pau maiā Pele mai. Hele mai nā mea apau mai ke ahi mai.[4]

(He is out. JULIA *still is deep in stunned shock.* SEVERINO *moves to her, a bit scared, slowly.)*

SEVERINO: Julia . . . Miss Julia . . . what is the matter? What has happened?

JULIA: *(From somewhere beyond shock.)* My fingers searched her wrist for a pulse of Life and—there was none. . . . A corpse—the corpse of an old woman, moving among the living. . . . *(She sits against the first step, her head against the newel post. There is an enormous clap of thunder, instant lightning, as if right in the living room.)* Oh, God! (SEVERINO *crosses himself.)* Oh God, Oh Merciful God!

SEVERINO: Deliber us from Ebil! And prom things that go boom-boom-boom in the night!

---

[3]AH KIU: Fire for the goddess of fire. And I wish there were offerings from the sea and from the mountains.

[4]AH KIU: All is Pele. All comes from Pele. All comes from fire.

(An inferno of a thunder and lightning storm breaks loose. It is too much. JULIA *cracks, weeping hysterically.)*

SEVERINO: Miss Julia . . . *(He comes to her quickly, sits beside her.)* No more, Miss Julia. . . . No more. . . . Come. . . . *(He gets up, supports her as she rises, still sobbing.)* Come . . . come . . .

(One of the flashes of lightning "locks" at the level of the actor's general lighting. SEVERINO *helps the sobbing* JULIA *off at downstage left. As they go,* JAMES ACTOR *comes into view from behind the stairs. In profound pity, he watches them go. Then, alone, he goes over to the end table and opens* JAMES' *manuscript. He reads in a quiet, resigned daze.)*

JAMES ACTOR: The actor who plays James enters from behind the stairs. In profound pity, he watches Julia and Severino go off at downstage left. Then, alone, he goes over to the end table and opens James' manuscript. He reads in a quiet, resigned daze. *(He sits, placing the script on his lap.)* He sits, placing the script on his lap. *(Reads on:)* He knows now. And he is overwhelmed by anguish: how is he to justify this appalling cruelty to the others? He stares, stunned, terrified, motionless, straight ahead.

*(*JAMES ACTOR *stares, stunned, terrified, motionless, straight ahead.* SEVERINO ACTOR *enters from the left.)*

JAMES ACTOR: *(Reading.)* The actor who plays Severino enters from the left. He stops near the actor playing James. *(Which* SEVERINO ACTOR *does.)*
SEVERINO ACTOR: What are you doing? What are you saying?

*(*JAMES ACTOR *looks at him for a moment, then hands him the manuscript.* SEVERINO ACTOR *takes it.)*

JAMES ACTOR: Read this.
SEVERINO ACTOR: *(Reading.)* The actor who plays Severino enters from the left. He stops near the actor playing James . . . which Severino Actor does. The Severino Actor says, "What are you doing? What are you saying?" . . . The James Actor looks at him for a moment, then hands him the manuscript. The Severino Actor takes it. The James Actor says, "Read this. . . ." *(He is overwhelmed.)* My God, the words are appearing at the same time I—you—

JAMES ACTOR: *(Interrupting, hard.)* I know. *(More calmly.)* Keep reading.

SEVERINO ACTOR: *(Reading.)* He is overwhelmed. "My God, the words are appearing at the same time I—you." The James Actor, interrupting, hard. "I know." More calmly. "Keep reading." *(Stunned, he moves to above the* pūneʻe, *behind the table, giving the manuscript to* JAMES ACTOR *as he goes.)*

JAMES ACTOR: *(Reading from the manuscript.)* Stunned, he moves to above the *pūneʻe,* behind the table, giving the manuscript to James Actor as he goes. . . . In a moment, he comes around and sits on the *pūneʻe,* not quite daring to look at James Actor directly. . . .

(All of which SEVERINO ACTOR *does as the words are read.* JAMES ACTOR *turns the pages rapidly, urgently, looking ahead. They are evidently all blank, adding to his mounting fear. He closes the manuscript, sets it aside on the end table. There is a fairly prolonged silence.)*

SEVERINO ACTOR: *(In a small voice, lost.)* What is it?

JAMES ACTOR: Everything we've said—done—as ourselves, actors, as characters in this play—everything—is all written down up to this point, then—nothing—just blank pages . . .

SEVERINO ACTOR: *(Urgently.)* What's happening? Who are we?

JAMES ACTOR: I know what I'm going to say in the next scene . . . *(Points to the script.)* But it doesn't know. And it won't until I say it. Then it'll become part of the script. . . . *(Looks at the script again, picks it up, opens it, finds the right page. He reads in a flat, resigned tone.)* . . . But it doesn't know. And it won't until I say it. Then it'll become part of the script.

(A rage wells up suddenly and, rising, he hurls the manuscript onto the pūneʻe. *He moves upstage, his back to* SEVERINO ACTOR, *who stares at him in dread realization.)*

SEVERINO ACTOR: You're lying. . . . You don't know what you're going to say in the next scene. . . .

JAMES ACTOR: *(Too hard.)* The hell I don't!

SEVERINO ACTOR: Okay. Your opening line. Say it!

JAMES ACTOR: What'n hell's the matter with you?

SEVERINO ACTOR: Say it! Say it!

*(*JAMES ACTOR, *tense, trapped, only stares at* SEVERINO ACTOR, *as if to outface him.)*

SEVERINO ACTOR: You—don't—know! My God, you don't know . . .

JAMES ACTOR: How do you expect me to play the scene—without Julia—and the telephone—the telephone starts it all . . .

SEVERINO ACTOR: I'll be the telephone. . . . Brrrrinnggg brrrinnggg brrrinnggg. . . . Your opening line, James. What is it? Say it! . . . Brrrinnggg brrrinnggg brrrinnggg!

(JAMES ACTOR *turns on his heel, moves to the left.*)

JAMES ACTOR: *(Calling offstage, irritated.)* Julia! We're going to start! *(Louder.)* Julia! Julia! *(To* SEVERINO ACTOR:) Where the hell is she?

(JULIA ACTRESS *appears on the porch, moving in from upstage left. She is in a gardening frock, and she carries a basket of freshly cut flowers.*)

JULIA ACTRESS: Right here. Where the hell should I be?

JAMES ACTOR: Oh. . . . Well. . . . We're ready to start. . . . *(To* SEVERINO ACTOR:) I'll show you. *(He goes off at the left.)*

JULIA ACTRESS: It's about time.

(*She, too, goes off, on the porch.* SEVERINO ACTOR *moves to the side table by the* pūne'e. *He waits as the play lights come on. Then he moves to the right, always facing the set as he goes.*)

SEVERINO ACTOR: *(The telephone.)* Brrinnggg! Brrinnggg!

(*He continues backing to just off right, where he goes on making the telephone sound, intent on the play. He stops as* JAMES, *now in a smoking jacket, enters from the left, hurries to the phone, picks the receiver up.*)

JAMES: *(Into the phone.)* Hello—oh, hello, Ray. . . . No, no, I was just in the coffee making some kitchen. . . . No, nothing, really. . . . Just—out of breath—running for the phone. . . . Yes, Julia said you had the papers all ready for signing this after—three o'clock?

(*During the preceding,* SEVERINO ACTOR *moves in close to* JAMES, *intent on him, all the time making the telephone sound—"brrinngg brrinngg!"—right in* JAMES' *face.* JAMES *pays no attention; it is as if* SEVERINO ACTOR *did not exist.* SEVERINO ACTOR *waves a hand back and forth close to* JAMES' *eyes. Nothing.*)

JAMES: Yes, she said you would. . . . But Ray, Ray, listen. Something has happened, something very—well—crucial—and—no, no, nothing's gone wrong. No, really. . . . It's just that something has happened and I can't see you this afternoon. . . .

(He does not notice that, behind him, on the front porch, JULIA has entered with her basket of flowers. She puts the basket down and listens. SEVERINO ACTOR sees her, moves to the front door, blocking it. As she listens, JULIA moves to the door, eyes intent on JAMES at the phone, oblivious of SEVERINO ACTOR. Meanwhile:)

JAMES: Well, something out of the ordinary. . . . Damn it, Ray, nothing's wrong with me. Or Julia. . . . It's just that, well, I've got second thoughts about selling the house. . . .

(At the door, JULIA reacts with shock at this. She does not seem to be aware of SEVERINO ACTOR's presence at the doorway by her side. He stares at her face.)

SEVERINO ACTOR: (Yelling very loudly directly at JULIA.) Julia!

(No reaction of any kind from JULIA, who is intent on JAMES, appalled.)

JAMES: (Into phone.) No, that's what I said. . . . Ray, just give me three or four days to—
SEVERINO ACTOR: (Another loud yell inches from JULIA, who still doesn't hear.) Julia!
JAMES: (Continuing over the yell.) . . . What do you mean you can't wait? . . . Well, if that's their attitude, tell them the deal's off. . . . (JULIA charges into the room for JAMES.) No, I mean it. It's off, Ray. Off!

(He hangs up in agitation. JULIA stares at him in utter disbelief. Seeing her now, JAMES is all irritated, self-righteous, phone-pointing, nearly shouting.)

JAMES: Can you believe that Ray Tanaka? Trying to armtwist me into a snap decision. "My people can't wait, Jimmy boy!" . . . Where does he come off? (As if spitting.) Jimmy boy!
JULIA: I can't believe my ears . . .
JAMES: He was going to bring a whole bunch of his friends up here for the signing—and a party! Tokyo big shots, he says. . . . Can you imagine? I sign away my heritage, they throw a party . . .

JULIA: You gave your word!

JAMES: That was before . . .

JULIA: Before what?

JAMES: Before my people's most sacred goddess came to me! (*Moves to the chair by the* pūne'e *and sits.*) I'm sorry. I'm not selling the house.

SEVERINO ACTOR: (*To* JULIA.) You don't hear me, you don't see me . . . (*Points to* JAMES.) He doesn't either. . . . I don't exist.

(JULIA *crosses to the* pūne'e, *sits not too near* JAMES. *We can see now that she is still quite shaken from her previous ordeal with the* OLD WOMAN.)

SEVERINO ACTOR: I'm not real.

JULIA: (*A big attempt at calmness.*) James . . . I know what that— whatever—it—is—is . . . It's a horror, a horror from out of the grave, James. . . .

JAMES: (*Noticing that something is really wrong with her.*) Hey. . . . What's the matter?

(JULIA *covers her eyes; she has begun to weep quietly in terror and confusion.* JAMES *comes quickly to her, sitting close.*)

JAMES: Hey . . . hey! . . .

(JULIA *reaches for him, and he gathers her in his arms. She hangs on frantically.*)

JAMES: What's happened? What is it?

(*She quiets down a little. He lets her calm herself. Meanwhile:*)

SEVERINO ACTOR: (*To* JAMES.) And you, too! Both of you! You can talk to each other, but you can't talk to me. . . . (*Yells, very loud, right in* JAMES' *face:*) Talk to me! (*Not the slightest reaction, of course, from* JAMES.)

JAMES: (*To* JULIA.) Feeling better? (*She nods, not quite "together" yet; he pats her hand gently.*) Take your time. (*He gives her the time.*)

SEVERINO ACTOR: It's not me. . . . It's you! Oh, my God, it's you who aren't real. . . . (*He backs away for downstage left as the realization deepens.*) You're . . . you're just characters in a play, saying speeches someone wrote for you. . . . But I'm not in the play now. I'm not Severino now. Nobody wrote me. . . . I'm—*(He stops abruptly, now remembering.)* I'm—*(He sits at the proscenium downstage left, increasingly befuddled.)* I'm—*(He sits there, in deep troubled thought, staring out front. With quiet, desperate insistence:)* I'm not in a play, I'm not in a play, I'm not in a play . . . *(He draws his knees up, presses his face against them, withdraws into silence.)*

JAMES: Want to tell me now?

(She nods.)

JULIA: *(After a moment, softly; it's hard.)* James . . . a little while ago —after you went up with that old—young—woman . . . the old woman came down and— *(A sudden spasm of horror makes her stop.)*

JAMES: Hey . . . hey . . . *(He takes her hand, rubs it tenderly.)*

JULIA: I felt her hand, James. Her wrist. *(Another spasm stops her. He reaches for her.)* No, no. Really. I'm all right.

JAMES: Don't go on, don't, you don't have to.

JULIA: She had no pulse, James.

(SEVERINO ACTOR kneels in prayer, eyes closed. JAMES only looks at JULIA, as if not understanding.)

JULIA: She—had—no—pulse, James. She isn't alive. . . . She's—a horror.

JAMES: Honey . . . honey. . . . You can't just grab a wrist like that and expect to feel a pulse. . . .

JULIA: She offered her wrist to me. As if to dare me.

JAMES: A pulse isn't that easy to find.

JULIA: You don't believe it!

JAMES : It isn't a matter of believing, Julia. It's just—you're so over-wrought, needlessly, and—

JULIA: You don't believe me! *(She is on her feet, headed for the stairs.)*

JAMES: What are you doing?

JULIA: Calling her. Getting her down here. Feel for yourself.

JAMES: You can't do that!

JULIA: Why not?

JAMES: I mean—it's so—undignified. It's—silly—calling somebody down just to feel his pulse. Her.

JULIA: All right. You go up and get her.

JAMES: Julia, what's gotten into you? Why are you acting so— unreasonably?

JULIA: I'm acting unreasonably! *(She calls out the hallway downstage left.)* Ah Kiu! Ah Kiu!

JAMES: What're you doing now?

JULIA: If you won't go up and get her, Ah Kiu will. *(Calling.)* Ah Kiu!

(AH KIU appears at the head of the stairs.)

AH KIU: Whaaat?

JULIA: *(To JAMES.)* Tell him.

JAMES: *(Sighing, giving in.)* What is the old woman doing, Ah Kiu?

AH KIU: No ol' woman. . . . Only girl now—pretty girl.

JAMES: Can she come down for a minute?

AH KIU: No. Pretty girl very busy.

JAMES: *(To JULIA, relieved.)* There you are. She's too busy.

JULIA: Busy doing what?

AH KIU: Puttin' on dress. White dress. Blue dress. Red dress.

JULIA: My clothes! She's trying on my clothes!

AH KIU: White dress, very pretty.

JULIA: Tell her to take it off! Right now!

AH KIU: Oh yes. More better no dress. Very pretty girl. *(He turns to go.)* Nice ʻōkole.

(He goes off. JULIA, boiling, comes back to JAMES, who is now on the pūneʻe.)

JULIA: The nerve! The unmitigated nerve! *(She sits on the pūneʻe, boiling.)*

JAMES ACTOR: *(Mumbling, really sore.)* Get it right, for Christ's sake! "The goddamned nerve!" That's the line.

JULIA ACTRESS: *(Between her teeth.)* No decent Hawaiian would say a word like that.

JAMES ACTOR: No goddamned Hawaiian would use a word like "unmitigated." You ever hear a goddamned Hawaiian say "unmitigated"?

(A moment. She looks at him with withering scorn.)

JULIA ACTRESS: Asshole. You mind if we go on with the play? You're supposed to take my hand, okay?

JAMES ACTOR: Okay. But please get the lines right!

JULIA ACTRESS: *(Exploding.)* Who the hell do you think you are? You the writer, you the playwright?

JAMES ACTOR: *(Exploding.)* No!

JULIA ACTRESS: You want to get lines right, get it right back there in my scene with Severino and Ah Kiu!

JAMES ACTOR: Oh, Jesus! What scene?

JULIA ACTRESS: The one back there. Before. Where they tell me it wasn't you came up to my bed last night, it was a Hawaiian man. . . .

JAMES ACTOR: What now? What's wrong with it?

JULIA ACTRESS: How did they know? All of a sudden they know. What were they doing? Looking through the keyhole? The only person who knew the Hawaiian man came up to the bedroom was the playwright. And what? The playwright told them?

JAMES ACTOR: Why not? It's his play. He can put any words he likes in anybody's mouth!

JULIA ACTRESS: It isn't done that way in a play! Knowledge has got to come logically in the world of the play. . . . It doesn't come out of nowhere, like it's straight from God. Gods have got to play by the rules, too.

JAMES ACTOR: *(Wild, mocking.)* Listen, listen to her! Listen to the big words. Now who's the friggin' playwright! "Knowledge has got to come logically in the world of the play!" Where do you come off?

(She pauses, gathers herself. She draws herself up, points a very deliberate finger at him.)

JULIA ACTRESS: Just don't shoot your mouth off about getting lines right. Okay?

(A moment.)

JAMES ACTOR: *(Mumbling.)* Let's get on with it.

(He takes his place; she joins him. He takes her hand as she starts to speak.)

JULIA: The nerve! The unmitigated nerve!

JULIA ACTRESS: Oh, God. No, no. I say the line—then you take my hand.

JAMES ACTOR: *(Withdrawing his hand.)* I know.

JULIA ACTRESS: Then let's get it right!

(A moment.)

JULIA: The nerve! The unmitigated nerve!

(He takes her hand.)

JAMES: *(Gently.)* Julia . . . Julia honey, listen.
JULIA: My clothes! She's putting on my clothes!
JAMES: Julia, listen.
JULIA: Sell the house, James.
JAMES: No.
JULIA: Let the new owners worry about her.
JAMES: *(Big.)* No!

(It stops her.)

JAMES : Now, listen to me. . . . In this house, up there, is a Hawaiian goddess. The first. The most sacred. The builder. The
creator. Pele. Up there, Julia. In that bedroom. In this house.
. . . We've heard of people seeing Pele, but never, never of her
moving in, living with—very well, sleeping with them . . . and
it's happening to us, Julia. . . . She's here.
JULIA: *(Now on her feet.)* And I'm going!

(She heads for the stairs. JAMES is after her.)

JAMES: Where?
JULIA: Out! Out of this house, out of your life! As soon as I get my
clothes back!
JAMES: Julia, Julia—listen: Of all the people, of all the Hawaiians
on this earth, we—we, Julia—have been chosen. . . . Why, Julia?
Don't you want to find out?
JULIA: No!

*(She turns again to go up the steps, but JAMES runs past her, up a couple
of steps, and blocks her way.)*

JAMES: Julia! Julia! No! Think!
JULIA: Get out of my way!
JAMES: Think, Julia! Our gods have chosen us! Doesn't that mean
anything to you?
JULIA: Your gods may have chosen you, but I won't have anything
to do with this travesty of a—

JAMES: *(Loud, furious.)* Then, goddamn it, what kind of a god do you want? *(The fury of the question and its import stop* JULIA *cold. He goes right on, passionately, but in control.)* If you find this a vulgar—

JULIA: —disgusting—

JAMES: —disgusting caricature of what a Hawaiian god should be like, then—Julia— *(She turns away to go.)* Julia— *(Reluctantly she looks back again.)* It is important you answer that. *(A pause for emphasis.)* What kind of a god do you want? Do any of us want? *(She cannot answer. She sits.)* Don't you see now? Don't you see why she came?

JULIA: *(Silently.)* No.

JAMES: It isn't that she's disgusting, Julia. No, no. That's not fair. Gauche, perhaps. Naive, primitively so. But surely not disgusting.

JULIA: *(Softly.)* She's disgusting.

JAMES: *(Oh so reasonably!)* She's pitiful, Julia! Call her a caricature if you like. But who did that to her? Who reduced that awesome figure of fire and fury to this—shriveled, ashen mockery of her former greatness, her former majesty, Julia?

JULIA: *(Right at him, but gently.)* You're an ass, James.

JAMES: *(Pressing.)* Us, Julia! We—

JULIA: You really are. . . . A pompous—

JAMES: —we ourselves—

JULIA: —self-infatuated

JAMES: —we Hawaiians—

JULIA: —ass.

JAMES: And she has come here to us so that we might teach her how she might once again be—

JULIA: *(More voice now.)* James?

JAMES: —a god or goddess relevant to our people at this time, and—

JULIA: *(Stronger.)* James! *(He stops.)* I said: you're a pompous ass!

JAMES: *(Undeterred.)* No no, Julia. You must try, you really must try to understand. . . . *(He sits beside her.)* If she came down those stairs now, and stood before you, and asked you: "What do you want me to be like?" What would you say? *(No response from* JULIA.*)* There's nothing pompous or asinine about that. . . . What would you like god—your god—to be like, Julia? *(He gets up and goes to the downstage left hall entrance. Calls:)* Severino! Ah Kiu! Severino! . . . I want you in here!

(At the first call of his name, SEVERINO ACTOR *gets up and goes off between the downstage left tormentor and curtain.)*

JULIA: What are you doing?

JAMES: Severino and Ah Kiu should be asked the same question. She came to them, too.

JULIA: And after you've heard our druthers, you'll just put them all together in a little list, hand it to her, and say, "Be this!"

JAMES: Of course not. She probably can't read.

(SEVERINO *appears in the hall downstage left.*)

JAMES: Ah, Severino! Come in, come in . . .

(SEVERINO *moves to the foot of the stairs.* AH KIU *appears at the top.*)

JAMES: Come on down, Ah Kiu. We're going to have a little talk down here. A very important little talk. (*To* SEVERINO:) Sit, sit.

(SEVERINO *sits at the bottom of the stairs,* AH KIU *at the top.* JULIA *remains on the* pūne'e. *And* JAMES *has all of the center stage to himself—and does he use it.*)

JAMES: Well . . . here we are. . . . Now, Severino, Ah Kiu, it is my contention that Pele has come to us for a reason so important that it challenges our very right to live.

(SEVERINO *and* AH KIU *just stare at him, now puzzled, but as* JAMES *continues, with growing incomprehension.*)

JAMES: Now—let me review with you what has happened.

JULIA: (*Sinking back with a groan.*) Oh, God!

JAMES: Last evening, at dusk, Ah Kiu was building a fire, and—ah yes! (*Goes to the piece of wood at the fireplace.*) Here it is! . . . When Ah Kiu placed this piece of wood in the fire, the whole house was filled with the most agonized, heartbroken sobbing. . . .

JULIA: (*Sitting up.*) I didn't hear any sobbing.

JAMES: Ah Kiu, tell her.

AH KIU: Yes. Wahine cry. Whole house cry.

JULIA: Ridiculous! I didn't hear anything.

AH KIU: 'Cause you haole, 'ass why. You one white Hawaiian.

JULIA: (*To* JAMES.) Are you going to allow him to talk to me like that?

JAMES: Oh come on, come on . . . both of you. . . . This is serious. Look at that. (*Hands her the piece of wood.*) Look at that. Carefully. See? A woman's face. . . . (*She studies the piece of wood, not too impressed.*) So! She announced herself . . . I emphasize again . . . in unbearable grief. Like a voice from the dead, crying death, not only her death but our death, too, . . . the death of a people. . . .

SEVERINO: (*The beginnings of hysteria.*) But flease, I am Pilipino, I am not Hawaiian. . . . I do not wish to—

JAMES: (*To* SEVERINO.) Wait! Wait, brother! We are all brothers! Wait! You will see! (*Once again lecturing.*) And so, Julia's Volkswagen—bang in the 'ōkole—the old lady is brought in—Pele.

(*Unnoticed by the others—so intent are they on* JAMES *and so intent is* JAMES *on himself—*JULIA *goes to the fireplace, lights it.*)

JAMES: Now! Now! What kind of god is it that visits us? Eh, Severino, what kind?

SEVERINO: *Māhū.* . . . One naughty *māhū* . . .

JAMES: Right! A smelly, dirty, alcohol-swizzling old crone who is also a beautiful, sexually sa-tis-fac-tory girl. . . .

SEVERINO: Oh, yes sir!

JAMES: A man. A virile one hundred percent throbbing phallus of a man. . . . Then, if you've got a female god who is also a male god, what about the god from whose thigh his only true begotten son was born? What about him, her, it? What about it, them, us? All in one! Trinity, the true trinity! (*He has whipped himself up into quite a state.*) Don't you see why she came?

SEVERINO: She's all mixed up!

JULIA: Oh, for God's sake! Of all the asinine—!

(*She is about to get up, to go, but* JAMES *says to her:*)

JAMES: No, no. He's right. . . . He's right! . . . Poor Pele, she no longer knows what she is, what to be! . . . Poor us! Poor Hawaiians, we no longer know who we were or who we are. . . . How then can we live into the future if—if—

(JULIA *has already put the piece of wood into the fire, has been watching it catch on fire.* . . . JAMES *moves to her, seeing, concerned.*)

JAMES: What the hell are you doing?

JULIA: Just—seeing . . .

JAMES: Seeing what, for Christ's sake? Damn it, the thing's on fire! Really on fire! Ah Kiu, help me, get it out, quick, quick!

(He keeps reaching into the fire to retrieve the piece of wood, and each time withdraws his hand in pain. AH KIU *rushes down to his side.)*

JULIA: I was just—seeing if it would cry. Like you said. . . . It isn't crying.
JAMES: Get a cloth, get a—something—here—no—grab it from this side. . . . (AH KIU *keeps reaching in, pulling his hand back in pain.)* Grab it! Grab it!
AH KIU: No can . . . no can . . .

(And they can only watch in growing despair.)

JAMES: *(Softly, heartbroken.)* Oh, my God, oh, my God . . .
JULIA: She didn't cry! You said she would cry! She didn't!
JAMES: *(Snapping, hard.)* Oh, shut up! *(He moves away, sits, staring at the floor.)*
JULIA: *(Hurt.)* What did you say? *(He just stares at the floor.)* I only wanted to see if—if what you said was true. . . . James, I wanted to hear it. I didn't believe you, but I wanted to hear it! *(No response in any way from* JAMES.) Damn it, James, I'm sorry! *(In anguished self-defense:)* All right. A damned piece of firewood. So, I burnt it! . . . So it's burnt! So what?

(She turns on her heel and stomps away defiantly. She sits left of the pune'e. *The silence grows, and it makes her feel even more guilty. Finally:)*

JULIA: *(Exploding.)* Well, why doesn't anybody say something?

(She slumps in despair. AH KIU *moves down to* JAMES, *concerned for him. He touches* JAMES' *cheek gently.)*

AH KIU: *(Gently.)* Kimo . . . Kimo . . .
JAMES: *(Quietly.)* I had—I had the strangest feeling then, as the wood burned. . . . A voice, but maybe more feeling than sound, like talk in a dream, saying silently, " 'Ua noa."
AH KIU: *(Always gently.)* Yes. Ah Kiu hear too.
JULIA: Hear what?
AH KIU: Pele. She say, " 'Ua noa."
JULIA: And what's that supposed to mean?
SEVERINO: *(Like a quiet realization.)* They're free!
JULIA: *(To the heavens!)* Suddenly it speaks Hawaiian! Great! Okay, Mister Mary Puku'i, what does it mean?

SEVERINO: I don't know. I jes' speak!

JULIA: Oh, Jesus! Jesus! (*To* AH KIU:) Free of what? Who?

AH KIU: I think so they goin' away now . . .

JULIA: Good riddance!

JAMES: (*To* AH KIU.) Go . . . go upstairs! See where they are, if they're really going . . .

(AH KIU *moves for the stairs, not hurrying but as if drawn there. He looks back at* JAMES *in sorrow as he goes.*)

JAMES: Go on, go on. . . . Hurry, Ah Kiu . . .

(JAMES *still stares at the floor, as if in a trance.* SEVERINO *rises, steps in* AH KIU*'s way, scared.*)

SEVERINO: Ah Kiu, no. Don't. Stay here.

JULIA ACTRESS: (*To* SEVERINO.) What the hell is he talking about?

SEVERINO ACTOR: He doesn't need them anymore.

JULIA ACTRESS: Doesn't—need—? Who?

(SEVERINO ACTOR *and* JAMES ACTOR *exchange a look across the stage.* SEVERINO ACTOR *moves to* JULIA ACTRESS *at the* pūneʻe, *sits with her.*)

SEVERINO ACTOR: He who created us, made us . . .

JULIA ACTRESS: Why are you dragging God into this? What's God got to do with anything anyway?

JAMES ACTOR: You misunderstand. Try. Try to understand. Calmly.

(JULIA ACTRESS *looks at* SEVERINO ACTOR *for her answer. He averts his eyes.*)

SEVERINO ACTOR: (*Simply, almost apologetically.*) Well, okay. He who wrote us.

JAMES ACTOR: That's better.

JULIA ACTRESS: (*To* SEVERINO ACTOR.) He who wro—? I can't believe what I'm hearing, what I think I'm hearing. . . . Say it again, say what you said again. . . .

SEVERINO ACTOR: (*As simply as before, but right at her now.*) He who wrote us.

JULIA ACTRESS: *(Quiet incredulity.)* You're nuts. . . . *(Protest grows.)* You're out of your friggin'—wrote us? You said, Wrote us!

(JAMES ACTOR has turned to the window and is looking out.)

JAMES ACTOR: Yes.

JULIA ACTRESS: *(Getting it straight.)* You're telling me—wait, wait—you're telling me I'm not in a theater, that there aren't signs out there, seats, lights, that these aren't flats—that I'm not me, that I'm—I think I'm going out of my mind—written! *(She starts to laugh. It's a bit hysterical.)* Written! *(The hysteria grows as the laughter grows.)* C.A.T. Cat, me. P.E.R.S.O.N. Person. Hey, Ma, looka me, looka me, I'm written. . . . I.M.P.L.A.U.S.I.B.L.E. Ridiculous, me. A.N.T.I.D.I.S.E.S.T.A.B.L.I.S.H.M.E.N.T.A.R.-I.A.N.I.S.M. Antidisestablishmentarianism. Mama, Mama, I'm a big word. . . . *(The hysteria dies down as:)* W.O.R.D. Word. . . . I'm a— *(She reaches out to SEVERINO ACTOR in vague supplication.)* And you—?

SEVERINO ACTOR: *(Softly.)* In the Beginning, there was the Word. . . . Written . . .

JULIA ACTRESS: *(To JAMES ACTOR.)* You—?

JAMES ACTOR: And the Word was with—

JULIA ACTRESS: *(Snaps!)* Okay! All right! Amen!! *(She moves to go, babbling low.)* That's it! That ties it! I'm outa here!

JAMES ACTOR: You can't!

JULIA ACTRESS: And why the hell not? I'm getting outa this booby hatch! *(She gets as far as the door to the porch.)*

JAMES ACTOR: *(Suddenly shouting, out of patience.)* He isn't finished with you!

JULIA ACTRESS: *(Right back at him.)* But I'm finished with him! So, I tell you what I'm going to do: I'm going to walk out of this theater like I should've done long before this. And don't wait up for me. It's going to be a long, long wait!

(She starts to go. JAMES ACTOR reaches through the porch window and grabs her hand.)

JAMES ACTOR: Wait! I'll tell you what you're going to do.

JULIA ACTRESS: Let me go. *(She tries to free her hand; he has too firm a hold.)*

JAMES ACTOR: You're going to walk off this porch, go around behind that wall . . . *(And with her free hand, he indicates the wall to the left of them.*) . . . and reenter through that hallway entrance. *(He has let her go, as he points to the hallway arch downstage left. She steps back glaring at him.)* You will come back in here, in terror, and sit on that chair—*(The one by the* pūneʻe.*)*—and you won't remember going from this exit to that entrance. A blank. Because off this stage, you don't exist. There is no you. And you will sit in that chair, and you will say only one thing: Holy Mary, Mother of God, in whom, like Him, we have our being and our becoming, help me.

JULIA ACTRESS: *(Holding her look of cold contempt, leaning closer to his face.)* Drop—dead! *(She goes along the porch and off at upstage left.)*

SEVERINO ACTOR: Are you sure?

JAMES ACTOR: Yes.

SEVERINO ACTOR: How? How do you know?

JAMES ACTOR: I don't.

SEVERINO ACTOR: You sounded so sure.

JAMES ACTOR: I know. The words just came.

(SEVERINO ACTOR goes to the chair by the pūneʻe. *He straightens it. Then:)*

SEVERINO ACTOR: What if—one time—I made up my own mind not to say the words he puts in my mouth but—

JAMES ACTOR: I know: other words, your own words, of your own free will . . .

SEVERINO ACTOR: Yes.

JAMES ACTOR: *(Shaking his head.)* You have no will of your own. Only the illusion that you are the one thinking, choosing, deciding. But all that is in his mind, not yours. . . . It's still—his words.

(They stop—for JULIA ACTRESS has appeared in the hallway entrance at downstage left. She seems to "come to" there: she looks back where she came from, thinks, seems befuddled, increasingly so, then terror hits her. She comes to the chair by the pūneʻe *and sits. She is trembling, very near a severe "break." Finally, in abject horror:)*

JULIA ACTRESS: Holy Mary, Mother of God, in whom, like Him, we have our being and our becoming, help me.

(And the break comes. A low wail rises, her hands come to her face as the sobbing begins, and then she bends forward, face to her lap, as the sobs keep

coming, shaking her whole body pitifully. Nearby, SEVERINO ACTOR *and* JAMES ACTOR *sit turning away, looking down—out of sympathy and respect.*

But from the start of her sobbing, the PELE ACTOR *has appeared offstage, downstage right, and is moving up to the improvised dressing table offstage at upstage right. He seats himself there and, for the rest of the scene that follows, busies himself removing his wig, makeup, costume, all of which he places precisely where they were when he first entered in Act 1 and began to put on makeup and costume.*

Then, gradually, the awful sobbing is over. There is a very slow stirring into life from SEVERINO ACTOR *and* JAMES ACTOR. JULIA ACTRESS *slowly raises her head; she stares straight ahead, forlorn, spent, numbed.)*

JAMES ACTOR: *(Softly, with great sympathy.)* How are you?

JULIA ACTRESS: *(Almost inaudibly.)* All right.

JAMES ACTOR: Truly?

JULIA ACTRESS: *(Inaudibly.)* Yes. *(But she nods slightly, slowly.)*

JAMES ACTOR: What do you remember?

JULIA ACTRESS: Only—only walking off the set, and then suddenly standing down there.... *(She indicates the downstage left hall entrance.)* Nothing else.... It is as if I didn't exist in between. *(A little life returns to her voice.)* But I do exist.... I'm an actress. In a theater. Playing the part of Julia.... Julia was written. I am real. I am really real. In a real theater. *(Again a pause. Again she is staring out front.)*

JAMES ACTOR: What do you see?

JULIA ACTRESS: I can't see, for the darkness.

JAMES ACTOR: What did you think you would see?

JULIA ACTRESS: People perhaps. An audience ... *(Pause.)* Is there an audience?

*(*JAMES ACTOR *doesn't answer.)*

JULIA ACTRESS: Are there people?

JAMES ACTOR: *(Softly.)* I don't know. *(To* SEVERINO ACTOR:*)* There could be. Perhaps, even, there should be. But—*(He shakes his head; he really doesn't know.)*

SEVERINO ACTOR: Even if there were, there's no use trying to talk to them.... It would be like your trying to talk to Julia, or me trying to talk to Severino.... They wouldn't hear. They can't talk back to you. . . . (*Gestures toward the audience.*) We can't talk back to them, can't hear them. . . . Can only hope and pray that they are there . . .

JAMES ACTOR: I don't think they are. . . . (*To* JULIA ACTRESS:) I'm sorry.

(*She only looks down. Pause.*)

JAMES ACTOR: Are you afraid?

JULIA ACTRESS: Are you?

JAMES ACTOR: (*After a moment.*) No. I don't think so.

JULIA ACTRESS: (*After a moment.*) Written . . .

JAMES ACTOR: Yes.

JULIA ACTRESS: No. I think I am—well—not afraid, but—well— it's like waiting—waiting to be afraid, or maybe not—I think, I think the only way you can be afraid is if there's a you that knows what it is to be afraid. . . . And—if there's no—me—? (*A pause. A shudder seems to run through her, then she is quiet.*)

JAMES ACTOR: Sometimes, walking at dusk or at dawn, in another country—England, Denmark, Scotland, France, Italy—I would turn a corner and, there, suddenly, before me would be a view, a building, a little chapel, a great cathedral—monuments of the indomitable playing and singing of the human spirit—and then, as suddenly, the frightening thought would overwhelm me: I wasn't real, I was dead: I had made myself up, a fiction. It kept happening over and over, each time more frightening than before. . . . I kept saying to myself: Be proud. You are a Hawaiian, an ancient and proud people, conquerors of the Pacific, discoverers and settlers of half the world. . . . But still it happened, still I felt lost, still I lived in increasing terror. . . . I started asking, what does that mean? What does it mean to be a Hawaiian? . . . I started to strip away all my pretensions and fantasies about myself. . . . The false wig, the false face, the fake costume. . . . And finally, beneath it all, there was a nothing. . . .

(*At his dressing table, the* PELE ACTOR *is all but finished divesting himself of his makeup and costume. He is not Hawaiian, nor is there the least hint of "female impersonator" about him. He busies himself hanging up his costume and putting things back as they were before the play started.*)

JAMES ACTOR: You can only define a Hawaiian today by what he has lost—by what he no longer is or can ever be again. I learned that.

(He sits close to JULIA ACTRESS, addressing her in deepest sincerity. She is completely pulled in by him, but something very troubling has hit SEVERINO ACTOR. He gets up, moves to the porch window, looks out. He is struggling to find the words for something.)

JAMES ACTOR: And that is a death beyond all hope. . . . And I thought: If you go home, you might find that you were wrong. . . . And so I came home. . . .

JULIA ACTRESS: And—? *(No answer.)* What did you find?

JAMES ACTOR: That I wasn't wrong. But then, in this old house, sitting here among the things my parents had loved, and their parents before them, I slid quite naturally into a solution. . . . You see, if I really admitted to myself that we were finally and utterly dead, I would go uncontrollably mad. . . . I watched the other Hawaiians, and do you know?

JULIA ACTRESS: What?

JAMES ACTOR: They were wonderfully and delightfully mad, but controllably mad! They have all assumed roles, as if in a play they are all acting out, author unknown. . . . They are all fictions, inventions, words—even the angry protestors, perhaps worst of all, the angry protestors . . .

JULIA ACTRESS: *(Getting angry.)* And you—?

JAMES ACTOR: I put my costume back on and rejoined my people, James Dixon-Wentworth Alama!

(During the preceding, JAMES ACTOR has slipped gradually into the voice, diction, gestures of JAMES.)

JAMES ACTOR: We remake ourselves. Death masks that can yet sing, speak, smile—and smile—and smile. . . . *(He begins to sing, in Hawaiian, a popular old hula; his hands begin to dance.)*

JULIA ACTRESS: Stop it!

JAMES ACTOR: *(Imitating.)* Oh, I got so much aloha for you, my dear!

(He sings and dances for a moment or two longer before JULIA ACTRESS' hand lashes across his face. She is on her feet and moving away. At the window, in tremendous rage, she whirls around, yelling at JAMES ACTOR.)

JULIA ACTRESS: You sonofabitch!

(JAMES ACTOR *remains seated, rubbing his cheek, withdrawn. Strangely moved to a kind of awe,* SEVERINO ACTOR *comes to him.*)

SEVERINO ACTOR: What made you speak like that?
JAMES ACTOR: Speak like what?
SEVERINO ACTOR: Like you just did.
JAMES ACTOR: How was that?
SEVERINO ACTOR: Like you were James.
JAMES ACTOR: Just—words . . . *(He shrugs.)*
SEVERINO ACTOR: No. It was different. It was James who was here. It was James who was talking. Not you.

(JAMES ACTOR'*s look—uncomprehending, a little dazed—works on* SEVERINO ACTOR.)

SEVERINO ACTOR: Oh, my God! You don't even know.

(JAMES ACTOR *looks down, avoiding* SEVERINO ACTOR'*s look.* SEVERINO ACTOR *moves away, overwhelming feeling welling up rapidly.*)

SEVERINO ACTOR: Then it's possible! Miracles are possible! *(He sits, deeply moved, and crosses himself.)*
JULIA ACTRESS: What the hell are you doing?
SEVERINO ACTOR: It can't just be words! I know that now! I know, I know!
JULIA ACTRESS: Then what is it? What happened to me back there?
JAMES ACTOR: You were written going offstage and written reappearing at downstage left. You weren't written in between . . .
SEVERINO ACTOR: *(Quiet conviction.)* But you existed. Oh, I know now! You were held in his mind.
JULIA ACTRESS: Whose mind?
SEVERINO ACTOR: He who made us.
JAMES ACTOR: He who wrote us. Who is writing us. Even now. At this moment.
JULIA ACTRESS: If some jerk is writing us, all this is—this whole silly business is—he's shooting his mouth off. His hangups, that's all this is.

JAMES ACTOR: He's working himself out. To find himself. Create himself. And in that work, he needs us. He becomes himself, through us. . . . He needs us, desperately. *(He and* SEVERINO ACTOR *are "locked" across the room.)* I take comfort in that.
JULIA ACTRESS: *(Her confusion rising in rage.)* Oh, bullshit! Bullshit! . . . Why, oh why, why did I ever get mixed up with—this—you! *(She sits, covering her eyes with one hand.)*
JAMES ACTOR: It's why we were made, why anybody is made. . . . To be mixed up—in this—with him.

(There is a longish pause.)

SEVERINO ACTOR: *(Always quietly.)* You said it would all end in laughter. Howling laughter.
JAMES ACTOR: It will.
SEVERINO ACTOR: She doesn't feel like laughing. . . . Do you?
JAMES ACTOR: It hasn't ended yet. *(He rises to help* JULIA ACTRESS *up.)*
SEVERINO ACTOR: Do you know how it's going to end?
JAMES ACTOR: No. Of course not. . . . Anyway, it's too soon for endings—if there ever are endings. *(He touches* JULIA ACTRESS *gently. She looks at him submissively, takes his offered hand, rises.)* Come. . . . We have to go back to the beginning.
JULIA ACTRESS: *(Terribly exhausted, a weak protest.)* Oh, why? Why can't we just exit?
JAMES ACTOR: We can't.
JULIA ACTRESS: I'm tired. I can't go through all this again. . . . Why can't we just disappear, like that *māhū* with the maile wrapped all around him? . . . I need to rest.
JAMES ACTOR: He needs us. . . . He has made some mistakes that have to be corrected, different new tacks to try, those rewrites you wanted, a new way of hoping. . . . *(To* SEVERINO ACTOR:) You coming?
SEVERINO ACTOR: I'll be there.
JAMES ACTOR: Right.

(He takes JULIA ACTRESS *off at the left, above the stairs.* SEVERINO ACTOR *is still seated, lost in thought. He is only vaguely aware that* PELE ACTOR *has moved in and has stopped a little way from him. Finally, without turning to him,* SEVERINO ACTOR *raises his head, facing the front.)*

SEVERINO ACTOR: I know now. . . . Just as he writes us, so is he written. . . . The Creator who has created him creates us through him—so that He may, one day, with our help, achieve Himself . . .

PELE ACTOR: Don't think about it. . . .

SEVERINO ACTOR: But if He needs us, then He must try to reach us, from time to time. . . .

PELE ACTOR: You'll only make yourself the more unhappy.

SEVERINO ACTOR: But—for a little while, minutes ago, James was allowed to cross over into our world—I saw—I heard! A miracle! And if James could—then— *(He is intent on the cordless prop telephone.)* —then even if all the wires are cut, even if there are no wires, we can speak to Him, and He will speak to us. . . .

PELE ACTOR: Don't hurt yourself this way. . . . We have to start again, try again. . . . Now come . . .

SEVERINO ACTOR: He must, He must! It'd be too cruel for Him to remain silent like this. . . .

PELE ACTOR: Don't. Let's play again and, in our playing, perhaps one day—

SEVERINO ACTOR: *(Heartbroken.)* Father, O my Father, it has been so lonely without you.

(He covers his face, and PELE ACTOR *comes to him.)*

PELE ACTOR: You must have the courage to be happy. . . . *(No response.)* Let me tell you a story. Nothing real, just words put together to make a story. *(Sits beside* SEVERINO ACTOR, *putting an arm around his shoulder.)* Once, in a country, far far away, there was a young hunter who paused by a mountain pool to drink. As he bent forward, and just before his lips touched the water, he saw, right there, inches from his eyes, the reflection of a beautiful bird. *(Very slowly,* SEVERINO ACTOR *raises his face to* PELE ACTOR.) The colors of gold and sapphire, emerald and ruby and amethyst. The sheen of star and moon and sun. And on its breast, the purest white he had ever seen. . . . He turned quickly to look at the branch directly over his head, for that was surely where the bird stood—or should have. There was nothing there. There was no bird anywhere. An empty tree, an empty sky. . . . And so taken was the young hunter with that beauty that for the rest of his life, hunter became seeker. . . . He went everywhere, searching—searching for that beauty. . . . What was it? What had come to him, from beyond all dreaming and beyond all imagining? What? What? . . . And so he searched. . . . Finally, a great distance from home, alone, old and dying, his search a failure, he climbed to the peak of a mountain so high its peak was barren of all life. . . . And there, in final defeat, he would die. . . . Life started to ebb away. And just before the last light died out of his seeing, he called out the name of the other most beautiful thing he had ever known in his life: his mother's name. . . . *(He holds out a hand.)* And, like a gift from heaven, down from the sky, there fell into the palm of his dying hand, a single feather of purest white . . .

(With a slow, graceful upward move of his hand, he "captures" the imagined feather. He offers it tenderly to SEVERINO ACTOR, *then runs his hand gently along* SEVERINO ACTOR'*s cheek.)*

PELE ACTOR: Come. Let us try again. *(He helps* SEVERINO ACTOR *up, then leads him off.)* Gifts happen. Like miracles.

(He leads SEVERINO ACTOR *offstage above the stairs at the left. But just before they are off,* SEVERINO ACTOR, *who has been intent on the prop phone, reaches for it; his hand makes the same "feather catching" gesture that* PELE ACTOR *had made.)*

SEVERINO ACTOR: *(Like* SEVERINO, *very softly.)* Oh, fleece!

(And they are off. The stage is empty and nothing happens for a long time. Then the lights begin to fade, slowly, spots highlighting the cordless prop phone throughout the fade. Now the rest of the stage is spotlighted. Then those spots fade. And a moment before the spots are gone, the actors' general lighting bumps in abruptly.

The door of the closet by the lanai opens and, as at the start of the play, JULIA ACTRESS *steps out. She closes the closet door, comes down to the end table by the* pūne‘e, *takes the playscript from it, and exits downstage left with the script. The lights change to dusk, lanterns and lamps coming on.* JAMES ACTOR *enters, as in Act 1, pours sherry into two glasses. Then* JULIA ACTRESS *enters from the left holding the playscript against her breast. The lights begin to fade.)*

JAMES: Well—? How do you like my new play?

(As the lights fade to black, JAMES *and* JULIA *only mouth their dialogue. They raise their glasses for* JULIA'*s toast. We are in black.)*

Afterword: A Portrait of John Kneubuhl

John Alexander Kneubuhl was a complex man whose writing linked his Samoan roots, the New England literati of the late 1930s, and behind-the-scenes Hollywood. Known as Sione Nupo to his countrymen, Kneubuhl was a playwright, historian, and self-taught anthropologist whose work was meant to awaken Polynesians to their vanishing culture. With his lyrical command of English, he used words as weapons—prodding the sensitivities of his people, as well as those of his adopted Hawaiian home—in plays that brought together Polynesian characters and existential explorations of identity and the life force itself.

John Kneubuhl was a man of dichotomies: a realist but also a visionary; a historian but also a man tussling with contemporary Polynesian ways. A sage and a mystic at times, Kneubuhl was a bicultural Polynesian who used the medium of theater to explore identity, loneliness, and the craft required to bring them to the stage. By his own reckoning, using a phrase as honest as it was humorous, he was "the world's greatest Swiss/Welsh/Samoan playwright."

John Kneubuhl lived many lives. The first, in Samoa, featured lavalava in the village *fale* and crystal goblets in town. His mother's genealogy boasted a long line of highborn Samoan women who were related to one of the ruling royal families of Samoa, the Tupuas. It was that branch which intermarried with missionary stock involved in Christianizing the South Pacific from Tahiti to Tutuila, Kneubuhl's home island. His mother, whom Kneubuhl called a "dark-haired Greer Garson," was a talented pianist, singer, and painter who was sent to New Zealand at a very young age for a very British education. Kneubuhl's father was a navy surveyor from Iowa who settled in Samoa, opened a store, and found prosperity in the shipping business.

Kneubuhl was considered a special child from birth. Two stories marked that event. A number of native people claimed to have seen his grandmother's ghost leaning over his cradle to impart a shadowy kiss, then depart as quickly as she had appeared. Moreover, it was Samoan custom to take the newborn's umbilical cord, chant over it, then place it in the rafters of the Christian church. If it was left intact for a week, that meant the gods accepted the child, who would now grow up to be a good person and "a nice Christian." If it disappeared, that meant the rats dragged it away and Satan was rearing his ugly head. Kneubuhl's was gone within a half hour! Both stories point to the commingling of native sensibilities and deeply rooted Christian ideas that lived side-by-side in Kneubuhl's Samoa in the early 1900s.

John was a sickly child and was often sent to his maternal grandfather's village to shed his Western garb and romp with the native boys. At his father's table, however, he was expected to be a good little English-speaking American. The home at the edge of the naval base in Fagotogo boasted an impressive library of literary classics. As there were no children's books in the home, young John sated his curiosity with *The Merchant of Venice* and *The Jew of Malta*, his first readings in English. Secretly his mother collected his scribbled attempts at poetry in English and Samoan. Years later he commented that he was troubled at an early age by his bilingualism: "What bothered me was, what language did God speak? Because I did not know what language to pray to him at night. He can't speak English, I mean he knows how to speak English, but he wouldn't be listening to all the people, you know." These early stirrings heralded the beginning of Kneubuhl's discomfiture with his dual heritage.

When he was thirteen, John was sent to Hawai'i's elite Punahou School, where he became an outstanding athlete and concert pianist. He was known for running hurdles for the school's track team and playing piano at Honolulu Symphony rehearsals. He met his future wife, Dorothy Schenck, in the eighth grade at Punahou when she directed him in a class play. Her job was to make him whistle on his exit—an impossible task in John's eyes. Fifty years later, he was still talking about falling in love with "Dotsy" while she patiently tried to get him to squeak out a whistle. Their union was to become a lifetime partnership.

A major influence on John Kneubuhl during his Punahou years were his loving Hawai'i hosts, the Judds, who were of upper-crust missionary stock that ran in Hawai'i's Big Five business circle and socialized with Princess Kawananakoa. It was a "pampered life." Summer breaks were spent in Samoa, filled with visits to the *fale* of his childhood and a return to the duality of town formalities and village freedom.

High hopes for the aspiring pianist led Kneubuhl to Yale University, an educational tradition in the Judd family. It was Kneubuhl's dream to be one of the select students who worked year-round with the noted avant-garde composer Paul Hindemith. A class assignment led Kneubuhl to write a one-act Polynesian opera, but Hindemith rejected it immediately and urged Kneubuhl to try the creative writing program instead. He was admitted to Yale's Workshop 47 playwriting program, the only undergraduate to be allowed into the highly competitive clique. Within a few weeks he knew that he had found his life's work.

Under the masterful guidance of Walter Prichard Eaton, playwriting teacher at Yale, Kneubuhl became a protégé of the celebrated playwright Thornton Wilder during his senior year. He had previously seen Wilder's *Our Town* and was deeply taken by what he called "magic theater." Wilder was a loving taskmaster who decided that Kneubuhl would submit a one-act play to him each day for a month. Recounting those days, Kneubuhl said:

> He'd read it. He'd never say if it was good or bad or indifferent or whatever. He'd just say, "When are you going to learn to write freely? FREELY, FREELY, FREELY?!" . . . O.K., fine. So I'd go and write freely, freely, freely. I'd hand it to him. "Damn it! You MUST write with discipline. DISCIPLINE, DISCIPLINE, DISCIPLINE." He acted like a ping pong ball between freedom and discipline until all of a sudden I realized . . . where else does stylistic power come from? It is this constant attempt to resolve this tension between freedom and discipline, and that tension is what makes for power. . . . You learn how to think metaphorically. If the title contains something you can use metaphorically, you seek out the metaphor, and all of a sudden, there it is.

Success at Yale with two plays—particularly *The Sunset Crowd*—focused much attention on the young playwright. The idea of loneliness took on a poignant dimension in the play as teenage Samoan alcoholics live out their fantasies in the Sunset Bar. As they drink and drink, they find escape by jumping on a beer-soaked table and becoming an airplane to fly away. Kneubuhl described the action as "an escape from loneliness; an escape from pain; an escape from not knowing who they are. At the end of the play . . . they get on the airplane again and the mute sings, he suddenly sings, and they fly off to wherever Never-Never Land is."

John and Dotsy, now a student at Wellesley, married in 1942, two days before his graduation. He soon began a stint with U.S. Navy Intelligence as a Japanese language specialist. Then, after his discharge in Honolulu, the dream of every young writer began to unfold: a position was created for him as assistant director and resident playwright in Honolulu's premier community theater. Kneubuhl's early years at the Honolulu Community Theater were acclaimed as groundbreaking because he placed island life and island issues on the stage. Fresh out of Yale and the military, at age twenty-six, he had a lot to say about his craft when interviewed in a Honolulu newspaper:

> [He] feels there is a place for the new young writer, especially here in the islands of the Pacific where there is such a wealth of material that has so often been misrepresented by those who have not the understanding of Hawai'i's history nor know the truth of its future. He has a great respect for the technical proficiency of Broadway playwrights but says "they have been repeating themselves since 1930." His point concerning these playwrights is that they live in urban centers which force them to write out of psychological bankruptcy for audiences that are socially unproductive.[1]

Kneubuhl's 1946 production of *The Harp in the Willows*, written for the Honolulu Community Theater, was "hailed as the possible greening of island-created drama, praised in newspaper reviews and editorials, and sold out at the theater."[2] It was the story of missionary Lorenzo Lyons and his invaluable contributions to Hawaiian music. The Kaumakapili Choir sang the tunes and, as Kneubuhl explained, "spoke Hawaiian all over the stage."

Kneubuhl's characters spoke Creole English (Hawaiian pidgin) in the 1947 production of *This City Is Haunted*. He wrote the play after bristling at an editorial that demanded a ban on pidgin in schools, since he felt pidgin to be "a very poetic thing." The audience exploded in laughter at the first pidgin line—"Eh, Albert, howzit?"—and followed with a standing ovation for that very line. Kneubuhl was delighted.[3] His tutelage under Wilder was put to good use in *This City Is Haunted* with the metaphorical use of the title. As Kneubuhl said, "You realized it's just not the city of Honolulu that's haunted, it's the golden city of heaven. The moment you stumble on that, you say, 'I've got it!' It's about a preacher going crazy."

The year 1948 brought *The Sound of Hunting* to the Honolulu Community Theater, an adaptation of Harry Brown's Broadway play written for the 442nd Regimental Combat Team of Japanese-American soldiers. The response from the community was minimal —until reviews hit the newspapers and audiences from the Japanese community began to pack the theater. Indeed, it was popular enough to tour the state with a cast of eight neophyte actors. It was an energizing experience for Kneubuhl, who was hoisted aloft by the audience in Kaua'i as they cheered and wept in response. It was, he said, "one of the most thrilling things that has ever happened to me, the hold that *theater about themselves* could have on people."

Praise was heaped upon Kneubuhl for his scripting and direction in 1950 of the feature movie *Damien*, which was filmed on location in Kalaupapa with local actors and premiered at the Kūhiō Theater in Honolulu. It was a sign of good things to come in this new medium. The last play Kneubuhl wrote in this era, *Point Distress*, was called "an edge-of-the-seat thriller" by a *Honolulu Advertiser* writer, Edna B. Lawson.[4] Kneubuhl called it a psychological melodrama set on "some South Sea island."

Four busy years had passed in Honolulu before Kneubuhl left for Los Angeles with two cents in his pocket and high hopes. It took a few years of disappointment in Hollywood, including comments that he "wrote too well" for television, before one of his scripts was sold: a television half-hour script that was intended as a little birthday gift for a friend's daughter was bought by Douglas Fairbanks, Jr. One script led to another and soon Kneubuhl was working fulltime, seven days a week, for the next twenty years. Kneubuhl made a name for himself in Hollywood through countless scripts created for major television productions of the 1950s and 1960s. His long list of credits included *Playhouse 90; Mannix; Adventures in Paradise; Mission Impossible; Ironsides; Hawai'i Five-O; The Wild, Wild West; Gunsmoke; Have Gun, Will Travel; Star Trek; Ben Casey; Dr. Kildare; Wagon Train; Hallmark Theater; Kraft Playhouse; Medic;* and *Markham.* Yet in his own words: "I was successful, but nothing could compensate for the essential hollowness of the work. I ended up feeling more alienated than ever. I quit and came home to Samoa in 1968."[5]

For more than a decade after Hollywood, Kneubuhl shifted his focus to education in his homeland. He was instrumental in organizing the American Samoa Community College and initiated the program in Samoan-Pacific Studies. He created and then directed the bilingual/bicultural program for the American Samoan Department of Education. His energies focused on lecturing on Polynesian history, culture, linguistics, and ecology. He fought a system that used English as a foundation when in fact Samoan was the language of the home. He worked tirelessly in American Samoa to change the educational status of the young people of his homeland. His payback was an increase in Samoan pride and a growing number of Samoans who were now motivated to seek an education.

Kneubuhl did not put aside his writing during this period. In fact, he tightened his focus on what he termed his "Hawaiian plays," working to complete those he had started earlier and initiating the final works in a proposed trilogy. Although he had spent most of his career writing for the commercial markets of television and the movies, these stage works were everything *but* commercial. His effort to change the native education in the Pacific seemed to have sharpened his aim. His plays set out to awaken island audiences to realities they perhaps did not want to face but could not deny when confronted with their dwindling cultural identity. He wanted them to feel their responsibility, their role in the loss of cultural memory and the subsequent erosion of ancient spirituality. His last decades were a return to roots—to American Samoa and Hawai'i—for the reestablishment of pride in language and culture vital to those locales.

The Kneubuhl plays offered here are the culmination of a lifetime of thought, put to paper by a writer whose bicultural heritage haunted him and drove his art. They are well-told stories with vibrant characters and masterful layers of metaphor. History interweaves with mythology, social commentary, and philosophical musings. His language is lyrical, passionate, and base at times without apology. He was not afraid of sexual innuendo or sexual directness. He often flirted with the concept of the madman—and woman—as sage, protector, and catalyst. The release that comes from alcohol often unties the tongues of his characters. Ever present is the poetry of English and the Polynesian languages he sprinkles throughout to characterize those who have not relinquished that part of their identity. Also present are the retelling of historical truths, a passionate belief in the majesty of Polynesian culture, and the themes of alienation, spirituality, and allegiance to family that mark most of Kneubuhl's works. Here, however, a new element comes into play in the form of stylistic challenges that question reality and the world created by the writer. In fact, the writer is at the heart of all.

"My first requirement of theater," said Kneubuhl, "is not that it be insightful, true to human 'whatever.' My first gut demand is that it be theatrical." In keeping with this belief, Kneubuhl would lure the audience into a slice of Polynesian life—then disrupt that familiarity by a character who addresses the audience directly and simply steps into the scene. Or actors come on stage before the "real" play begins and put finishing touches on the set. Further, he believed that "the most important thing besides theatricality is a sense of play, even silly play, rather than grim straight line tragedy." So his characters and situations are often comedic, with a teasing maid or befuddled gardener thrown in to lighten the drama.

Although it was the last play written by Kneubuhl, *Think of a Garden* is the first play in this trilogy. In a letter written a year before he died, Kneubuhl confided:

> Everyone here thinks it is a straight autobiographical play, and I guess it is, but only in a very special sense. I have to insist that writers *shouldn't* ever write their autobiographies because they will inevitably fictionalize. The responsibility of the artist is to take a set of facts and, true to his creative hubris and obedient to the disciplines of the genre in which he is working, realize the potential that is in that set of facts. So, autobiographical facts become the starting points for acts of the imagination.
>
> I tell anybody interested that the three plays are really about the making of plays, specifically *these* three plays. And so they are really about The Writer and his search. That is why, despite their actual order of composition, the plays must be presented, in print or on stage, in this order:
>
> 1. *Think of a Garden*—in which the source, the font, the first cause of the itch that sets the Writer a-scratchin' is presented.
>
> 2. *Mele Kanikau: A Pageant*—in which a Stage Writer takes the Real Writer's set of autobiographical Samoan facts and shows us how he has realized them by converting them into a Hawaiian play of a "legendary" cast and mould. Facts are turned into a theatrical fiction (that is "truer" than the facts) before our eyes.
>
> 3. *A Play: A Play*—The Writer comes to realize the glory, sanctity, and limitation of the very thing his life (all life) is based on: Language; Words. And so on, and on.[6]

Think of a Garden is much more than the "itch" Kneubuhl refers to. It is an artful weaving of history, family memory, and subjective observation. He does not merely tell a story: he interprets historical facts through the personal lives of those the facts have touched and

radically changed. It is Kneubuhl's last play, written as a culmination of the writer's art, but intended to explain the early influences
that set him writing. Premiered in Samoa on the day he died, the
play has since been produced in Aotearoa and Hawai'i.

Kneubuhl's prefatory note to the four-scene play celebrates the
heroes not included as characters but implied by the events fore-
told. He offers an apology for the autobiographical nature of the
play. Yet it is that very autobiographical approach which lends cre-
dence to the telling and triggers our understanding of the forces
that led Kneubuhl to take up the pen. For that reason, *Think of a
Garden* is the most Samoan of all John Kneubuhl's plays. The
Samoan view of family, deference for the dead, behavior in times of
mourning, even concepts of time—all are deftly etched beside the
story of Samoa's early move toward independence. The effect is a
story as textured as a fine mat.

Kneubuhl was known to say that a play about the United States
president would be ever more effective if written through the
perspective of the scullery maid and butlers assigned to the White
House. That "once-removed" approach is used to great effective-
ness in *Think of a Garden.* We mark the paces of the liberation and
assassination of Tamasese, hero of the Mau Movement, the independence underground of Western Samoa, by hours spent with the
Kreber family, whose matriarch is a distant cousin of Tamasese. The
impact of the injustices wrought by New Zealand High Commissioner Allen reverberates through the Krebers as it no doubt
resounded through the Samoan population. In highly dramatic
moments, bloody events in the Mau Movement physically manifest
themselves within the writer-as-a-young-boy, David. Thus, the play
is highly political, readily exposing the bigotry of the colonial powers
who were responsible for Tamasese's death and its ramifications.

There is no question that this is John Kneubuhl's story. He is
David—not a typical Samoan child, but a mixed-blood, sensitive
young man caught in a triple dilemma: his dark Samoan skin, the
attempts to educate him in an upstanding Christian way, and a
family that was moving to the outside of Samoan life. When
Kneubuhl was writing *Think of a Garden*, he was disturbed that it
was "a relentlessly sad play."

The character called "The Writer" is prominent as a narrator/
Greek chorus throughout *Think of a Garden*, reflecting on family
history and social conditions, reminding us that he is the young
boy, David, trying to make sense of his bicultural life. His mother is
the regal, bicultural Lu'isa, educated in New Zealand and fiercely

proud of her chiefly lineage. His "blunt, open, friendly" father, Frank, is an American who is not beyond calling his son a "half-savage" and worrying about him "running around the village so much, night and day, like any other native kid." It is no wonder that these varying heritages create confusion in the young boy.

As real as the other characters in the play may be, they too are metaphorical representations of true Samoans. Lilo is Lu'isa's brother, dashingly good looking, hard drinking, devoted to David. He can be seen to represent Samoans who bravely stood their ground, but eventually succumbed as a people. There is anger within him, but also a soul-searching that demands truth. His tragedy is expressed in the unfathomable sadness of having lost the hero who was to be the answer to all the ills of his people.

Pito is David's nursemaid and the household help—an old Samoan who had raised the previous generation, giving her the privilege of speaking her mind whenever she sees fit and only in Samoan. Pito is David's link to his Samoan past, often spending time with the young boy, relating stories of his heritage, and imparting cultural wisdom. She is the epitome of tradition, wrapped in the visage of an even older Samoan tradition, the clown of the *faleaitu*, a native formal theater. Her jovial ways belie the truths she speaks to David behind closed doors. These truths reinforce David's Samoan identity, as she urges him to "promise me, promise me that you will always remember who you truly are."

Brother Patrick, David's tutor, has a deep love for the boy, tempered by a deeper love for the liquor decanter, and represents the well-intended missionaries who populated the Pacific at the turn of the century. While he seems to appreciate David's bicultural dilemma, he is terrified by David's connection to a spirit world that is tied up in Samoan lore. Protective yet helpless, he must defer to the stronger tie of family opinion once matters get out of hand.

The tale of Tamasese, of David, of all Samoa, unravels in Scene 4 into several threads. The underlying message, uttered by Lu'isa, is that Samoans must take personal responsibility for their present and for their future. David will be removed from the conflict, along with Lilo, who chooses his own way. The once-noncommittal father figure has redefined himself, as did many outsiders to the Samoan cause, in fighting for those who fought the injustices. The threads are rewoven at the penultimate moment by The Writer, who, in a moving apex, calls upon the image of Tamasese to inspire his sense of "who he truly is."

While there is no doubt that John Kneubuhl wrote *Think of a*

Garden to explain why the writer writes, at the same time the play itself is a gift to the people of his homeland. He captured a crucial event in their history, immortalized it through his pen, and keened openly for all that was lost by Tamasese's untimely death.

Mele Kanikau: A Pageant, completed in 1975, is another dirge, but one of entirely different origins. The title means "anthem of lamentation." In its three acts, Kneubuhl places characters he created out of events witnessed in childhood. The writer appears as The Author, the character who introduces the play and also the idea of the writer-creating-the-story-which-in-turn-creates-the-writer. Kneubuhl is almost timid in his use of his alter ego in this instance —a stark contrast to the adult David in *Think of a Garden* or his later work, *A Play: A Play*, in which writer and work are intricately fused. In *Mele Kanikau* the writer tosses his ideas into the air, juggles them a bit, then deftly bounces them back into the arena of the story, pondering his role in the unfolding of events—a performance that draws us deeper into *Mele Kanikau*. The story has such a strong life of its own that The Author's musings are forgotten until he steps in, unobtrusively, and comments on the process of writing, of creating poetry, of letting "hard facts" speak for themselves.

To the Samoans, Kneubuhl gave a gift; to the Hawaiians, a warning. *Mele Kanikau* is Kneubuhl's strong exhortation to Hawaiians to wake up to the fragile state of their culture. Now, nearly twenty years after it was written, the play is still bold in its name-calling. Yet, *Mele Kanikau* is more palatable today to the people of Hawai'i than it was to those of the 1970s. "Hawaiian Pride" is a fact of the 1990s. Hawaiian identity has been greatly strengthened since the dawn of the Hawaiian renaissance some two decades ago, with its "back to roots" movement emphasizing language, culture, and sovereignty. There are fewer "Pageant Hawaiians" to point a finger at these days. Conversely, there are many more Hawaiians who have traced ancestral ties, explored ancient ways, and found modern-day relevance for values from the *wā kahiko*, the ancient times. Still, the play resonates with powerful themes. Indeed, it would still create a maelstrom if produced in today's Hawai'i.

Disconnection from roots, as well as the erosion of family and religious ties, lie at the core of *Mele Kanikau*, along with the question that appears throughout Kneubuhl's Hawaiian plays: "What is a Hawaiian?" Kneubuhl's own early experiences brought him face to face with alienation from his dual heritages, an alienation that haunted him throughout his life and became the grist for his Hawaiian plays:

And the old, lovely, gentle chief—it was nighttime—turned around and asked me, very nicely, who I loved better, my father or my mother. Tears just streamed down my face. I'd never been asked that because he was asking me to make a choice. He expected an answer and of course I'm going to say I love my mother better because she's Samoan. I remember I ran out of the hut, sobbing. And I think I'm still running, still sobbing. . . . And it's one of the kinds of things I write about—alienation—how do we get to belong again?

Kneubuhl's story, at the outset, sets about debunking the Hawaiian image proffered by the tourist industry. The hula dancer, Ginger Lei, decked in slick hula attire, enters eating a sandwich and then proceeds to paint her toenails! Already we realize that myths will be exposed and reality questioned.

The setting is a pageant somewhere in Honolulu, very likely in Waikīkī, complete with surrogate king and queen. Noa Napoʻoʻanaakalā has arrived from his retreat far in a valley on the north shore of Oʻahu to take the pageant in a new direction. His entourage includes his haole companion, Frances, and a youthful corps of dancers, all of whom speak Hawaiian fluently, which immediately separates them from the city folk. They are out of their element in the pageant setting, but definitely in power, exuding a *mana* that is unquestionable.

The story that unfolds is complex, running parallel to a tale of lovers fleeing civilization to escape predictable lives. It is tinged with concerns over Noa's mental and physical health and the very idea of possession. An exorcism does take place, but it is of a cultural rather than a personal sort. Noa reacts to his old friend, Carl, who questions why Noa drinks so much, so boldly, in front of all the pageant performers whose job it is to recreate Hawaiian history and represent Hawaiian monarchy, albeit in a glitzy Hollywood style:

NOA: Why? Because I don't want to pretend that what's rotten and cheap is good and beautiful? Because I don't want to pretend that these awful people really represent my people?

The exorcism continues by returning to the question at the core of Kneubuhl's concern: What is a Hawaiian? Carl, the spurned lover and, now, king of the pageant, answers:

CARL: What's wrong with that? Don't look down your nose at me. People like me—we're the real Hawaiians. We take the world as it is, we go out, we try. We don't sit around, whining and belly-aching about some great past that we've lost. We work. We cope. The best way we can. In the real world. And we make it . . . You listen to me: I'm more Hawaiian, any minute of any day, than you've been in your damned drunk crybaby life.

But Noa disagrees:

> NOA: *(Always simply.)* You don't know what you've lost, Carl. And if you don't know that, you're not a Hawaiian.

Kneubuhl plays with daring sexual behavior and wraps it in mystical trappings in *Mele Kanikau*, harking back to stories of *faleaitu* and *poula* evenings in Samoan villages long ago. In what Kneubuhl called "Rabelaisian" gatherings, villagers would assemble for dancing that eventually led to a kind of sexual frenzy. In some instances, a call would be heard, "It's him—he's coming; he's coming," a warning that the ghost was entering the hut, causing all to scatter to the surrounding forest to fulfill their sexual desires. In *Mele Kanikau*, Noa's behavior, too, is triggered by forces beyond his control.

In a stirring play-within-a-play (or pageant-within-a-pageant), Noa cajoles, then forces, the king to face his inner pain. It is a brilliant mélange of hula, fierce chant, and manipulation. This high point in the play is inherently lyrical for its use of Hawaiian names to denote caste. The lowly *kauwā*, or untouchables, are named Malalo (Underneath), 'Aikelekele (Eater of Filth), and Kapihe (To Mourn). It is appropriate that the character playing the queen is named Lydia, the English name of the last ruling monarch of Hawai'i, Lili'uokalani.

Finally, the meaning of Noa's name itself seals the significance of the catharsis forced upon the characters. Napo'o'anaakalā (Setting of the Sun) signifies the closure wrought by Noa and his daring antics: in turn, each of the Waikīkī pageant members' responsibility in the death of The Hawaiian is pranced before the players. By extension, Kneubuhl turns the tables on us all and has Noa set the sun of condemnation on *Hawai'i* for its own demise. Kneubuhl blamed the "spiritual death" of the Hawaiian people on the Hawaiian chiefs' neglect of their responsibility to their subjects. He felt that the chiefs had lost sight of the true meaning of *'āina*—which should be *family*, as found elsewhere in Polynesia. To that end, he pitted the *hālau* from the hills against the city dancers.

Kneubuhl's niece, Honolulu playwright Victoria Nālani Kneubuhl, speaks about *Mele Kanikau* as the play in which she sees "more of Uncle John . . . than in any other play. David in *Garden* is what he tells us he is but Noa in *Mele Kanikau* is really as close as it comes." She sums up the play as a "beautiful love letter to Dotsy."[7] Love that was cherished, lost, and deeply mourned does pulsate through *Mele Kanikau*. Its power emboldens some of the characters in the play and embitters others. Kneubuhl's niece, Victoria, admits a strong attachment to *Mele Kanikau*, whose message underscores "that our personal acts towards one another count for something." In her reckoning:

> Pageant Hawaiians in *Kanikau* carry the ideas of what John felt Hawaiians thought about themselves—the golden age/the glorious *ali'i*, while Noa *ma* carries the raw energy and spirit of Polynesia. Who really is the protagonist here? Who goes through transformation? I think it's Carl—that's who we are meant to identify with, that's who Noa comes back for—to *ho'oponopono*, through a release of anger so that we can embrace our grief and Love. What a moment of theater it is when Carl comes to that gift, "how their spirits went, even in Death, in human form to the *ali'i* Kahililoa, to remind him once again of Love."[8]

Act 3 of *Mele Kanikau* is startling. Lessons are learned, but not without sacrifice. Contrasts between what is truly Hawaiian and what is manufactured to be "Hawaiian" carry us to the last refrain: *Ha'ina 'ia mai ana ka ka puana*, "the story is told." . . .

A Play: A Play is the most structurally complex of Kneubuhl's Hawaiian plays. It is disconcerting from the beginning when we are made to see the finishing details of set dressing before the play commences. Kneubuhl's deep admiration for Pirandello's *Six Characters in Search of an Author* seems to resonate just beneath the surface.

Once *A Play: A Play* begins, the dialogue is clipped, terse, leaving the impression that we are watching an old black and white film with vacuous Cowardesque characters moving blithely about the space. But this is Volcano, Hawai'i, home to Pele and an assortment of others who seem clichés of their lineage: the *hapa*-Hawaiian James Alama, owner of the estate; his *hapa* adoring lover, Julia; the Filipino yardman, Severino; the Chinese servant, Ah Kiu. It is not until we are caught up in strange occurrences in James Alama's home that the production snaps and we are jolted into the reality of the actors playing these roles. Much to our chagrin, in this play The Writer does not appear to explain why the actors slip out of character. Instead we are led into a fascinating maze of a story that turns back on itself again and again. The irony is that the playwright is indeed ever present, not as a character but as The Creator himself.

Is this the "glory, sanctity, and limitation" of language and words Kneubuhl referred to in characterizing this drama? Is it a Polynesian *Twilight Zone*? It certainly is a detailed look at the power of writing: putting word by word on a page and hoping each syllable will bring life to the story. And this is what indeed occurs in *A Play: A Play*, a direct spin on the idea that the playwright "brings the character to life." But it is unsettling, even terrifying, for the actors watching their story unfold. Kneubuhl summed it up:

> Seeing the *becoming* of a work, a created work, is as important as a prayer, because it sets theological surges. In that sense, for me, writing a play is a kind of a sacred, religious act. In addition to alienation and whatever, I have *become*, the plays have *become*, things that say, "Look, this is about the writing of a play." And in that writing of a play we have our search for which there really are no final answers, because answers have no finality. In that process of searching you are seeing a live playwright, a live poet, whatever, at work doing this living thing which I now present to you on this stage tonight.

Some of Kneubuhl's central concerns resurface in the storyline. We come to question James Alama's Hawaiianness when we find that he is going to sell the family estate. We watch the change as he comes to grips with his Hawaiian heritage. We get a smattering of Hawaiian mythology with the story of the volcano goddess, Pele, and Kamapua'a, the mutable pig demigod and Pele's nemesis. Pele's commentary on modern ways—including the licensing of pet white dogs—underscores, through the form of a modern allegory, what Hawaiian culture has lost. There is a generous smattering of Hawaiian language and diverse plays on words uttered with various ethnic accents.

Kneubuhl is at his most daring in *A Play: A Play* when he tramples upon the Hawaiian religious icon, Pele. Her portrayal includes her unquenchable thirst for liquor and her ability to change form and gender in order to cause voices to rise and human beings to grovel in fear, sexual defensiveness, and sexual delight. While she seems pathetic in her most common disguise, that of an old woman, she elicits deep compassion when she utters:

> OLD WOMAN: All dead. . . . All my *mo'opuna* and the *mo'opuna* of my *mo'opuna* and their *mo'opuna*. . . . No home. . . . An' my great-great-great-great-great-gran' chirren too. . . . All dead, everybody. . . . All the fires dead now; all the old ways gone. . . . Wandering now. . . . Only wandering. . . . Looking for a home. . . . And nobody cares any more. . . .

Such thoughts lead to unsettling questions. If the powerful fire goddess can be subdued by modern life, is there any hope for us mere mortals? (Mere Hawaiians?) Are we living lives scripted by The Creator? (By the colonialists?) How do we redeem ourselves? (Take back control of our lives?) Kneubuhl does not offer pat answers to these questions:

> If the play works, if it is successful, what I have elicited from you is your confession about your nature rather than a common agreement about anything. I have existentially succeeded in singling out each one of you and made you react so that if there is someone around they will say, "You're not commenting on the play. The play has trapped you into saying something about yourself by making that reaction to the play." So, in that sense, I've kept that kind of ambiguity going all the way through. There are no answers, no anything, which I think is more honest. I think plays are situational things. In the real deep human situation as you interact you widen consciousness and you never pin it down to anything.

And so *A Play: A Play* does work: it reveals our own frustations about who we are and the extent of our influence in the creation of our lives. We come to question the role of fate and the tug of spiritual forces beyond our mundane existence.

Kneubuhl was joined in his efforts to help American Samoa survive the inevitable changes of modernization by many who felt passionately about education, language, and the very art of writing. The writer's group he founded in American Samoa, O Le Si'uleo o Samoa, continues to promote native writers. To these "disciples" and others across the Pacific, Kneubuhl left two directives. The first is a strongly worded command: "So, you young people, I urge you that it is your moral duty as a Polynesian to learn one Polynesian language that is dying." The second comes from years of cease-less thinking and writing:

> One of my last missionary things—before angels come and go with me to Hell, because I prefer the society there than in the other place—is to try to get this over to our young Pacific writers: that they have too much to draw on to waste their time on bootless angers, fruitless angers. They're not turning their energies to what is magnificently there and what is useful in their search for identity. . . . And we're not doing that. We have a lot to offer and a lot to say. There is a rich, wonderful, multicultural heritage we have now in Hawai'i where democracy really works. It's the one shining example in the world to me where different cultures mix and work and it works.

There is a cadre of people in Samoa, Hawai'i, and New Zealand who knew John Kneubuhl, worked with him, and deeply admired his art and his life's work. There is great hope among us that John Kneubuhl's vision will continue to educate, continue to challenge, and continue to inspire. Through the examples set by John Kneu-buhl's plays, we Pacific people have been moved to make our voices heard as his is still being heard, throughout Polynesia.

JACKIE PUALANI JOHNSON

Notes

Direct quotes attributed to John Kneubuhl were obtained in video and audio inter-views conducted by Professor Johnson at the University of Hawai'i at Hilo in April and December 1990 unless otherwise noted.

1. "Movie Firm Makes Offer for John Kneubuhl Play," *Honolulu Star Bulletin,* 7 January 1947, p. 3.
2. Pierre Bowman, "Lyons' Legacy of Song," *Honolulu Star Bulletin,* 24 August 1976, p. C4.
3. Victoria Nālani Kneubuhl, personal letter, July 1994.
4. Edna B. Lawson, "Point Distress Proves Edge-of-Seat Thriller," *Honolulu Advertiser,* 21 June 1950.
5. Frederic Koehler Sutter, *The Samoans: A Global Family* (Honolulu: Univer-sity of Hawai'i Press, 1989), p. 211.
6. John A. Kneubuhl, personal letter, 16 February 1991.
7. V. N. Kneubuhl, 1994.
8. Ibid.

Glossary

'ae (Hawaiian): yes.

'āina (Hawaiian): land.

ali'i (Hawaiian): chief.

'aumakua (Hawaiian): family or personal gods that assumed the shape of various objects or animals.

fale (Samoan): thatched hut.

faleaitu (Samoan): native formal theater indigenous to Samoa. The male clown creates skits that incorporate village gossip, problems, and parodies of villagers and chiefs. Issues are explored, and often resolved, in a comedic way. The clown plays male or female roles.

hālau (Hawaiian): hula school.

hānai (Hawaiian): to care for, to adopt.

haole (Hawaiian): literally, stranger, foreigner. Popular usage: white person.

hapa (Hawaiian): literally, half. Popular usage: mixed blood.

hāpai (Hawaiian): pregnant.

heiau (Hawaiian): temple.

hikie'e (Hawaiian): large Hawaiian couch.

holokū (Hawaiian): a loose dress styled after missionary garb.

ho'oponopono (Hawaiian): literally, to correct. Also: family conferences in which relationships are set right.

hula (Hawaiian): Hawaiian dance.

'ilima (Hawaiian): small native shrub bearing delicate yellow-orange flowers.

kāhili (Hawaiian): feather standard, symbolic of royalty.

kala (Hawaiian): prayer to free one from sorcery.

kauwā (Hawaiian): untouchable.

kōkua (Hawaiian): help.

kumu (Hawaiian): teacher, source.

ku'u ipo (Hawaiian): my sweet heart.

lavalava (Samoan): length of fabric artfully tied about the waist to create a skirt.

lehua (Hawaiian): flower of the *ohi'a* tree.

ma (Hawaiian): literally, and others.

mā (Samoan): embarrassed.

māhū (Hawaiian): homosexual of either sex.

make (Hawaiian): dead.

malo (Hawaiian): male's loincloth.

mana (Hawaiian): supernatural or divine power.

mele kanikau (Hawaiian): a dirge, a mourning song.

mō'ī (Hawaiian): sovereign, monarch.

mo'opuna (Hawaiian): grandchild.

noho (Hawaiian): various meanings, among which is possession by a spirit.

'ōhelo (Hawaiian): berries found on a small shrub abundant in the Volcano region and sacred to Pele, the volcano goddess.

'ōkole (Hawaiian): buttocks.

'opihi (Hawaiian): limpet.

Pākē (Hawaiian): Chinese.

pau (Hawaiian): finished.

piko (Hawaiian): navel.

poula (Samoan): "teasing nights" that included dancing naked and clandestine sexual activity.

pūne'e (Hawaiian): moveable couch.

pupule (Hawaiian): crazy.

Sione Nupo (Samoan): transliteration of John Kneubuhl.

tālofa (Samoan): greetings, hello.

tūtū kāne (Hawaiian): grandfather.

'ukulele (Hawaiian): stringed instrument brought to Hawai'i by the Portuguese.

vave (Samoan): quickly.

wā kahiko (Hawaiian): literally, the ancient time.

Production Credits

Think of a Garden was first produced by O Le Si'uleo O Samoa in Pago
Pago in 1992.

CAST

THE WRITER	Frank Pritchard
PITO	Naomi Oney
DAVID	Daniel Hunkin
LUISA	Kathleen Kolhoff
BROTHER PATRICK	Robert Moore
FRANK	Dale Long
LILO	Harold Si'ufanua

Directed by Patty Page

Since then, *Think of a Garden* has been produced in Auckland (1994), Wellington (1995), and Honolulu (1995).

A Play: A Play was first produced by the University of Hawai'i at Hilo
Theater in 1990.

CAST

HAWAIIAN MAN	Kenneth Lee
JAMES ALAMA	Peter Charlot
JULIA	Debra Fuller
AH KIU	Randall Wung
SEVERINO	Robbie Tingcang
FERN-WRAPPED MAN	Keoki Kapelewina
OLD WOMAN	Earnest Morgan
YOUNG GIRL	Kelly Hamora

Directed by John Kneubuhl